The Amateur Historian's Guide to
The Heart of England

"If you wish to pursue the most enjoyable of historical rambles through medieval and Tudor London, then the one indispensable adjunct to such a trip is this Holy Grail of Guidebooks."

—RENAISSANCE MAGAZINE

◆ ◆

PRAISE FOR THE Amateur Historian's Guides

*"For following in the footsteps of Shakespeare's kings and nobles . . .
indeed for tracking the Bard himself . . . there is simply no better guide."*
—MICHAEL KAHN, artistic director,
The Shakespeare Theatre, Washington, D.C.

*"The lively book is full of the history that seemed so boring in high school
as it lays out trips throughout the counties of Kent, Sussex, and Surrey."*
—ROCHESTER DEMOCRAT AND CHRONICLE

*". . . this comprehensive guide pinpoints all the known specific sites
and artifacts from the years 1066 to 1600. In addition, it gives
historical information—often written in a humorous fashion—
about the people and events associated with the sites."*
—PORTLAND OREGONIAN

*"After tracing your London ancestor, use this book to view his or her
city. Retrieve dates of historical events and building construction
(1066–1603) from its timeline. Locate medieval and Tudor sites on
its overview map. Read the descriptions of multiple sites and note
their access information. Wonder at the 'did you know' commentaries
on historical persons associated with each site. Finally, follow
the excursion plans for one, two, three, or five-day trips . . . Or,
you could just enjoy an effortless virtual tour with a cup of
Earl Grey at your side and the opened book in your hands."*
—ANCESTRY MAGAZINE

+ The Amateur Historian's Guide to +

The Heart of England

Sarah Valente Kettler
&
Carole Trimble

Capital Books, Inc.
Sterling, Virginia

Capital Books, Inc.
P.O. Box 605
Herndon, Virginia 20172-0605

Design and composition by Melissa Ehn and Megan Geer
at Wilsted & Taylor Publishing Services

Illustrations and maps by Chadwick Design, Inc.

LIBRARY OF CONGRESS CATALOGING-IN-PUBLICATION DATA
Kettler, Sarah Valente.
    The amateur historian's guide to the heart of England : nearly 200 Medieval
& Tudor sites two hours or less from London / Sarah Valente Kettler &
Carole Trimble.—1st ed.
        p. cm.
Includes bibliographical references and index.
    ISBN 1-892123-65-7 (alk. paper)
        1. England—Antiquities—Guidebooks.   2. Historic buildings—
England—Guidebooks.   3. Historic sites—England—Guidebooks.
4. England—History, Local—Guidebooks.   5. London Region (England)
—Guidebooks.   I. Trimble, Carole.   II. Title.

DA90.K45   2003
942.03—dc21

                                                                2003011986

Printed in the United States of America on acid-free paper that meets the
American National Standards Institute Z39-48 Standard.

First Edition

10 9 8 7 6 5 4 3 2 1

In memory of our dear friend
Janis B. Mucka:
"Happy Travels, Jan!"

✝

CONTENTS

ACKNOWLEDGMENTS

With three books now behind us, we can't say enough about the support, encouragement and *patience* of our friends and families. Without their constant cheerleading (and occasional martini mixing), our "one-book-a-year" output would have been nigh impossible! In the words of Shakespeare, "thanks and ever thanks . . ."

Kathleen Hughes of Capital Books has our endless gratitude for continuing to believe in our ideas and back our enterprises. Our agent, Gail Ross, has lent us perspective and wise advice throughout. Technically speaking, Hector Benedi—computer guru extraordinaire—has landed us in the 21st century . . . not easy to do when your client is rooted in the Middle Ages! Thank you one and all.

"Across the pond," we owe more thanks than we can list . . . to Gillian Hawkins of Duckworth Publishing for representing us so ably abroad . . . to the superlative staff at the Franklin Hotel for providing us a home (and office!) away from home . . . to the countless tourist information center personnel, docents, unofficial tour guides and congenial passersby who welcomed every question these Yanks could conjure, no matter how elementary or complex. The warmth and enthusiasm that's greeted us in England has been amazing and *greatly* appreciated.

Finally, a very special thanks—and a very poignant farewell—to our driver, Roy Adair. When Roy first opened his door for us almost three years ago, little did he know that he'd be adding "restaurant critic, security guard-charmer, disc jockey, diplomat, chaperone and amateur historian" to his resume. So often did he unerringly "sense" the way to ancient sites—some even *we* had written off as lost—that he earned the sobriquet "Radar Roy." Roy is about to embark on a well-earned retirement. We wish him all good things—and plan to hold him to his pledge of driving us through Aquitaine!

INTRODUCTION

One of the things we have always loved about historical research is the way in which one thread leads to another and then to another and so on until an entire pattern is spread before you. It's like putting together a puzzle, one piece at a time, until a whole picture is formed. We are never so excited as when we have started on the hunt for missing pieces or loose threads and then found the exact bit that pulls the whole pattern together.

That happened time and time again as we were researching and writing this book, *The Amateur Historian's Guide to the Heart of England*. It was like a treasure hunt in which a person or an event would pop up in one place and then another, and in a third and a fourth, until the history of the sites in this book was woven together in a smooth mosaic. Mental lightbulbs were flashing continuously as we found new pieces of the historical puzzle and cried, "Eureka! That's how that fits together!"

As we did in our last book, *The Amateur Historian's Guide to Medieval & Tudor England: Day Trips South of London*, we have grouped the sites according to their geographic and historic connections. The sites are packaged as "trips," most of which can be considered "day trips" from London. This means that, using London as a base, you can depart in the morning and return in time for dinner or the theater.

A few of the trips are really too far or too packed with compelling sites and history to make for a comfortable "day trip." We recommend that you consider taking a break from London and immersing yourself in an overnight medieval and Tudor experience in the English countryside. Several of the trips also include many more sites than can be covered easily in a day (*al-*

though you'd be surprised how many we can pack in when we're on a mission!). This is because many of the sites in this book have widely divergent—and often extremely limited—open hours, so you will have to pick and choose which sites best meet your special interests and whose hours of operation best fit your schedule.

As we also did in our last book, we wanted to share with you a couple of points about our approach to this book and thereby, we hope, answer your questions before you ask them.

WILLIAM WHO?

Anyone who has done much reading about medieval and Tudor history knows there is considerable confusion about ancient names and their spelling. People occasionally are known by their proper names only (spelled in a variety of ways), by their titles (which often changed) and by nicknames (often a play on a physical attribute). Hence, "William the Conqueror" also is known as "William of Normandy" . . . or William, *Duke* of Normandy . . . or "William the Bastard" . . . or "William I." Likewise, Henry II is known as "Henry Plantagenet" . . . or "Henry Fitzempress" . . . or "Henry of Anjou." A king by any other name . . . we tend to use them all.

In most other instances, when a person is known to history by more than one name—such as Empress Matilda (a.k.a. Maude) or King Stephen's wife Maud (a.k.a. Matilda)—we have chosen the name we like best and stuck with it.

In the case of Henry VIII's many wives, we *do* realize that each of the "Catherines" also was known as "Katherine" and, occasionally, as "Kathryn." For the sake of clarity, we refer to Katherine of Aragon, Catherine Howard and Katherine Parr. Apologies to those of you who might strongly prefer another spelling.

BUT WHAT ABOUT . . . ?

As much as we tend to joke about "leaving no ancient stone unturned," we have a confession to make: there are a handful of sites (*mere pebbles in the historical landscape*) that we have not investigated, and several that we have "turned," but have decided, for various reasons, to cast aside for purposes of this book. *The Heart of England* offers a wealth of medieval and Tudor buildings and villages—more than could be covered conveniently in the time and space allocated to this project. Since our interest and expertise is in the realm of history, rather than architecture, we have tended to place primary focus on sites of historical importance—places connected to the people and events that shaped England from 1066 to 1600. Secondary focus has been given to "lesser" sites that can be visited conveniently in tandem with the major sites. Finally, we have included a smattering of attractions we found just too unique (*or too peculiar*) to overlook. (*And, for the guy who asked the question at the Travel and Leisure Books signing: yes, there are a couple of medieval barns in this book.*) In your travels, you will probably come upon a guildhall or two, several manor homes, many churches and perhaps even a village that you feel was a "glaring omission" on our part. Rest assured: we probably know *of* it, but felt there wasn't enough to say *about* it to make it worth our while—or yours.

RUN THAT BY ME AGAIN ...

Certain historical people and events had such a dramatic impact on English history that you will find them cropping up time and time again throughout this book, our previous two books and all of our future books (*we assume!*). It's that "domino" effect again—the people and places of medieval and Tudor England bump into each other endlessly. Frankly, we find it a wee bit taxing to test our talents by continually penning short, pithy and fresh recaps of these people and events on the off chance that you might have missed a previous reference. We bet you grow weary of the repetitive reading, too! Assuming you already have some basic background about the people and events that pepper our books, we've opted not to insult your intelligence by repeating Ancient History 101 any more than is necessary. No longer will you always find multiple explanations of exactly who Empress Matilda was and why she engaged in a 19-year struggle for the English crown with her cousin Stephen of Blois. No more will you have to reread the play-by-plays of every civil war and family feud that rent medieval society during the reigns of the Plantagenet kings. Henry VIII's conflict with the Church is a well-worn topic — one brief recap should jog your memory. However, if you become confused or encounter a reference you don't understand, or you simply crave the telling *one more time*, check the index of this book or hurry out and buy the first two volumes in this series (*that is if — heaven forbid! — you don't already own them*). We can almost guarantee you'll find the story you're looking for — with all the necessary facts . . . and the added bonus of our erudite interpretation!

WHAT TIME WAS THAT?

For years, the accepted method of historical dating has been to use "BC" ("before Christ," for those years before the birth of Jesus, arbitrarily designated as year 1) and "AD" (Anno Domini: the years following Jesus' birth). Many religions, however, do not recognize the birth of Christ, and some cultures use other methods of historical dating. In recent years, an increasing number of authors and historians have adopted the more inclusive "Common Era" dating system. We have chosen to follow suit. When you see "BCE" (Before Common Era), know that we are referring to the years familiarly known as "BC." Similarly, "CE" refers to the period of time traditionally known as "AD."

～

Needless to say, we had a great time working on this book, and we hope you will enjoy it equally as you trace the historic threads of the *Heart of England* either from your armchair or by way of a trek through this wonderful part of Great Britain.

TIME LINE

1066 *October 14*
William, Duke of Normandy, defeats the last Saxon king of England, Harold, at the Battle of Hastings and begins the Norman Conquest of England.

1066 *Christmas Day*
William the Conqueror is crowned King of England.

1087 William II succeeds to the throne of England.

1100 Henry I succeeds to the throne of England.

1135 Stephen of Blois usurps the crown of Empress Matilda, Henry I's daughter and designated heir. Stephen ascends the throne of England.

1139 Empress Matilda arrives in England to begin pressing her claim to the English crown.

1142 Just as Stephen is on the verge of capturing Matilda and thus ending the civil war, the empress escapes from a siege of Oxford Castle during a blizzard. She and four companions sneak by Stephen's sentries to reach the frozen Thames. They walk down the Thames to Abingdon Abbey, where they mount horses and ride for the protection of Wallingford Castle.

1153 The barons of England force a peace agreement, signed at Wallingford Castle, that ends the civil war that has raged for 14 years. The agreement provides that Matilda's son, Henry Fitzempress (a.k.a. Henry Plantagenet), will succeed Stephen as King of England.

1154   Henry II, son of Empress Matilda, succeeds to the throne of England.

1167   Henry II bans English students from attending the University of Paris, an action that helped fuel the growth of Oxford University.

1170   Thomas à Becket, Archbishop of Canterbury, is murdered in Canterbury Cathedral by knights who believe they are acting on the wishes of King Henry II.

1173   Thomas à Becket, Archbishop of Canterbury, is canonized by Pope Alexander III.

1189   Richard the Lionheart succeeds to the throne of England.

1199   John succeeds to the throne of England.

1215   Magna Carta is signed by King John at Runnymede. John retreats to Windsor Castle, reneges on the agreement and withstands three months of siege before an end is negotiated.

1216   France's Prince Louis invades England at the invitation of barons rebelling against King John. Later that year, King John dies of dysentery and his nine-year-old son ascends the throne as Henry III.

1258   A council of barons meets to produce the "Provisions of Oxford," a set of recommendations meant to curb the power of King Henry III.

1263–1265   Barons, led by Simon de Montfort, Earl of Leicester, revolt in an effort to force Henry III to abide by the Provisions of Oxford.

1272   Edward I succeeds to the throne of England.

1291   Edward I commissions construction of the "Eleanor Crosses" to commemorate the stops made in 1290 by the funeral cortege of his beloved wife as it made its way from her death site in Nottinghamshire to Westminster Abbey.

1307   Edward II succeeds to the throne of England.

1327   Edward III succeeds to the throne of England.

1348   Edward III establishes the Order of the Garter at Windsor Castle.

1377   Ten-year-old Richard II succeeds to the throne of England.

1381   Peasants' Revolt occurs.

1399   Henry Bolingbroke usurps the crown of Richard II and ascends the throne of England as Henry IV.

1413   Henry V succeeds to the throne of England.

1422   Henry VI succeeds to the throne of England.

1461   Edward IV deposes Henry VI and ascends the throne of England.

1470   The House of Lancaster wins back the Crown for Henry VI; Edward IV flees in exile.

1471   Edward IV returns from exile and deposes Henry VI a second time. Henry is subsequently murdered in the Tower of London.

1483   Edward V inherits the throne of England, but is never crowned because his uncle Richard, Duke of Gloucester, claims the Crown as Richard III.

1485   Forces led by Henry Tudor defeat the royalist forces of Richard III at the Battle of Bosworth. Henry ascends the throne of England as Henry VII; his marriage to Elizabeth of York, daughter of Edward IV, ends the Wars of the Roses.

1509   Henry VIII ascends the throne of England.

1533   Archbishop of Canterbury Thomas Cranmer convenes an ecclesiastical court at Dunstable Abbey to rule on Henry VIII's request for a divorce from Katherine of Aragon. The divorce is granted and Katherine informed while staying at Ampthill Castle. Henry marries Anne Boleyn.

c. 1535–1539   The Dissolution of the Monasteries occurs.

1536   Anne Boleyn is executed on charges of treason; Henry VIII weds wife number three, Jane Seymour.

1539   The fourth wife-to-be of Henry VIII, Anne of Cleves, arrives in England.

1540   Henry VIII marries (in January) and divorces (in July) Anne of Cleves and then marries (also in July) his fifth wife, Catherine Howard. Henry and Catherine were first married in June— before his marriage to Anne was declared officially "null and void"—in a secret ceremony at Hampton Court. (*It was a busy year for Henry.*)

1542   Catherine Howard is arrested at Hampton Court and charged with committing adultery. She is taken to the Tower of London, where she is executed after her trial and conviction.

1543   Henry VIII marries his sixth—and last—wife, Katherine Parr.

1547   Edward VI succeeds to the throne of England.

1553   Lady Jane Grey is declared Queen of England and reigns for nine days before the Crown is rightfully claimed by her cousin, Princess Mary Tudor.

1555   Nicholas Ridley, Bishop of Rochester, and Hugh Latimer, Bishop of Worcester, are burned at the stake in front of Balliol College in Oxford for their refusal to renounce Protestantism.

1556   Archbishop of Canterbury Thomas Cranmer is burned at the stake in front of Balliol College in Oxford for his refusal to renounce Protestantism.

1558   Elizabeth I succeeds to the throne of England; she receives the news at Hatfield House.

1564   William Shakespeare is born in Stratford-upon-Avon.

1587   Mary, Queen of Scots is executed at Fotheringhay Castle.

1603   Elizabeth I dies at Richmond Palace.

The Amateur Historian's Guide to
The Heart of England

CONTENTS

Getting There & Getting Organized

THE HEART OF ENGLAND

he nine counties encompassed in this book are known throughout Britain as "The Heart of England," and it's easy to see why. Not only are they centrally located, more or less in the middle of this sceptered isle, but there's an ambience in this region's scenery and hospitality that is genuinely heartwarming. As much as we knew in advance about the ancient sites that lay just north of London, we were continually surprised—and often elated—by how welcoming and engaging the Heart of England proved to be.

We are, however, London diehards. To us, London will always be the *true* "heart" of England. As we did in our last *Amateur Historian's Guide*, we used London as our home base when working on this book, leaving the capital city early in the morning, touring for a full day, and returning to London in time for

3

dinner. In some cases, this made for a very long day—you'll find several trips in this book where we encourage you to consider a night at an outlying ancient inn or B&B. In most cases, however, this "have it all" method works well, a perfect blend of bucolic countryside and cosmopolitan verve. A day of ancient history capped with 21st-century sophistication and a nightcap . . . what's not to love?

Tip!

Even though you theoretically will be moving "against traffic" when heading into the Heart of England, you will still encounter rush hour slowdowns in and around London. If you're intent on a full day of touring, our suggestion (*actually Sarah's suggestion; Carole recoils at the very idea*) is to depart London around 8:00 a.m. and plan to wind up at your last site no later than 4:00 p.m. Of course, if you're planning a light day, or have no particular schedule for returning to London at night, you can accommodate accordingly.

~~

Having said all that, let us begin with a few caveats. The first involves mode of travel. As you read this book, you'll see that we have grouped most of the sites into "day trips." Travel time to most sites is less than two hours (in many cases, much less) and some—though by no means *all*—of the attractions can be reached by train. If you're English, or if you're handy with a map and confident driving in a foreign country, heading off on your own by car is always an option, albeit one we've never tried. Typically, we engage the services of a car and driver. While we recognize this can be quite expensive, it's a luxury worth considering if you are traveling with several companions who can help share the cost, or if you have a specific deadline for returning to London—such as a 7:30 p.m. curtain for a *not-to-be-missed* play.

The second caution involves "quality" vs. "quantity." While we have never (*well, hardly ever*) seen a medieval or Tudor site we didn't at least *appreciate*, we have found there inevitably comes a point when even we suffer from historical overload. You can absorb and enjoy only so much before all those abbeys start to blur together and the castle ruins become interchangeable. These trips offer you a cornucopia of options, but trust us: you will find it far more pleasurable if you pick and choose among the sites, particularly if you face a busy evening back in London. We also recommend you build some "surprise" time into each day's touring, rather than scheduling visits back-to-back. Every day we stumbled across the unexpected—an ancient church, an inn, a shop, a pub or a friendly resident—and wished we had time to simply *linger*.

Whether you opt to "see it all," leaving no ancient stone unturned, or choose to venture outside of London to see just a few well-chosen diversions, we're certain you'll enjoy the varied delights that await you in the Heart of England.

BEFORE YOU LEAVE HOME
(assuming home is not England)

This book assumes that you will be traveling *to* London and using that city as your base from which to explore the Heart of England. Because you will want to have the maximum amount of time to enjoy medieval and Tudor sites—and the minimum amount of time consumed with in-London hassles—we offer you some tried-and-true advice to help your trip run smoothly. Years of London travel have proven that this system works for us. (*Friends and readers who have had the good judgment to take our words of wisdom to heart swear that it works for them, too!*)

~ Make your hotel reservations in advance

Trial and error have led us to the London hotel that works best for our needs, whether it be business or relaxation (*we take both very seriously*). If you are a regular visitor to London, you have probably found the hotel that suits your fancy. If not, there are plenty of travel books and websites that can help you find a London hotel to match your budget and preferences. The impor-

tant thing is to do this well in advance. London remains a tre-
mendously popular tourist destination, and it's not uncommon
to find "your" hotel booked months ahead of time. Making your
room reservations as early as possible not only gives you the widest choice of hotels, it also gives you immediate access to your
hotel's concierge service, which will help you with our next
two suggestions.

~ If you have a "must" on your restaurant list, book it now
If you do not hail from a big city, you may find this hard to believe, but trust us: many of London's most popular restaurants
fill their premium dining hours (7:30 p.m.–10:00 p.m.) weeks or
even months in advance. Keep some flexibility in your evening
plans—you don't want to have to race back from every day trip
just to *eat*. However, if a restaurant on your list has come highly
recommended—one you'll be bitterly disappointed not to experience—book it when you plan your trip. Chances are your hotel will be glad to make these reservations for you.

~ Purchase tickets for at least one performance ahead of time
Again, you do not want to fill every evening with written-
in-stone plans (*we've heard a rumor that spontaneity can be
fun . . .*). Still, if you feel your trip will be less than perfect without an evening at the hottest West End show, then by all means
buy in advance! Several great Internet services offer on-line theater tickets; we use *www.whatsonstage.com.* You can also call
the box office directly or prey upon your congenial hotel concierge when you make your room reservations.

Tip!

One of the primary attractions in this book is Stratford-upon-
Avon, home (at least for the time being) of the Royal Shakespeare Company. As you'll read, we firmly believe the primary
reason for any trip to Stratford is to enjoy a Shakespeare performance—but you *must* book your tickets for both matinee and
evening shows well in advance. To determine what's playing,

visit the R.S.C. website, *www.rsc.org.uk*, or call the box office, 01789-403403. You may be tempted to try your luck the day of the show, but we feel this is just too important to leave to chance!

~ Local currency

While it is not necessary to turn all of your cash into British currency before you leave home, you will want to have at least a day's worth of spending money in your wallet when you arrive in London. That can be at least £100, depending on your "day one" plans—more if you're traveling with "goody-hungry" children. Be sure to factor in transportation from the airport and tips for drivers and hotel staff.

Day trips into the Heart of England will require more cash (as opposed to "plastic") than a day in London. Whether you bring your pounds from home or acquire them in the UK is a matter of preference. If you are planning to bring traveler's checks, we highly recommend that you bring them in pounds sterling* rather than the currency of your homeland. Although *bureaus de change* and most banks will cash traveler's checks in foreign currency, many shops and restaurants do not. Be advised that most tellers will require you to present your passport when cashing traveler's checks. If the idea of jaunting around England, passport in hand (as opposed to secure in your hotel safe), makes you nervous, you will need to cash your traveler's checks before you depart London for the day or upon returning in the evening.

Nearly every London establishment takes credit cards, and the exchange rate usually works in your favor when you pay with plastic. However, as you venture from London, your need for ready cash increases. Many sites do not accept credit cards or large-denomination traveler's checks for entry fees. Likewise,

---

*As we were going to press, there was still some uncertainty about whether and when England would be converting to Eurodollars. We urge you to check with your local bank before departure and make the necessary adjustments when ordering your currency and traveler's checks.

many pubs and some ancient inns and eateries function on a cash-only basis.

Automatic teller machines abound in London and are not hard to find in most towns in the Heart of England, but we've run into a glitch with foreign ATMs and are reluctant to endorse them unreservedly. However, when they work properly, they can be a convenient way to obtain ready cash. If you choose to go this route, check to be sure that your bank card is recognized in foreign countries and that you have obtained — and memorized — your PIN in advance.

~ Pack wisely

Ah, there has been many a day when we wish we heeded that "pack wisely" advice! To us, packing wisely means bringing half of what we own and buying a matching amount in England — then whining about our overwhelming mountain of luggage. We know better, and so do you. But just to be on the safe side, let us run through our most commonsense suggestions.

* *Slightly upscale leisure clothes.* As you venture out of London by day, dress for comfort, particularly if ruins are on the agenda. By the same token, jeans that are *too* comfy and shorts that are *too* short are not the wisest choice if you're planning to visit a cathedral or privately owned manor home. There is not a dress code per se, but you will feel more at ease and be treated with more respect if you dress with respect.

* *At least one "smart" outfit for evening.* London is a cosmopolitan city, and attire — at least in the evening — tends to be "smart" rather than super-casual. Even if you're planning on spending the evening outside of London — perhaps in one of our suggested ancient inns — you'll want to bring along a nice outfit and change out of your "touring . . . clothes" before dinner.

* *Walking shoes — a pair and a spare.* Although we pride ourselves on clambering over ruins and rubble without ever resorting to "sensible shoes," this is not something we're

inclined to recommend! Many of the sites in this book
involve negotiating stone stairways that are exposed to
the elements. Surfaces can be slick and footing less than
secure. Your shoes should be comfortable for both standing
and walking. Take the time to find shoes that don't look like
they've run too many laps round the block and break them
in *ahead of time*. Also, since you are very likely to encounter wet weather, we recommend a spare pair of walking
shoes, unless yours are particularly waterproof.

• *Mad dogs and Englishmen.* Both may be able to ignore the
elements! You, on the other hand, will find it easier to scoff
at the inevitable rain if you've packed a waterproof wind-
breaker (preferably with a hood) and a well-made (i.e.,
wind-resistant) umbrella. (*However, unless you are native to
England, leave the "Wellies" at home!*) Should you forget—
or choose to ignore us—the gift shops at most sites sell
these, along with the ubiquitous can't-have-too-many-of-
them souvenir sweatshirts.

• A *lightweight pair of binoculars.* Why do we *always* forget
these? Particularly on the trips in this book, with so many
painted ceilings and intricately carved gargoyles, you'll
want to be able to get the closest possible look!

• A *roomy, collapsible tote.* We never leave home without this
extra piece of luggage because we always leave England
with *way* more than we carried upon arrival. If you have a
weakness for guidebooks, postcards, history tomes, biogra-
phies and free fliers (*not to mention funky jewelry and cute
shoes!*), trust us—you'll need a way to get those goodies
home. (*Much as we'd like to believe this book replaces the
need for all that extraneous literature, we know too well the
temptations of on-site bookshops.*)

• *Last, but not least, this book!* And if you're planning on
spending some of your days in London, you'll also want to
be sure to pack our first book in this series, *The Amateur Historian's Guide to Medieval & Tudor London.* You'll thank
us for that bit of self-serving promotion, believe us! We can

almost guarantee there are sites you've not stumbled upon and historical anecdotes you've not enjoyed—we're here to pass them along!

NOW THAT YOU'RE THERE, HOW TO GET *THERE*

No doubt about it—getting in and out of London was definitely easier when all one had to do was hop on your trusty steed and take to the old Roman road. Ah, well. Gone are those days . . . and so are the Robin Hoods, roving wolves and mud slides that were part and parcel of such convenience. In reality, travel from London to the Heart of England is really fairly easy. Here are some tips from those of us who've made it there—and back again!

* *Trains.* Each section of this book is divided into day trips and each assumes that London is your point of departure. Many, but not all, of these day trips have at least one anchor site that is accessible by train. For these sites, we've provided the station from which you'll depart London (Euston, Victoria, Paddington, etc.) as well as the name of the station for which you're bound. We have not provided you with train schedules or fares, however. These you can easily research on your own, once you've plotted your basic itinerary—that way you'll get the very latest information. The fastest and most efficient way to do this is via the Internet. Go to *www.raileurope.com* and click on Brit Rail, or visit *www.railtrack.co.uk*. Enter your departing city (i.e., London) and your destination (i.e., Oxford); you will be given all of the schedules for the day you wish to travel. Alternatively, you can call Brit Rail from home (in the USA, call 1-877-456-RAIL) or Rail Track when you arrive in London (020-7557-8000). Most hotel concierges also keep a current rail directory on hand, although we have yet to become adept at reading it.

Alas, in some cases, the primary town you are visiting is accessible by train, but the other sites you want to see are farther afield. You will need to use a taxi service for these trips. Most train stations have cab service on hand; all have phones from which you can dial the local cab company if no taxis are waiting.

Tip!

Unless you live in England—and perhaps even in that case—there is one site we suggest you *only* tackle via train: Reading. As you will read in that chapter, Reading is nearly impossible to navigate by car. Luckily, train service to Reading is frequent, and the trip there is relatively quick.

* *Motorcoach/bus.* Many sites are also accessible by motorcoach (upscale buses that run specialty tours to specific destinations) or by bus (by which we mean your basic public transportation). Since we have not tried this method of traveling in England, we have not generally provided motorcoach or bus details in this book. However, a relatively easy way to check it out, if you're interested, is to call the site . . . which we *always* urge you to do before you stop by, for reasons we explain later.

* *Car rental vs. car hire.* Some people don't think twice about landing at a foreign airport, hopping into a rental car and heading out on the motorway, armed with nothing more than great maps and a healthy dose of derring-do. We are not some of those people. We find that European drivers travel at breakneck speeds, which makes it rather dangerous to make a spur-of-the-moment stop when an ancient ruin (*or appealing pub*) catches your eye. Nor have we quite mastered that "opposite thing" England has going—not only do the cars travel in the left-hand lane, but the steering wheel is on the right-hand side of the car. We pre-

fer to sit back, check our manuscript and leave the driving to someone else. However, if you are one of those people who appreciate both the autonomy and the economy of driving yourself, go to it! We have provided you with the most direct route from London to each of the featured sites, using main arteries and the best-marked roadways. Still, you will want to invest in at least one — and possibly two — great maps. We recommend both the A–Z series, which produces regional as well as county guides, and the Great Britain Ordinance Survey. Both do a grand job of giving you landmarks and obscure markers that will help you get your bearings.

Another option is to hire a car and driver. Convenience is the advantage here — you will be picked up at your hotel, driven directly to the sites of your choice and returned to your hotel as close as possible to your specified time. Cost is the disadvantage. You can expect fees to run in the range of £30–£35 per hour, or a flat rate of about £225 for a full day of touring. Should you choose this method of travel, ask your hotel for recommendations. Most hotels have a service they use on a regular basis, although they may add a mark-up, so ask. Do not hesitate to request several recommendations so you can comparison shop. You can also use the Internet to search for firms. We used Google to search for "Car & Drivers, London," checked references, bartered bids and discovered a driver who was top-notch in every way. You can, too.

LEARN TO LOVE BRITISH TELECOM

You will note that almost every site in this book has a phone number (the exception being some ruins, a smattering of ancient churches and some ancient inns and eateries). USE IT! We cannot stress how important it is to get into the habit of calling sites ahead of time. The numbers we give you in this book are preceded by a zero (0); this is the number you will use when calling a site from London or anywhere else in England. If you wish to call from another country, drop the zero and add the international code and country code. For example, when calling from the USA, dial 011-44-(drop zero)-number.

Why is it important to call ahead? For several reasons. One is to verify opening hours. Although we have made every attempt to give you accurate, up-to-the-minute opening times, these can (and do!) change. Many a time we have stood before a locked gate or closed door and wished we'd made that simple call before leaving London. Another reason to call is to see whether any special events are occurring during your visit; they may dictate a change of plans. Festivals, reenactments, lectures, workshops, concerts and elementary school field trips are but a few of the "surprises" you might encounter at a site. Knowing about them ahead of time will allow you to join in—or avoid them. Perhaps you'll want to call and get details about bus or motorcoach service from London—most sites have this printed and will fax it to you at your hotel if you ask. Most staff also can give you directions on how to best travel from one site on your agenda to the next, provided these sites are fairly close to one another (and the sites in this book are). Finally, we have found the staff at sites throughout the Heart of England to be knowledgeable, helpful and genuinely enthused by amateur historians. If you call a site ahead of time, you may be able to arrange a special tour or gain access to a part of the property that's "officially" closed. With advance notice, most sites will try to accommodate your needs and interests.

INSIGHTS, ASIDES AND OTHER HANDY TIPS

~ Admission fees

For the sake of brevity, we have listed the basic adult and basic child admission for each attraction, *as we went to press*. Like open hours, these can and do change. We also have let you know if there is a "family ticket" or discounted admission for families. Please note, however, that every attraction seems to have a different policy on discounts (also known as "concessions") for seniors, students, group tours and visitors with special needs. Don't hesitate to ask at the ticket window—you may find you qualify for a concession that will save you a few pence over the price we quoted.

In addition, there are widely divergent policies on the age of a "child" (anything from over 3 to under 15 years of age) and what constitutes a family (two adults and two children, two adults and four children, etc.). You can pretty well assume that the price we quote is the highest price an adult or child would have to pay (as of the time of publication). In many cases, you'll be in for a pleasant surprise in the form of a lower-priced ticket!

You will want to note as well that although most churches do not officially charge an admission fee, a donation is both encouraged and appreciated. Let's face it: the cost of maintaining these ancient buildings is staggering. In most instances, we have found a donation of £2.00 per person is about right. The prices for church literature range from 50p to £1.50 per handout.

Finally, both **English Heritage** and the **National Trust** have overseas membership opportunities. Essentially, you make a donation to the organization and, depending on the amount of your contribution, you obtain reduced admission to several (or all) of the sites maintained by that group. For our purposes, these plans tend to include too many "après-Elizabeth" sites to be of value to us. However, if (*for some unfathomable reason*) your interests extend beyond the medieval and Tudor period, check it out. From the USA, call 011-44-333-1182 for English Heritage's member services department or check the website, *www.english-heritage.org.uk*. The National Trust's Royal Oak Foundation for American members can be contacted at 1-800-913-6565 or at *www.royal-oak.org*. The National Trust website address is *www.nationaltrust.org.uk*.

~ Open hours

Let us be *very* clear: the farther you go from London, the more "flexible" the open hours . . . that's our euphemism for wildly inconsistent. We've had more than a small number of disappointments after showing up at a site with clearly posted open hours, only to find the gates shut tight. On the other hand, we've also happened by sites that supposedly were closed (and in one rare case, supposedly "vanished"!) only to find them . . . open! We've visited castles where the portcullis started to groan threateningly because it was a) raining, b) dusky, c) within an hour of the posted closing time for that day. Some sites close if a large group—say, a wedding or a conference—has booked the facility for a special function. And due to the age of all these sites, closures for maintenance are not uncommon. We don't mean to sound negative—we're *hugely* grateful that these sites are open at all! However, if there is a site you simply must see, we recommend you call in advance—both when planning your itinerary and again before you depart London.

With regard to holidays, it is safe to assume that all sites are closed on December 24 and 25; most sites are closed on Good Friday, Easter Sunday and New Year's Day as well. Then there's the maddening issue of Bank Holiday Mondays. Some sites that are typically closed on Mondays are open on Bank Holiday Mondays. Others that are usually open on Mondays are closed due to the holiday. All together now: "CALL IN ADVANCE!"

Here are some rules of thumb that will help you as you start to plan your trip. Generally, most attractions in England have "summer" hours and "winter" hours. The summer season tends to stretch from Easter Monday through mid to late October. Winter hours are generally in effect from November 1 through Easter. In almost every instance, historic attractions (and Tourist Information Centres) are open more days of the week, for longer hours each day, during the summer.

You will note we have not included the open hours for Tourist Information Centres. By and large, they follow their "hometown's" business hours. Weekend hours may be more limited. All Tourist Information Centres post their hours; if you arrive too early, check back later in the day.

Tip!

Despite the stated "closing" hour, last admission to many sites is actually one hour before closing. That means if a site "closes" at 5:00 p.m., the latest you will be admitted may well be 4:00 p.m. Plan accordingly!

~~

~ House and garden

We make no bones about it—the great outdoors, by and large, is not our cup of tea. However, many of our readers are fascinated by English gardens, and many of the manor homes listed in this book boast the most beautiful gardens you'll ever see. Often, the gardens of a manor home open earlier and remain open later than the house itself. Also, in some cases there is a discount ticket for those who only care to stroll the grounds. The hours and prices we include in this book are for the house or the combined house/garden package. Should you be interested in seeing only the flora and fauna, check the policy when you call ahead (*which we know you'll most certainly do!*).

~ Churches

In your travels, you will certainly happen upon a host of churches with medieval traces that are not mentioned in this book. Consider them a bonus—particularly if you can gain access! The Heart of England abounds with ancient churches, many, many more than we could possibly list . . . or you could possibly visit. Most are open on an extremely limited basis, if at all. Nor is showing up on Sunday, hoping to join the service, necessarily the answer. In towns with more than one church, the churches tend to split their worship schedules, with one offering weekday service and the other Sunday service. (*We stum-*

bled upon one church that served as both a Roman Catholic and an Anglican house of worship. We can only imagine the later Tudors' reaction to that!) Of course, we have not given ancient churches short shrift. We have included compelling churches, close to primary sites, where the history, the architecture or the access is out of the ordinary.

ANCIENT INNS AND EATERIES

Okay, okay, we admit it! We love our history, but we're rather partial to our cushy Knightsbridge hotel and the cosmopolitan cuisine (*not to mention the vodka cosmopolitans*) of London. After a long day of sightseeing, we're more than ready for the 21st century. We realize, however, that many of you can't get enough of all things medieval and Tudor. For you, we have nosed around and come up with a list of B&Bs, country hotels, inns, pubs and restaurants where you can indulge in a total immersion experience. We are confident you'll enjoy every minute. At the end of most sections, you'll find a list of **Ancient Inns and Eateries**. These are establishments where at least *part* of the public areas dates from the Middle or Tudor Ages. In cases where we have actually experienced the hospitality on offer, we indicate as much, waxing eloquent . . . as we are prone to do. In the vast number of cases, however, we have NOT visited the listed establishments. Therefore, please don't assume that a listing in this book is a "Sarah and Carole" endorsement of the spot. It is not. Much as we pride ourselves on our, ahem, finely tuned sensibilities, we are amateur historians, *not* hotel/restaurant critics.

If you are keen on an even more in-depth "slice of life" experience and your vacation schedule allows, be sure to check out the many intriguing overnight accommodations operated by the **Landmark Trust**. The Trust maintains a host of ancient buildings where you can spend an evening or a week, depending on the property. None of these facilities offers meals; "self-catering" (you shop, you cook, you clean up . . .

or you find a restaurant in town) is the name of the game. Still, the chance to stay in close-to-original period surroundings is one you may not want to miss. To obtain listings, prices and terms, you must purchase the Trust's guidebook, which costs about $25. In the USA, phone 1-802-254-6868 or go to *www.landmarktrust.co.uk.*

Tip!

We have encountered some B&Bs that do not have in-room or public phones for their guests. If it is important for you to be available by phone, check the policy before checking in. A cell phone with an international calling plan should solve this problem.

CAROLE AND SARAH'S GREATEST HITS

For those of you with limited touring time or who want only to dip a little into the medieval and Tudor treasures of the Heart of England, we offer up our very subjective list of *not-to-be-missed* sites. One of the joys for us in writing this book was that most of the trips offer a cornucopia of attractions that run the gamut of the Middle and Tudor Ages. However, we recognize that such a wide swath is not everyone's cup of tea. We also found common threads running through the trips that historically linked sites in one area with those in another. Therefore, we decided to pull together some of these particular attractions in "theme" trips. We hope this will make it easier for those of you with special interest in a particular period or person to enjoy your visit to the Heart of England.

~ Best close-in day trip . . .
No doubt about it—go to **Windsor Castle**. It's just a half hour train ride from London, and we can't say enough good things about it. It's one of our very favorite spots in England.

~ Castle crazed . . .

If you truly love castles, add **Kenilworth** to your itinerary. The ruins are extensive and very evocative; the history is incredible.

~ Best cathedral . . .

St. Albans is our candidate here. It is a beautiful and deeply moving place. We lingered much longer than we had intended on our visit because it was difficult to tear ourselves away.

~ A night out of town . . .

If you're looking to escape the city for a night, we recommend you combine a trip to **Oxford** with an overnight stay at **The Mill and Old Swan Hotel in Minster Lovell**. You really need two days to truly appreciate all the medieval and Tudor wonders of Oxford. Close-by Minster Lovell is too special to be missed and makes for a nice bucolic break from the more intense atmosphere of Oxford.

~ So you're a Richard III fanatic?

The Heart of England is crammed with sites connected to Richard III, starting with **Minster Lovell Hall** and **The Mill and Old Swan Hotel** mentioned above. Richard visited his good friend, Francis Lovell, at Minster Lovell Hall. His retainers stayed at The Mill and Old Swan Hotel, and the hotel boasts some interesting graffiti associated with that visit. Other sites in this book with Richardian connections include **Warwick Castle, the city of Leicester, Bosworth Battlefield** (*of course*), **St. Mary Fotheringhay** and **Fotheringhay Castle ruins**.

~ Forget medieval, let's go Tudor!

Although we are loathe to admit it, we do recognize that some amateur historians are devoted to the Tudors rather than the Middle Ages. Just for you, we have put together a list of the major sites in this book with Tudor affiliations. **Windsor Castle** is an absolute *must* for you; Henry VIII is buried in **St. George's**

Chapel, along with Jane Seymour. Close to Windsor is **Donnington Castle**, once a favorite of Elizabeth. If you've got a full day to devote to your Tudor passion, we suggest you take in the Warwick trip, which is packed with Tudor memorabilia, including **Lord Leycester Hospital, Beauchamp Chapel at St. Mary's Collegiate Church, Kenilworth Castle** and **Baddesley Clinton Hall**. With more time to tour, other sites you can add to your itinerary include **Greys Court, Christ Church College and Cathedral** and **St. Mary the Virgin Church in Oxford, Stratford-upon-Avon, Bradgate Country Park, Castle Ashby, Holdenby House, Boughton House, Kirby Hall, Fotheringhay Castle, Dunstable Abbey,** and **Hatfield House**.

~ Feeling spiritual?

One of our great passions in tracing the history of the Middle and Tudor Ages is visiting the many ancient churches and abbeys with links to this period that abound in England. (*We have to admit, however, that we occasionally do run out of adjectives to describe wondrous corbels when we've hit the fourth or fifth church of the day.*) This book is chockablock with magnificent ones. For those of you who share this interest in ancient religious establishments, we have put together a list of those that are unique and have such special features that they count as *not-to-be-missed* attractions. Combined in a theme trip, they would make for a truly rewarding venture into the Heart of England.

- *St. Mary the Virgin Parish Church* in Ewelme; burial site of Alice de la Pole, granddaughter of Geoffrey Chaucer
- *Dorchester Abbey*, good-quality medieval wall paintings and a wealth of other medieval treasures
- *St. Peter ad Vincula*, South Newington, one of the most outstanding collections of medieval wall paintings in England
- *Beauchamp Chapel at St. Mary's Collegiate Church*, Warwick, burial site of Robert Dudley, Earl of Leicester and other noble notables

- *Dunstable Abbey*, site of the ecclesiastical court that declared the marriage of Henry VIII and Katherine of Aragon "null and void"
- *Elstow Abbey*, founded by a niece of William the Conqueror
- *St. Albans Cathedral*, a truly magnificent and very spiritual place

OXFORDSHIRE, BERKSHIRE

NORTHAMPTONSHIRE

WARWICKSHIRE

⌂ Sulgrave Manor

Banbury •

Broughton
Castle ♜

BUCKINGHAMSHIRE

• Chipping Norton

Key

♯ Cathedral
⌂ Abbey or Priory
♜ Castle
⌂ Notable building or structure

This map provided for orientation purposes only.
You will need to acquire a detailed roadmap of
The Heart of England if you plan to drive.

Minster Lovell Hall ⌂

• Witney

• Oxford

Dorchester
Abbey ⌂   Ewelme •

• Abingdon

0 Miles   5
0 Kilometers 8

Wallingford Castle ♜

⌂ Grey's Court

• Maple Durham

• Reading

Windsor Castle ♜
Eton

⌂ Dorney
Court

WILTSHIRE

Donnington ♜
Castle

SURREY

HAMPSHIRE

Berkshire & Oxfordshire

CONTENTS

Windsor

Majesty and Matriculation

e are very pleased that Windsor and Eton are the first trip in this book. This is one of our favorite day trips from London. It is close and convenient; travel time is just over a half hour and train service is frequent. The sites and history are superb, and there are several interesting restaurants listed in Ancient Inns and Eateries. So hop on a train and travel back in time for a day visit to the largest and one of the most majestic medieval castles in England, a spectacular church with a treasure trove of medieval and Tudor tombs, and one of the country's oldest private boys' schools housed in a host of ancient buildings.

✺

 ## Royal Windsor Information Centre/ Town and Crown Exhibition

Windsor High Street
Windsor

>>>

PHONE
 01753-743900

LOCATED
 22 miles west of London; M4 to junction 6 to A355; second exit onto A308; or M3, junction 3

TRAVEL
 Frequent train service from Paddington and Waterloo stations; travel time is approximately 35 minutes. Bus service (Green Line) from Victoria Station.

OPEN
Daily, year-round

ADMISSION
£1.00 Adults
50p Children

TIP!
If you want to enjoy the towns of Windsor and Eton on wheels rather than by foot, guided tours on double-decker buses are available. For information, contact the Guide Friday Head Office in Stratford-upon-Avon; phone 01789-294466; e-mail *info@guidefriday.com*.
>>>

✝ Windsor Castle

>>>
PHONE
01753-831118

E-MAIL
windsorcastle@royalcollection.org.uk

OPEN
9:45 a.m.–5:15 p.m. daily, March–October
9:45 a.m.–4:15 p.m. daily, November–February

ADMISSION
£11.50 Adults
£6.00 Children
£9.50 Seniors
Family ticket available

CONVENIENCES
Gift shops in each ward; guided grounds tour every half hour
>>>

The roots of Windsor Castle's history are deep indeed, reaching all the way back to the mists of Camelot, when King Arthur and his knights of the Round Table were alleged to have met regularly at Windsor. In fact, they supposedly conducted their sessions on chivalry on the site now occupied by the Round Keep, an 80-foot-high tower dominating the castle's landscape.

Whatever the truth of the Arthurian legend, it is fact that the Saxons had a castle on the site high above the River Thames and that William the Conqueror was quick to realize its strategic importance after the Norman Conquest in 1066. He had a castle built here in about 1070, approximately 3 miles upstream from the old Saxon palace, to guard the western approach to London. This was one of nine fortresses ringing London that William had built to make sure those independent-minded and unruly Londoners would stay conquered. His "ring-around-London" castles were about 20 miles apart and each was within a day's march of the City.

The Conqueror's castle at Windsor was enlarged and expanded by his successors. Henry II greatly increased its strength by rebuilding it in stone, starting sometime between 1166 and 1170. Edward III "modernized" the palace with a major reconstruction program in 1344. That consummate redesigner of palaces, Henry VIII, also left his mark on Windsor: he replaced the main gateway and, of course, named it for himself.

The basic layout and design of the castle you see today were

☛ Did you know?

Birthplace of Edward III (b. November 13, 1312), Windsor also was his favorite castle. He spent a great deal of time here, making it the site of many of his festive Christmas and Easter courts, spending lavish amounts on reconstruction and refurbishment and lodging his highest-ranking prisoners in the Norman Tower. It may even have been Windsor and its associations with the Arthurian legends that inspired Edward (who rather fancied himself as a 14th-century King Arthur) to found the Order of the Garter, a chivalric fraternity that rewarded knights for their brave and gracious behavior.

created by these monarchs. You will find traces of them—and other medieval and Tudor monarchs—scattered throughout the palace's buildings and grounds. Unfortunately, many changes have stripped away large amounts of the medieval and Tudor features. George III and George IV were especially vigilant at "improving" Windsor Castle. A 1992 fire caused heavy damage to many of the castle's state apartments, but the restoration efforts that followed that catastrophe also uncovered some original medieval work and clues to daily life in the Middle Ages.

Windsor is the largest castle in England, covering more than 13 acres. It remains a principal residence of British sovereigns, just as it has been for the past 900 years. There is much to see and do at Windsor Castle, so put on your most comfortable walking shoes and prepare to have a great time.

Tip!

The Union Jack flies from the Round Tower unless the Queen is in residence. Her standard flies then.

THE CASTLE LAYOUT

Windsor Castle is divided into three areas—the Lower, Middle and Upper Wards. Most of what is of interest to the medieval and Tudor enthusiast is located in the Middle and Lower Wards, but there are a few structures and items of note from our period in the Upper Ward.

You'll enter the castle grounds through St. George's Gate into the outer bailey of the Middle Ward. On your right is the Edward III Tower, which was greatly modified during the renovation projects of the latter half of the first millennium. Next, you will pass through an exhibit about the castle's history. (*We particularly liked that one of the early panels in the exhibit is entitled "Laying the Foundation," a chapter in both of our earlier books. Too bad we didn't copyright that phrase!*) The exit from the exhibit puts you on a path to tour the Middle Ward first.

◆ ◆ ◆ ◆ ◆ ◆ ◆ ◆ ◆ ◆ ◆ ◆ ◆ ◆ ◆ ◆ ◆ ◆ ◆

☞ **Did you know?**

It was during a Christmas court at Windsor Castle in 1126–1127 that King Henry I, who had no legitimate male heir, tried to force his barons to accept his daughter, Matilda, as his successor. *The Anglo-Saxon Chronicles* reported "there he caused archbishops and bishops and abbots and earls and all the thegns that were there to swear to give England and Normandy after his death into the hand of his daughter." Swear they did, but they weren't happy about it. None of these men was interested in being the first in England and France to owe allegiance to a woman monarch. So the stage was set at that Christmas court at Windsor for a 19-year-long bloody struggle for the throne that tore England apart after Henry's death.

◆ ◆ ◆ ◆ ◆ ◆ ◆ ◆ ◆ ◆ ◆ ◆ ◆ ◆ ◆ ◆ ◆ ◆ ◆

~ The Middle Ward

As you enter the castle grounds, turn to your left and find the Henry III Tower, constructed in the early 13th century. On either side of the doorway of this tower, you will see stone bosses representing Henry III and his consort, Eleanor of Provence. Henry's shield is above the doorway.

Across the path from the Henry III Tower is the Store Tower (*we found it amusing that this tower now houses one of the castle gift shops*). Behind that is the Winchester Tower, built in the 1170s by King Henry II to serve as the official royal residence and Great Hall (as opposed to the private apartments located in the Upper Ward) and then rebuilt by William of Wykeham in 1357–1358 as part of Edward III's "modernization" program. The stone wall that runs between the Winchester Tower and the Norman Gate to the Upper Ward was part of Henry II's defensive strengthening of the castle. The tower in the middle of the wall, called the Magazine Tower, was added by Edward III, who also built the Norman Gate, complete with portcullis, and tower to guard the Upper Ward, where the royal apartments were located. The Governor of Windsor Castle still lives in the Norman Tower. The room above the arch in the gate was used as a prison in medieval times. It must have provided

> ♦ ♦ ♦ ♦ ♦ ♦ ♦ ♦ ♦ ♦ ♦ ♦ ♦ ♦ ♦ ♦ ♦ ♦ ♦
> ☞ Did you know?
> King John of France was captured by the Black Prince at the Battle of Poitiers in 1356. His ransom of £50,000, an enormous sum at the time, provided the funding for the lavish refurbishment of Windsor Castle.
> ♦ ♦ ♦ ♦ ♦ ♦ ♦ ♦ ♦ ♦ ♦ ♦ ♦ ♦ ♦ ♦ ♦ ♦ ♦

special accommodations because among the notable prisoners confined there were three kings — John of France and David II of Scotland (both prisoners of Edward III) and James I of Scotland. James spent 11 years at Windsor during his 18-year sojourn (1406–1424) as a prisoner of the English Crown.

Next to the Norman Gate and Tower is the Round Tower, the dominant feature of the Middle Ward, which is surrounded by a deep moat that has been converted into a lovely garden. The moat was dug in the 1070s, and the dirt from the ditch was used to build the mound on which the Round Tower sits. The first castle was a typical wooden motte-and-bailey Norman structure. Henry II replaced that with a stone keep, building the lower half of the structure you see today. George IV added another 30 feet to the top in the 1820s. Edward III actually lived in this tower for a short time in the mid-14th century while his royal lodgings were being renovated.

~ The Upper Ward

As you pass through the Norman Gate, look to your left to find a building constructed by Elizabeth I in 1583. Tudor roses decorate the front of the building and Elizabeth's initials are carved above the entrance to the "loo" and the path to the State Apartments tour. (*We'll warn you right now that there is little—if anything—on this tour to excite amateur historians dedicated to medieval and Tudor history.*) The most interesting feature of this building is a large gallery on the first floor that Elizabeth used during the winter for daily exercise; she was a fitness fanatic, dedicated to maintaining her health through vigorous walking as well as other forms of exercise.

Henry VII added the building's next section, up to the Side Door, in the 1480s. Now the site of the Royal Library, this section is not open to the public. Look for the Welsh dragons and fleurs-de-lis that decorate this building. To the side of the library, at Engine Court, is the King John Tower, a comparatively undisturbed medieval structure.

The private quarters of all Britain's kings and queens have al-

> **☞ Did you know?**
>
> Edward IV was a great reader and bibliophile. When his collection became too large to be transported conveniently during the court's frequent moves, Edward had the books stored at Windsor, creating the foundation for the castle's Royal Library.

> **☞ Did you know?**
>
> Henry VI was born at Windsor Castle at 4:00 p.m. on December 6, 1421, despite the fact that Henry V had ordered his queen, Katherine of Valois, not to go to Windsor for her lying-in. Henry was fearful of a prophecy that foretold "Henry of Windsor shall long reign and lose all"—a prophecy that was indeed fulfilled.

ways been in the Upper Ward of Windsor Castle. Henry II and Henry III both built stone buildings to house their families and retainers and Edward III expanded those facilities. Little is left of these medieval quarters today. Charles II had the living quarters largely rebuilt, then George IV carried out a major reconstruction program. Most everything that is open to the public in the State Apartments dates from later periods of history. It's grand and glorious, but not our cup of tea. The only thing of interest to us inside the buildings is the gargantuan suit of armor made for Henry VIII c. 1540 on display on the Grand Staircase. One wonders how he was ever able to mount a horse wearing that ton of metal. Incidentally, the staircase was built on the site of a medieval herb garden.

~ The Lower Ward

In addition to St. George's Chapel, several other buildings in the Lower Ward were constructed by medieval or Tudor monarchs. The wall that encloses this outer bailey was built as part of Henry II's expansion plan in the 1220s.

The oldest structure in this part of the castle grounds is the Curfew Tower, built by Henry III in the 1220s. The building is pretty much as it was then, complete with an awesome dungeon with a vaulted ceiling and

◆ ◆
☞ Did you know?
The Windsor Castle built by Henry II was a strong defensive castle that withstood siege many times, thrice in particular when it was under the control of King John. The first time it happened, John wasn't king yet. He was holding the castle as Count of Mortain and using it as a focal point for his efforts to stir up opposition to his brother, Richard the Lionheart, who was being held captive in Germany. Forces loyal to the king tried to coerce John into yielding the castle, but in the end it was John's mother, the powerful Eleanor of Aquitaine, who coaxed him out. The second siege came after John retreated to Windsor following the signing of Magna Carta at Runnymede and then reneged on the deal, causing his barons to break out into open rebellion. John held out at Windsor for three months before an end to the siege was negotiated. The third and final assault also occurred during the barons' revolt against John. Windsor was one of the few major strong points to hold firm for the king. That siege ended when John died and opposition to Henry III's assumption of the Crown melted away.
◆ ◆

13-foot-thick walls. The tower also contains eight bells from St. George's Chapel, moved here in 1477. Unfortunately, the Curfew Tower is not accessible to the public because it is located at the far end of the Horseshoe Cloister, which provides housing for castle staff. The cloister was built in 1478–1481 by Edward IV to provide offices and quarters for people associated with the College of St. George and the Order of the Garter. The conical roof of the Curfew Tower, added in 1863, can be spied above the buildings on the ground, but is best viewed as you walk around the outside of the castle walls.

Another building that is inaccessible because it is located on the other side of the Horseshoe Cloister is the Chapter Library, built in 1415 by Henry IV. Originally, the building served as a dining room for chapel clergy living in Horseshoe Cloister. Supposedly, this is where Shakespeare debuted *Merry Wives of Windsor* for the pleasure of Queen Elizabeth.

Across from St. George's Chapel is the Mary Tudor Tower. As you leave the Lower Ward, you will exit Windsor Castle through the King Henry VIII Gate, built in 1511. For your last glimpse of the medieval

* *
☞ Did you know?

Most likely, it was in the Curfew Tower dungeon that King John confined Matilda de Braose and her son Will and left them to starve to death in 1210. Matilda was the wife of William de Braose, a powerful baron from the Welsh Marches. De Braose was once John's close confidant and in a position to know the truth about the disappearance of Prince Arthur of Brittany. John's one-time rival to the throne of England, Prince Arthur was captured in battle and imprisoned by John in 1202. He vanished sometime in the next year.

A few years after the prince's disappearance, public rumors were rife that John had killed Arthur, and the king suddenly turned on de Braose. As a symbol of de Braose's good faith, John demanded hostages and was enraged when Matilda refused to surrender them, saying publicly that the king could not be trusted because he had killed Arthur. When Matilda and her son eventually fell into John's hands, he had them imprisoned in Windsor Castle and left them alone without food or water for 13 days. He was making sure that Matilda would tell no one what she knew—or thought she knew—about the disappearance of Prince Arthur.

* *

and Tudor history of the castle, look above the arch for a panel embossed with the Tudor rose and the pomegranate emblem of Katherine of Aragon.

✺

☩ St. George's Chapel
Lower Ward, Windsor Castle

>>

OPEN
   10:00 a.m.–4:00 p.m. Monday–Saturday, year-round

WORSHIP
   Sunday
      8:30 a.m. Holy Communion
      10:45 a.m. Matins with sermon
      11:45 a.m. Eucharist
      5:15 p.m. Evensong
   Weekdays
      7:30 a.m. Matins
      8:00 a.m. Holy Communion
      5:15 p.m. Evensong

ADMISSION
   Free of charge

CONVENIENCES
   Bookshop; special guidebook for children

>>

If you are like us and one of your major thrills in life is tracking down ancient dead kings, then you are going to enjoy St. George's Chapel. There's a real treasure trove here, including the grand prize for you Tudor fanatics—Henry VIII. He is buried here alongside wife number three, Jane Seymour, mother of Henry's only surviving male heir, the future Edward VI. Here also you will find the tombs of Edward IV and Henry VI, the champions of the White Rose of York and the Red Rose of Lancaster during the Wars of the Roses. Also to be found, at least in spirit, is Edward III, whose colossal battle sword, measuring 6 feet, 8 inches long, hangs on the wall of the south quire aisle.*

The College of St. George, of which the chapel is the focal point, was founded in 1348 by Edward III. Inspired by the legends of the search for the Holy Grail by King Arthur and his knights of the Round Table, Edward had established the Order of the Garter that year to reward his knights for displays of bravery and chivalry. When he cast about for a spiritual home for his new order, he settled on

••••••••••••••••••••••
☞ Did you know?

In 1416, the Emperor Sigismund presented the "heart" of St. George to the Chapel of St. George when he was installed as a Knight of the Garter.
••••••••••••••••••••••••

Windsor Castle and the chapel that had been built there in 1240, most likely because of the site's Arthurian connections. The name of the chapel was derived from the dedication of the Order of the Garter to St. George, England's patron saint. The insignia of knights who have been invested in the Order of the Garter since the 14th century line the panels of the Garter Stalls in the chapel quire. Investitures in the Order are still held here in an elaborate ceremony conducted every year on Monday during Ascot Week in June.

From its beginnings, the College of St. George has been entirely self-supporting, governed by a dean and canons who have a freehold to the chapel and its associated buildings and who are responsible only to the reigning monarch. The College of St. George was exempted by the Pope in 1352 from diocesan and provincial authority. This makes St. George's Chapel a "royal peculiar," one of a very elite handful of churches in England.

Construction of the church you see today began in 1475. During a lull in the Wars of the Roses, Edward IV decided to

---

*As usual with churches that have been in continuous use for centuries, there are many tombs (several of more recent kings and queens of Great Britain) and other features in St. George's that are not related to our favorite period of history. Again, as usual, we are skipping a recitation of these items, but you can peruse them, if you are so inclined, with the help of on-site brochures and maps as you wander through this magnificent church.

build a new, grander chapel at Windsor that would serve as his mausoleum. He put Richard Beauchamp, Bishop of Salisbury, in charge of the project. Unfortunately, Edward failed to predict how quickly he was going to need that tomb; he died in 1483 at the age of 41. The resumption of the Wars of the Roses that followed his death slowed construction of the new chapel. It was not until 1528, during the reign of Henry VIII, that the church was completed. The resulting structure is considered to be a masterpiece of late Perpendicular architecture. It is also a beautiful, reverential space.

While the building itself dates from the late 15th and early 16th centuries, don't be fooled by the outside decor. The gargoyles, grotesques and King's Beasts that can be seen on the south front exterior are mostly reproductions of original medieval designs. The statues of kings along the wall, dating from 1882–1883, are meant to represent (from east to west) Henry III, Edward III, Henry VI, Edward IV, Henry VII, Henry VIII, Charles I, George III and Bishop Beauchamp (he's the one holding the model of the church). On the lower wall of the third bay from the west, look for Edward IV's badge with a crucifix, rose and sun rays, one of the few original pieces of medieval art you will find on the outside of the chapel.

> ◆◆◆◆◆◆◆◆◆◆◆◆◆◆◆◆◆◆◆◆◆◆◆◆◆
>
> **☞ Did you know?**
>
> A "college" in the Middle Ages was defined as a group of secular clergy and laymen who lived communally and assumed responsibility for maintenance of a "collegiate" church. Today, there are only two such colleges within the Church of England—the College of St. Peter at Westminster and the College of St. George.
>
> ◆◆◆◆◆◆◆◆◆◆◆◆◆◆◆◆◆◆◆◆◆◆◆◆◆

On the inside, it's a different story. Badges, arms, symbols and signs of Edward IV, Henry VII and Henry VIII are scattered throughout the building on the ceiling, walls and windows. So are the badges and arms of Sir Reginald Bray, who contributed the money to complete construction of the chapel. The brilliant colors of the ceiling bosses also are original.

As you enter the chapel, you will be guided down the south nave aisle, where you will find the Beaufort Chantry. This chapel was founded in 1506 by Charles Somerset, Lord Herbert, who later became the first Earl of Worcester. Charles's claim to fame is that he was a bastard son of Henry Beaufort, Duke of Somerset, who was a descendant of John of Gaunt and a staunch supporter of the Lancastrian cause in the Wars of the Roses. The earl died in 1526 and it is his effigy, along with that of his wife Elizabeth, that you see on the tomb in the chapel. The screen surrounding the tomb dates from 1517. The words on the door translate as "I scorn vacillation and cowardice," which became a Somerset family motto.

Across the nave is the Urswick Chapel, founded in 1494 as a chantry, but endowed in 1507 in honor of Christopher Urswick, dean of the chapel at the time and a close friend of Henry VII. Urswick was instrumental in bringing about the culminating event of the Wars of the Roses—the marriage of Henry VII and Edward IV's daughter Elizabeth, thus uniting the Houses of Lancaster and York and ending the 32-year power struggle. Henry VII's badge can be found above the door of the chapel.

◆◆◆◆◆◆◆◆◆◆◆◆◆◆◆◆◆◆◆◆◆

☞ Did you know?

The tomb that dominates the Urswick Chapel today is not from our period of history. It is the tomb of Princess Charlotte, whose death in childbirth in the 19th century cleared the way for Victoria to inherit the throne.

◆◆◆◆◆◆◆◆◆◆◆◆◆◆◆◆◆◆◆◆◆

The next chapel you will encounter is the Rutland Chapel, founded in 1481 as a chantry by Sir Thomas St. Leger and his wife Anne, sister of Edward IV and Richard III. The tomb in the center is that of their only daughter, Anne, and her husband, George Manners, the 11th Lord Roos (d. 1513). On the north wall of the tomb is a copper memorial to the St. Legers and a brass one to Robert Honeywode, a canon of Windsor from 1504 to 1522.

Stone bosses in the ceiling of the north quire aisle represent Edward the Confessor; St. George; the badge of Thomas, Earl of Arundel; the royal arms; Edward IV; and the Yorkist rose surrounded by sun rays. Also depicted is the badge of Edward IV's close friend William, Lord Hastings (you know, the guy who lost his head on the green at the Tower of London in 1483 because he ticked off Richard III during a council meeting; we tell you all about him in our tour of Leicestershire). Lord Hastings is buried (*presumably with his head*) in the chapel named for him. The paintings in that chapel date from about 1490 and tell the story of St. Stephen, the first Christian martyr.

Close by the Hastings Chapel is the tomb of Edward IV and his consort, the notorious Elizabeth Woodville. The tomb was wrecked during the Commonwealth and then accidentally broken open when the aisle was being repaved in 1789. King and queen were reburied and covered with a black marble panel. Behind the tomb in the quire are ornate wrought-iron gates designed in 1482 to protect the king's grave. They give some hint of the fantastic design of the original tomb.

Between the Hastings Chapel and Edward IV's tomb is a window depicting the genealogy of the House of York. Across from the tomb is a piece of the font used in the baptism of Edward III, who was born at Windsor. In front of the tomb is a marble slab marking the graves of George, Duke of Bedford, and Mary, one of Edward and Elizabeth's daughters, who died in 1482.

Just behind Edward and Elizabeth's tomb is the Edward IV Chantry, built in the quire at the direction of Edward's will as a place from which priests could pray for his soul. (*He was planning on a long stint in purgatory.*) Henry VIII adapted the structure as a gallery with an ornate Tudor window from which wife number one, Katherine of Aragon, could watch the Garter ceremonies.

In the middle of the floor of the quire is Henry VIII's tomb. (*You were wondering when we were going to get there, weren't you?*) And we're not kidding, it's

• •
☞ Did you know?

Edward IV and Lord Hastings certainly were close friends. They were boon companions, drinking and carousing buddies who not only shared food and wine (*and plenty of it!*), but mistresses as well. The most infamous of these, thanks to reports written by Sir Thomas More, was "Jane" (real name Elizabeth) Shore. Supposedly Edward's favorite mistress (More wrote, "For many he had, but her he loved . . ."), Jane transferred her favors to friend William after Edward's death. (*Maybe they were just trying to console each other for the loss of their party pal.*)
• •

in the floor, covered with a black marble slab. It didn't even have a marker until the mid-19th century. Not only that, but Henry is sharing it with his favorite wife, Jane Seymour, and another king—Charles I, the one who was beheaded and was a Stewart, not a Tudor. How insulting is that for a man who had such a monumental impact on history?

The problem started when Henry died before his tomb was ready. He had intended to use costly and lavish materials, "confiscated" from Cardinal Wolsey, to create a memorial for himself in what is now the Albert Memorial Chapel. But the tomb wasn't finished before he died, so Henry directed in his will that his body be buried beside that of Jane, who was already interred in the floor of the quire at St. George's. No one ever got around to finishing the planned elaborate tomb and moving the body. Apparently, the filial devotion of Henry's children did not extend to constructing a "fitting" memorial for their father. (*Or maybe they did think that spending eternity in the floor before the altar was the appropriate spot for their oh-so-loving and concerned parent.*) Eventually, the partially completed tomb was destroyed and Henry was left in the floor of the quire.

Once you have finished ogling Henry's tomb, look around at the quire. The stalls that line both sides are a riot of color and pageantry with the banners, helms and crests of the knights who have been invested in the Order of the Garter since the 14th century. Most of the woodwork in the quire dates from the late 15th century, except for the organ loft and two stalls at the end, which date from the time of George III. Some of the most interesting carvings are on the arms and backs of the stalls' seats.

As you leave the quire, look straight ahead and admire the brilliant West Window. Most of the stained glass dates from the early 15th century. Figures depicted in the glass include Edward III, Edward IV and Henry VII. Henry VII's arms are carved in stone at the top of the window.

On display in front of the rood screen is a misericord dating from c. 1478. The elaborate wood carving depicts the meeting between Edward IV and Louis XI of France to finalize a peace treaty in August 1475.

The Bray Chantry, burial place of Sir Reginald Bray (d. 1503), a close friend of Henry VII who ensured that St. George's would be completed by leaving the bulk of his estate to the college, is located in the south transept. Bray's tomb was destroyed to make room for subsequent guests, but his presence is clearly felt throughout the church. Depictions of his badge, hempbray for crushing hemp, appear 175 times in the building. Today, the Bray Chantry houses the church's bookstore. It also contains the tomb of Giles Tomson (1553–1612), dean of the chapel and one of eight scholars chosen by James I in 1607 to translate the Bible into English.

Next in line is the Chapel of Oliver King, built around 1500. King was a canon of Windsor from 1480 to 1503 and then was Bishop of Bath and Wells. He also was a secretary for Prince Edward (son of Henry VI), Edward IV and Henry VII. Portraits of these royals, plus the boy king Edward V, decorate the wall opposite the chapel. Notice that the crown above the head of Edward V is suspended, indicating that he was never crowned king. Much of the glass in the windows of the chapel dates from the late 15th century. Features include a Tudor shield alongside the shield of Aragon, symbolizing the union of Henry VIII and Katherine of Aragon; red roses; the cross and shield of St. George; and the arms of Henry Stafford, Duke of Buckingham, a key supporter of Richard III. The wall paintings also are medieval.

● ●

🔖 Did you know?

Legend has it that King Edward III chose the name for his new chivalric order after an incident that occurred during a ball in 1347. According to the story, the king retrieved a garter dropped by the beautiful Joan of Kent, Countess of Salisbury, a.k.a. the "Fair Maid of Kent," with whom he allegedly was in love. In a dramatic gesture, the king tied the garter around his own knee, saying "Shame on him who thinks evil of it." Whether the story is true or not (and many historians think it is), the phrase did become the motto of the new order.

Joan has another connection with the spiritual home of the Order of the Garter. She was married to the king's oldest son, the Black Prince Edward, in St. George's Chapel on October 10, 1360. (*How's that for irony—capturing the heart of both father and son?*)

● ●

Now hold your breath, because next comes the awesome sword of Edward III. According to the chapel's history, Edward actually used this sword in battle and, when it was not in use, it hung over Edward's Garter stall in the old church. If you weren't intimidated by Edward's fearsome military reputation before seeing the sword, you will be after. Just imagining the strength it took to lift and wield that sword to maim and kill other men in chain mail makes us break into a cold sweat. Next to the sword is a painting of Edward III, but it is not contemporary; it dates from 1615. Across from that, a display of rare books begins. The books are from the chapel library and date back as far as the 12th century.

The next small chapel, the Oxenbridge Chapel, was built around 1522 and named for John Oxenbridge, a canon of Windsor and a high official in the courts of Henry VII and Henry VIII. The chapel was dedicated to St. John the Baptist, and the paintings in it tell the story of his death.

Close by the Oxenbridge Chapel, a stone marks the burial place of Charles Brandon, Duke of Suffolk. Brandon was left an orphan after his father, who was Henry VII's standard bearer, was killed in single combat with Richard III at the Battle of Bosworth, shortly before Richard himself was killed. Brandon was raised with the future Henry VIII and the two were close friends—at least they were until Brandon betrayed Henry's trust by secretly marrying the king's sister Mary. For this offense, Brandon was banished to his estates in Suffolk. Eventually, the king relented and the duke won favor again, so much favor that Henry interfered with a plan to bury Brandon at Tattershall and instead arranged for him to be interred at Windsor at the king's expense. The stone marking the grave (a 20th-century addition) is decorated with the duke's arms and those of his wife Mary.

As you continue along the south quire aisle, look for a plate from the stall of a Knight of the Garter. This one belonged to Thomas Howard, the fourth Duke of Norfolk, who, following the family tradition, was executed for treason in 1572. (His great-grandfather and father had both been executed for acts of treason, and his grandfather had been convicted and sentenced to death, but was saved from the ax by the timely death of Henry

VIII.) As part of his punishment for treason (*killing him wasn't enough?*), the fourth duke was stripped of his honor as a Knight of the Garter. His crest, banner and sword were ripped from his stall in the quire and thrown into the ditch outside the castle. But, clearly, someone retrieved at least the plate with the crest because it was returned to St. George's in 1955.

Across the chapel from Edward IV lies Henry VI, that poor, weak man who would have made a much better monk than king and whom Edward deposed. By Edward's order, Henry was first buried at Chertsey Abbey. From the start, Henry's grave was a place of pilgrimage, but it wasn't until 1481 that reports of miracles occurring at his tomb started circulating. In an apparent act of atonement, Richard III (*whom Shakespeare wrongfully charged with Henry's murder*) ordered the body moved to Windsor in August 1484. Pilgrims flocked to St. George's to pray there. Their contributions for this privilege were collected in an iron money box, crafted sometime around 1480, that now stands outside Henry's tomb.

The last small chapel you will pass by in St. George's is the Lincoln Chapel. This chapel also once was a pilgrim's shrine containing the tomb of Master John Schorn, a 14th-century cleric attributed with miraculous healing skills. Originally buried in North Marston, where he served as a rector and performed his miracle healing, Schorn was moved to St. George's at the request of Bishop Beauchamp, who was supervising construction of the new church. The Bishop was granted a papal bull authorizing the transfer in 1481 and an elaborate tomb was constructed for the miracle worker. Alas, Schorn lost some of his tourism appeal after Henry VI was relocated close by. In 1585, Schorn's shrine

☞ Did you know?

Henry VI was confined at Windsor Castle for 16½ months after suffering a mental breakdown in 1453 that left him catatonic. He came out of his stupor on Christmas Day 1454 "as a man who wakes after a long dream." He told contemporaries, "he never knew till that time, nor wist what was said to him, nor wit not where he had to be whilst he had been sick, till now." As soon as he could speak again, Henry ordered a mass of thanksgiving to be said at St. George's Chapel.

was dismantled to make room for a Knight of the Garter, Edward Clinton, the first Earl of Lincoln. His effigy and that of his third wife, Elizabeth Fitzgerald, are the main attraction of the chantry today.

As you cross the ambulatory heading for the exit, look to your right for the door that led to the chapel built by Henry III in 1240 as a monument to Edward the Confessor. The door is notable for its beautiful 13th-century ironwork.

Henry III's chapel was the original home of the Order of the Garter, but the church fell into disrepair after the new building was constructed. Only the north wall of the original structure remains. At various times the crumbling ruins were considered as possibilities for the burial sites of Henrys VI, VII and, as already discussed, VIII. Cardinal Wolsey definitely planned to build a major monument to himself there and imported luxurious items to make his grave comfortable. However, as we already discussed as well, Henry VIII decided that such an extravagant tomb was more appropriate for a king than for a disgraced cardinal and Wolsey was buried elsewhere. And because Henry never got to use the space or the materials, George III had them collected in 1810 and used for Lord Nelson's tomb in St. Paul's Cathedral in London. Once again, the old chapel was neglected until 1863, when Queen Victoria chose to make it into a memorial for her beloved Prince Albert (*and that is more than enough said about that!*). Today, the Albert Memorial Chapel is maintained separately from St. George's Chapel.

As you exit St. George's, you enter the Dean's Cloister. The medieval features of this area include the walls, a wall painting (c. 1251), possibly of Edward the Confessor, a 14th-century "counting" room with floor tiles dating from 1355 and a 14th-century "porch of honor" that once was the entrance to the cloister and the royal lodgings at Windsor. The Galilee Porch that now leads to the Albert Memorial Chapel has 12th-century walls and a 13th-century wall painting, possibly of Henry III. Fifteenth-century Tudor badges decorate the doorway into the chapel.

And now you've done it—you've joined Edward III's chivalric order, fought the Wars of the Roses and paid homage to a couple of medieval miracle makers! It's time for a break!

While you're in Windsor . . .

Particularly if you are traveling with children, you may want to pay a visit to the Windsor Brass Rubbing Center located at Parish Church on High Street. To make an appointment, call 01753-854808.

◇◇

CONTRASTING KINGS: HENRY VI AND EDWARD IV

Opponents in life, companions in death—there are few odder pairings in the selection of burial sites for medieval kings than that chosen for Edward IV and Henry VI. Of course, Edward had St. George's Chapel rebuilt to be an appropriately opulent site for his tomb and it was only after Edward's death and burial that Henry VI's body was moved there. Still, one can't help but wonder how easily Edward rests so near the king whose throne he usurped and whose death he ordered.

In life—and as kings—Henry and Edward were a study in contrasts. Henry was mild, meek and monkish. Edward was brash, bold and licentious. Henry inherited his crown as an infant and generally sat on a throne that actually was ruled by others. Edward inherited the mantel of leadership of the Yorkist cause at the age of 18. He quickly demonstrated his military prowess with a crushing defeat over the Lancastrian forces at the Battle of Mortimer's Cross on February 2, 1461. He then moved rapidly to consolidate his political power and control of the throne.

A puppet king for most of his life, Henry presided over a court rife with corruption, inefficient and split into factions deeply divided by greed and ambition. His personal prudity and piety caused many contemporaries to question whether a son born to Henry's queen, Margaret of Anjou, truly was Henry's son. Edward was a strong, authoritative and efficient king who restored order to the realm and fiscal prosperity to the throne. A lover of luxury, Edward dressed flamboyantly, ate and drank lavishly and partied ceaselessly. He was a notorious adulterer with numerous well-known mistresses. Although his court, too, was rent by factions, Edward was able to keep them in check until his death.

Henry was an inept military commander whose 1453 loss of the French domains won by his father, Henry V, led to a mental breakdown that left Henry VI in a catatonic state for more than 16 months. When confronted by a revolt led by his cousin Richard Neville, Earl of Warwick, and his brother George, Duke of

Clarence, in alliance with Henry VI's queen, Margaret of Anjou, Edward was forced to flee England in October 1470. He returned six months later, in April 1471, leading a force of about 1,200 mercenaries. With an army augmented by English supporters, Edward once again dealt a devastating blow to the Lancastrian forces at the Battle of Tewkesbury on May 4, 1471.

During the battle, Henry and Margaret's son, Prince Edward, was killed as were the strongest and staunchest of the Lancastrian military leaders. Queen Margaret was captured and Henry VI was imprisoned in the Tower of London. Determined not to repeat the mistakes of the past and leave the remnants of the Lancastrian cause with a rallying point, Edward ordered Henry's death. Poor, bewildered Henry was killed in the Tower of London on May 21, 1471, allegedly while at his prayers in a small chapel in the king's quarters.

Edward died in bed at Westminster Palace on April 9, 1483, at age 41. Contemporaries attributed the cause of this early death to his excessive lifestyle.

◇ ◇

Eton College

High Street

Eton

>>

PHONE

01753-671177

OPEN

Times and dates for the chapel, school yard and cloisters change annually according to the school calendar. Call ahead to check. Access to school buildings is by guided tour only; tours are scheduled daily at 2:15 p.m. and 3:15 p.m.

ADMISSION

£3.00 Chapel, school yard and cloisters
£4.00 Daily guided tour
£5.50 Extended tour
£7.00 Specialist tour (2 hours, for adults only)
£7.50 Connoisseur tour (specialist library tour, for adults only)

>>

Founding Eton College was one of the first independent actions Henry VI took when he reached his majority and the reins of government passed from the hands of his protectors into his. If one is looking for Freudian symbols that explain the reign of Henry VI, Eton College stands out. Dedicated to the Virgin

Mary and to providing a free education to poor boys, Eton is a clear indication of where the king's interests were centered— on religion and education, not on government and the exercise of power.

Henry VI himself conceived the concept for Eton College, laid the foundation stone in 1440 and oversaw the design and construction of much of the complex. He took a great personal interest in the well-being of the boys at Eton, often inviting them to visit him at Windsor, lecturing them on morality and watching over their general welfare.

The school started with 24 "poor and indigent" scholars, but the number was soon increased to 70. Henry richly endowed the school with 1,000 marks per year to support the students and awarded it control of numerous lands and privileges to ensure its ongoing prosperity. What Henry failed to provide for was the loss of his throne; when he was supplanted by Edward IV during the Wars of the Roses, Eton College almost failed. Edward had no love lost for anything with Lancastrian ties and actually shut down the school in 1465. But he changed his mind in 1467, regranted lands to the school and allowed it to resume.

The buildings of Eton College were constructed during the 1440s and into the 1450s. The tower, with its Tudor badge above the clock, was built in the 1500s. The statue of Henry VI in the center of the school's quadrangle was constructed c. 1700.

Guided tours of the campus include the College Chapel, School Yard, Lower School, Brewhouse Gallery and Museum of Eton Life. You are going to learn more than you ever wanted to know about the educational system and history of Eton on these tours; however, it is the only way you can get inside the Lower School, which dates from 1443 and is still used as a classroom. The names on the windows and pillars of the Lower School are those of students selected to go to King's College, Cambridge, in the days when that school accepted students only from Eton.

If you are willing to forgo a peek inside the Lower School, you can save some time—and some pounds—by heading straight for the chapel, the best part of a visit to Eton. Started in 1439, the chapel contains some truly fabulous 15th-century wall paintings of the miracles of the Virgin Mary. The paintings were covered by whitewash during the Reformation, but exposed again in 1847 and restored in 1923.

• •

☞ Did you know?

A legend of the college maintains that it was Edward's merry mistress Jane Shore who encouraged Edward to permit the school to reopen. However, there is no historical evidence the story is true. Even the portrait hanging at Eton that purports to be of Jane is not. It actually is a 16th-century painting of Diane de Poitiers, the mistress of King Henry II of France.

• •

Runnymede
Surrey

⟫⟫⟫

PHONE
01784-432891

E-MAIL
runnymede@trust.org.uk

LOCATED
4 miles southeast of Windsor, just north of Egham, off A308

OPEN
Daylight hours, daily, year-round

ADMISSION
Free of charge; fee for parking

CONVENIENCES
Tearoom

⟫⟫⟫

Okay, you caught us. Runnymede's not in Berkshire; it's in Surrey, which was covered in our second book, *Day Trips South of London*. However, we chose to include Runnymede in this book for *your* convenience; it's located closer to Windsor than to any of the medieval and Tudor sites we covered in that book. In addition, its history is associated more closely with Windsor.

In a way, a visit to Runnymede is rather anticlimatic. One of the most important legal documents in all of history was negotiated on this site, but all there is to show for it is a fairly minor monument. And that was sponsored by the *American* Bar Association.

Still, it was here (*in this very cow pasture!*), along the banks of the River Thames, that a somewhat humbled (*at least for the moment*) King John met with his rebellious barons to relinquish key royal perks . . . such as the lucrative "bennie" of dipping into the nobility's personal coffers at whim. Known as Magna Carta, this agreement was an important step toward limiting the might of the monarchy, defending the rights of subjects and creating a benchmark for democratic governments for ages to come. The text of the "Great Charter" is displayed alongside the memorial.

While you're at Runnymede . . .

Across the river from Runnymede you can find the ruins of the 11th-century **Priory of St. Mary**. If you are into nature, you can also seek out the Ankerwycke Yew, a tree thought to be more than 2,000 years old.

Tip!

If you'd like a little diversion from exploring medieval and Tudor times, you can arrange for a boat trip on the Thames from Runnymede and Windsor. Contact French Brothers in Windsor at 01753-851900.

While you're in Berkshire . . .

✝ Dorney Court
Dorney

>>

PHONE
01628-604638

E-MAIL
palmer@dorneycourt.co.uk

WEBSITE
www.dorneycourt.co.uk

LOCATED
Take the M4, junction 7. Proceed to Dorney, 2 miles west of Windsor
and Eton, on the B3026.

OPEN
1:00–4:30 p.m. random Sundays and Bank Holiday Mondays, May
1:30–4:30 p.m. Monday–Friday and Sunday, July–August

Note: Group tours of 20 or more people are welcome by appointment throughout the year.

ADMISSION
£5.00 Adults
£3.00 Children

CONVENIENCES
Tea served

TIP!
Dorney Court is a popular venue for corporate retreats, special
events and movie making. Be sure to call ahead and check opening
hours.

>>

Dorney Court was built in 1440 and has remained the home of
the present owners for more than 450 years. With a collection of
furnishings and decorative items that date back 600 years, the
gabled, pink brick Dorney Court has been hailed by *Country
Life* magazine as "One of the finest Tudor manor homes in England." (*Although you and we all know that 1440 is considered to
be "late-medieval" . . . not that we're nitpicking or anything!*)

While you're at Dorney Court . . .

Hard by the medieval-cum-Tudor manor home, you'll find the Norman church of **St. James** . . . Norman, that is, save for its Tudor tower. Inside, you'll find traces of a medieval wall painting depicting the Annunciation and a 12th-century baptismal font.

~

Donnington Castle
Donnington

>>

PHONE
  02392-581059

LOCATED
  Just north of Newbury on B4494

OPEN
  Daylight hours daily, year-round

ADMISSION
  Free of charge

>>

This ruin of a castle was once one of Elizabeth's favorites. The castle was built in the 14th century, but there's not much left except the remains of the gatehouse.

Donnington was built in 1386 by Queen Anne of Bohemia's chamberlain, Sir Richard Adderbury. The castle was owned briefly by Thomas Chaucer, son of the famous English poet, and eventually passed into the hands of the dukes of Suffolk, the de la Poles.

Despite this impressive medieval lineage, Donnington played its most significant role in history during the 17th-century Civil War. Refortification efforts made at this time enabled the castle to withstand several brutal onslaughts. Time and neglect since then have done much more damage.

ANCIENT INNS AND EATERIES

~ The Castle Hotel
18 High Street
Windsor
08704-008300
This is a 16th-century coaching inn located across the street from the castle. The restaurant serves lunch and dinner.

~ The Christopher Hotel
110 High Street
Eton, Windsor
01753-852359
Another old coaching inn, dating from 1511. Although not of our period, it's fun to know that the organic food restaurant in this hotel is named Lilly Langtry.

~ The Cockpit Restaurant
47–49 High Street
Eton, Windsor
This is a charming Italian restaurant with excellent food in a building dating from 1420.

~ The Manor Hotel
The Village Green
Datchet, Windsor
01753-545292
This ancient inn is located conveniently close to both Heathrow and Gatwick airports. It is a Tudor building with beamed ceilings in the restaurant and lounges.

~ Sir Christopher Wren's House Hotel
Thames Street
Windsor
01753-861354

Since we take issue so often with Sir Christopher Wren and the damage he did in renovating and remodeling medieval structures, we thought we would relent for once and throw in a plug for this hotel located in a house designed, built and lived in by Wren, even though the house dates from 1676.

CONTENTS

Wallingford

Squires and Spires

e've chosen this title for the introduction to this trip because it is chock-full of abbeys, churches and properties managed or owned by medieval and Tudor squires. This is one of our favorite trips. While the names of the sites may not be those that leap first to the minds of medieval and Tudor enthusiasts, their history will be quite familiar. The anchor site—Wallingford Castle—played a pivotal role in the Norman Conquest of England and in the 19-year-long civil war between King Stephen and Empress Matilda. The family of medieval poet Geoffrey Chaucer is closely associated with the area and its attractions. Dorchester Abbey is one of the most exquisite in England, and Greys Court has close associations with the kin of Elizabeth I. So, haul out the map and hit the road to enjoy one of the most intriguing trips close to London.

✝ Wallingford Castle and Town Defenses

Wallingford

>>>

PHONE

01491-826972 (Tourist Information Centre)

LOCATED

52 miles from London, 15 miles from Oxford via the M40, junction 6 or M4, junction 12; 3 miles from Ewelme

TRAVEL

Trains leave Paddington for Oxford; transfer at Oxford for Wallingford. Travel time from London is approximately 1½ hours.

OPEN

The town ramparts are accessible daily during daylight hours.
Castle grounds:
    10:00 a.m.–6:00 p.m. daily, April–October
    10:00 a.m.–3:00 p.m. daily, November–March

ADMISSION

Free of charge

TIP!

The Tourist Information Centre is located in the Town Hall at Market Place; the phone number is listed above. Using this as your starting point, follow St. Martin's Street out of the market area. St. Martin's becomes Castle Street. Follow Castle Street to Castle Gardens, immediately beyond the George Inn. Castle Gardens is a beautifully maintained public park, with the ruins of Wallingford Castle thoughtfully incorporated into the landscape—well worth your perseverance! As you leave the park, take a moment and follow the signs that lead you along the charming "Thames Walk." The bridge that arches over the river was built in 1530 and refurbished in 1571, when Elizabeth I allowed the town to charge tolls on traffic over and *under* the bridge.

>>>

Although Wallingford's lineage stretches as far back as the Roman era, the ancient town lies huddled within the fortifications believed to have been erected by Alfred the Great as protection against Danish invaders. Supposedly, these are the finest surviving Saxon earthwork defenses to be found in England. This was one of the country's largest Saxon burghs, guarding a strategic ford in the Thames, and particular attention seems to have been paid to construction of the defenses, allowing them to remain largely intact for nearly 1,200 years.

Just how critical was the Walling "ford"? The answer is perhaps best illustrated in the days following the Norman Conquest. Victorious at the Battle of Hastings, William of Normandy and his troops cut a devastating swath through southeast England en route to lay claim to London. The troops were repelled at Southwark on the south bank of the Thames. Never one to take no for an answer, the Bastard marched his men some 50 miles upriver, fording the Thames at Wallingford and approaching London from the north; their second attempt to enter the city went virtually unopposed. Remembering how easy their crossing had been, the Conqueror wasted no time in sending crews back to the fortified town, where a royal fortress was erected in the northeast corner of the ancient ramparts—the better to keep an eye over any other would-be Thames crossings! Under the supervision of one of William's most trusted supporters, Robert d'Oilly, Wallingford Castle, with its three water-filled moats, was complete by 1071.

Did you know?

The commonsense hospitality the citizens of Wallingford showed William of Normandy did not go unappreciated. The Bastard granted Wallingford an extra hour's leeway when he imposed his curfew on the rest of the conquered nation.

The castle played a key role in the civil war (a.k.a. the Anarchy) that raged between Henry I's daughter, Matilda, and her cousin Stephen for the English throne. Early in the struggle, Wallingford fell to Matilda's supporters and was garrisoned by Brian Fitz Count, who held out against King Stephen's troops during three brutal sieges. As you walk the town ramparts, you can look across the Thames and spot a siege platform that dates from this troubled era. It was to Wallingford, on a cold, wintry night, that Empress Matilda fled during a close-call escape

✦✦✦✦✦✦✦✦✦✦✦✦✦✦✦✦✦✦✦

👉 Did you know?

Robert d'Oilly was well rewarded for his loyalty to William of Normandy, holding the lucrative castles of Wallingford and Oxford. Clearly, the financial perks connected with this portfolio were not enough for the greedy—and savage—d'Oilly, who adopted the nasty hobby of plundering church lands for pleasure and profit. Finally, the monks of Abingdon Abbey had enough of d'Oilly's unwanted attention and they appealed to a Higher Power for revenge. Whether or not by divine intercession, d'Oilly soon found himself on death's doorstep. Miraculously recovered—and reformed!—d'Oilly set about making amends for his sacrilegious lifestyle. He endowed numerous religious foundations, including a priory church at Wallingford. The priory was dissolved in 1524 by yet another bane of the clergy's existence, Cardinal Wolsey.

✦✦✦✦✦✦✦✦✦✦✦✦✦✦✦✦✦✦✦

from Oxford in 1142; the fact that the Thames was frozen at the time made her crossing somewhat easier. Ironically, it was also at Wallingford that peace was achieved between the warring parties when Stephen—after a verbal mud-slinging match across the Thames—finally acknowledged Matilda's son Henry as his heir in 1153.

A number of later monarchs, particularly Henry II and John, expanded and improved the castle, making it one of the region's mightiest royal strongholds. Some of the castle's most compelling history is interwoven with the tumultuous reign of Edward II. Along with Berkhamsted Castle, Wallingford was one of several important properties gifted by the king to his controversial favorite, Piers Gaveston; Gaveston found it impressive enough to hold his own wedding tournament there. When the ill-liked Gaveston was arrested in 1312, his captor, the Earl of Pembroke, first intended to hold Piers at Wallingford—the prisoner's own castle! However, the earl's baser instincts foiled this scheme. While en route to Wallingford, Pembroke stopped at Brampton to enjoy marital privileges with his wife; Piers seized the opportunity and made his getaway.

✦✦✦✦✦✦✦✦✦✦✦✦✦✦✦✦✦✦✦

👉 Did you know?

Henry II held his first great council at Wallingford Castle in 1155. A year later, he awarded the town its first royal charter, 32 years before London received one.

✦✦✦✦✦✦✦✦✦✦✦✦✦✦✦✦✦✦✦

Later during Edward's rule, Wallingford was assaulted by rebel forces infuriated that Edward had imprisoned a number of their key supporters in the castle. Crossing the frozen Thames (*do we detect a recurring theme here?*), the rebels attempted to enter Wallingford by the postern gate. Their ruckus alerted the locals, who intercepted the attackers and kept the rebels contained until Edward's men, the Earl of Kent and Hugh Despenser, arrived with arms. This king's final link with Wallingford came after his deposition; his disaffected wife, Isabella, and her lover, Roger Mortimer, Earl of March, celebrated Christmas at the castle a mere month after Edward II lost his crown.

Edward the Black Prince, son of King Edward III, made Wallingford Castle his primary residence after marrying Joan, the Fair Maid of Kent. So fond was Joan of the castle that she continued to live there after the death of her husband until her own death, nine years later. Other noble women did not regard the castle with such affection: Wallingford served as a prison for two English queens of French birth. It was here that Henry IV, after deposing and executing Richard II in 1399, sent Richard's 9-year-old widow, Isabel. The new king needed a while to figure out what to do with her. Nearly two years later, Isabel was sent back to France—minus her dowry; Henry kept that to replenish his impoverished exchequer. Margaret of An-

◆◆◆◆◆◆◆◆◆◆◆◆◆◆◆◆◆◆◆◆◆◆◆

☞ Did you know?

Despite occasional periods of decline, Wallingford's buildings were frequently "recycled" in interesting ways. When the priory was demolished by Henry VIII, the proceeds went toward establishment of Christ Church College in Oxford, while half of its stones went toward the construction of a new town bridge. After Cromwell destroyed the integrity of the castle, much of its stonework was incorporated into renovations at Windsor Castle. Stones from the castle also have been found in the fabric of Wallingford's parish church, St. Mary-le-More.

◆◆◆◆◆◆◆◆◆◆◆◆◆◆◆◆◆◆◆◆◆◆◆

◆◆◆◆◆◆◆◆◆◆◆◆◆◆◆◆◆◆◆◆◆◆◆

☞ Did you know?

One of Anne Boleyn's alleged adulterous lovers was Henry Norris, whom Henry VIII had named constable of Wallingford Castle in 1535. Norris "confessed" to the crime while under interrogation at the Tower of London. He was executed for treason two days before Queen Anne.

◆◆◆◆◆◆◆◆◆◆◆◆◆◆◆◆◆◆◆◆◆◆◆

jou, consort of the hapless Henry VI, was also held in benign captivity at Wallingford after the Lancastrian cause was lost at the Battle of Tewkesbury in May 1471. She cooled her heels until 1475, when her cousin Louis XI made a down payment of £10,000 on her ransom.

The castle at Wallingford was largely demolished by Oliver Cromwell in 1670. Although the bulk of the remains are on private property, a small section of the castle wall and one round tower have been incorporated into a pretty public garden that is open during daylight hours. The town ramparts can be traced along three sides of Wallingford (as was often the case, there is no evidence of man-made fortification along the waterfront). They, too, are freely accessible during daylight hours.

☞ Did you know?

The jousting tournament is one of the images that spring to the amateur historian's mind when you mention the Middle Ages. In fact, jousting was banned by King Stephen during the Anarchy. When the ban was lifted by Richard the Lionheart, the sport was limited to five English sites, one of which was Wallingford.

Wallingford Museum
Flint House, High Street
Wallingford

PHONE
01491-835065

OPEN
2:00–5:00 p.m. Tuesday–Friday, March–November
10:30 a.m.–5:00 p.m. Saturday, March–November
2:00–5:00 p.m. Sunday and Bank Holiday Mondays, June–August

ADMISSION
£1.50 Adults
Children under 16 free of charge

If you are interested in exploring the Saxon and medieval history of this ancient market town, the museum offers an audio-guided walk that also takes in recent Roman excavations. The museum itself, located in a medieval house, features a model of Wallingford Castle.

While you're in Wallingford ...

Three of the 15 parish churches that dotted Wallingford in the 13th century are still in existence. Unfortunately, two of them, St. Leonards and St. Marys, are closed to the public. If you want to tour the third, **St. Peters**, a key can be obtained at the Tourist Centre in the Town Hall.

☞ Did you know?

A mint producing silver pennies from the reign of King Athelstan (924–940 CE) through that of Henry III (1216–1272) was located at Wallingford.

Ewelme Village
Oxfordshire

LOCATED

49 miles from London; approximately 4 miles east of Wallingford, off the B4009

Ewelme (pronounced "ewe-whelm") is a charming medieval village made famous by Geoffrey Chaucer, who praised in poetry the village well, located in the quadrangle of a group of 15th-century almshouses. In describing the spring that fed the well, Chaucer wrote:

In worlde is none more clere of hue,
Its water ever fresshe and newe,
That whelmeth up in waves bright
The mountance of three fingers height.

❖❖❖

THOMAS CHAUCER (C. 1367–1434)

Chaucer may have been inspired to wax lyrical about this well since the village of Ewelme was part of the holdings of his successful son Thomas. Thomas had an illustrious political career, made possible, in great part, because of his family connections; he was a nephew of John of Gaunt, father of the future King Henry IV. Thomas's mother was Philippa Roet, a sister of Katherine Swynford, who happened to be Gaunt's one-time mistress, mother of his Beaufort clan descendants and, later, his third wife.

Because of his royal relationships, Thomas was able to make a brilliant marriage that brought him extensive land holdings, including the manor of Ewelme. Through his own remarkable abilities as an administrator and manager, he greatly expanded these holdings by purchasing and leasing additional lands. He died in 1434, one of the richest men in England.

Along the way, he served his royal cousins loyally as a soldier, diplomat, parliamentarian and councilor through the reigns of Henry IV, Henry V and Henry VI. He was named steward of Wallingford Castle in 1399 and henceforth, made the village of Ewelme his principal seat. Among other offices, Thomas held that of MP from Oxfordshire 14 times, also being selected five times as Speaker of the House of Commons—a record not broken until three centuries later.

❖❖❖

✝ St. Mary the Virgin Parish Church
Ewelme

≫≫

PHONE
   None

OPEN
   Daylight hours daily, year-round

ADMISSION
   Donation requested

≫≫

This lovely little church was founded in the 1430s by William, Duke of Suffolk, and his wife, Alice de la Pole. Alice, who died in 1475, is buried here in an opulent tomb with an alabaster effigy of her on top. She is one of the few women to be awarded the Order of the Garter, and her effigy sports a carving of the garter on her left forearm. Look closely at the carving underneath the tomb and you will find a representation of a typical medieval outlook on life and death—a cadaver of an old woman, demonstrating that death is a physical as well as a spiritual transformation. Alice's father, Thomas Chaucer, who died in 1434, and his wife Matilda also are buried here in an equally elaborate tomb.

The tombs were constructed by the only son of the duke and duchess, John, born at Ewelme on September 27, 1442. John inherited the title Duke of Suffolk at age 8 after his father was murdered by fellow nobles who disagreed with the foreign policy Duke William propagated as chamberlain to the weak-willed Henry VI.

The rest of the church is a beautifully preserved work of 15th-century art. Some outstanding features include the medieval font (also a gift from Duke John), the vestry door and the corbels supporting the roof. There also are a few relatively well-preserved floor tomb brasses and some 15th-century heraldic glass.

THE ALMSHOUSES

Accessible from the west door of the church through a covered passage is a group of almshouses also built in the 1430s by the Duke and Duchess of Suffolk to provide care for poor men. The 13 houses arrayed round a square courtyard are some of the earliest brick buildings in this part of England. The houses are still occupied, so you can't peek inside, but you can wander discreetly around the courtyard and admire Chaucer's well.

EWELME FOUNDATION SCHOOL

Along with founding St. Mary and the almshouses, the Duke and Duchess of Suffolk established a school to educate the children of Ewelme. They appointed a grammar master in 1437 to begin the school and then, about 1450, built the building to house it close by the church, on the other side of the almshouses. The village claims that this is the oldest church primary school in England. At the very least, it is a well-preserved building featuring exquisite medieval glass windows and, on the exterior on either side of the windows, the shields of the duke and duchess. The building is still in use as a school so, again, you can't go inside, but the exterior is well worth a walk-around.

◆◆◆

ALICE DE LA POLE

Alice de la Pole, the granddaughter of Geoffrey Chaucer, was a brilliant and politically savvy woman who played an important role in the Wars of the Roses and was a close friend of Margaret of Anjou, Henry VI's queen. That Alice's astuteness was recognized and acknowledged in this male-dominated society is evident in the fact that she was granted the wardship of her son during his minority in a time when women were rarely accorded such rights. Her capacity to carefully assess the direction of political winds is demonstrated by her decision sometime before 1458 to marry her son to a sister of Edward IV, joining her son's fortune with the House of York despite the family's long and close relationship with the House of Lancaster. This kinship may be the reason why Edward IV appointed Alice to be the guardian of Margaret of Anjou after the May 1471 Battle of Tewkesbury in which Margaret was captured and her son, Prince Edward, was killed. Alice was paid the princely sum of five marks a week for watching over the former queen.

◆◆◆

Dorchester Abbey
Dorchester-on-Thames

≫≫

PHONE
  01865-340703 (abbey museum)

WEBSITE
  www.dorchester-abbey.org.uk

LOCATED
  Off the A4074; 5 miles from Wallingford; 8 miles from Oxford

OPEN
  Abbey
    1:00–5:00 p.m. Tuesday–Friday, May–September
    11:00 a.m.–5:00 p.m. Saturday and Bank Holiday Mondays, May–September

2:00–5:00 p.m. Sunday, May–September
Closed October–March
Museum
   Irregular hours, based on availability of volunteers; call ahead
ADMISSION
   Donation requested
CONVENIENCES
   Brass rubbings and tearoom open on weekends at 3:00 p.m.
»»

Although a spectacular example of Norman architecture, Dorchester Abbey is light in the "captivating history" category. Nothing of major import seems to have happened there, with the exception of how it was saved from destruction during the Dissolution of the Monasteries. Thanks to the intervention of one Richard Beauforest, Dorchester Abbey was spared the fate that befell many other abbeys and monasteries during the "reforming" zeal of Henry VIII's reign. Beauforest purchased the property in 1536 for £140 and donated the buildings to serve as the parish church, a function the abbey still fulfills. Nonetheless, we rate this as a *not-to-be-missed* attraction because of the beauty of the abbey and the wealth of medieval treasures it holds.

There has been a church at this site in Dorchester since 634, making Dorchester Abbey one of the oldest abbeys in England. Construction of the exquisite building you see today was begun in 1140, when Dorchester was refounded as an Augustinian abbey. The magnificently carved quire was rebuilt in the 14th century.

Of the many outstanding features of the abbey, its glorious stained glass windows take pride of place. One of the windows reputedly is set with some of the oldest glass in England, dating from the 13th century. In addition to a rare Norman lead font decorated with carvings of 11 apostles (*we assume the missing apostle is Judas*), the church contains several fine medieval effigies, including one of a knight drawing his sword from his scabbard. The effigy, c. 1300, is presumed to represent a crusading knight prepared to fight for the Kingdom of God, even beyond the grave. Also to be found in the Lady Chapel is a faded effigy of Sir John de Stonore (1280–1354), Lord Chief Justice of England under Edward III.

There also are a good quality 14th-century wall painting of the Virgin Mary and John the Baptist at Christ's Crucifixion, wonderfully preserved medieval floor tiles and a fabulous sedilia adorned with three miniature 14th-century windows. One amusing feature is a corbel, now decorating a pillar, that is a carving of sleeping canons being awakened by a horn-blowing devil. (*How's that for a bugle boy?*)

Just west of the abbey you will find The Old School House, which dates from the 15th century. The building may once have served as the monastery's guest house.

There is also a museum on the abbey grounds featuring exhibits about Dorchester's ancient past.

Abingdon Abbey
Thames Street, Checker Walk & Abbey Close
Abingdon

>>

PHONE
01235-525339

LOCATED
About 62 miles from London, 6 miles from Oxford, at the junction of A34 and A4183

OPEN
2:00–4:00 p.m. Tuesday–Sunday, April–September
Closed October–March

ADMISSION
£1.00 Adults
Children free of charge

CONVENIENCES
Unicorn Theatre

>>

There is little left of Abingdon Abbey, once an important and wealthy Saxon abbey. Founded in 675 in honor of the Virgin Mary by Cissa, King of the West Saxons, as a monastery for 12 Benedictine monks, Abingdon went the way of most religious houses during the Dissolution of the Monasteries in the 16th century. All that is left today are a heavily restored 15th-century gatehouse, a few domestic buildings, a long two-story building with a timbered gallery and vaulted undercroft and a 13th-century chimney that is part of the ruins of what is thought to have been the abbey's exchequer. One part of the former exchequer for the abbey is now a theater. The one significant part of the abbey that survives is the parish church of St. Nicolas, built in the 12th century to serve the religious needs of the people of the parish (a role it continues to play today) and to keep them from disrupting the monks' devotions.

☞ Did you know?

Thomas Pentecost, a.k.a. Rowland, was the last abbot of Abingdon Abbey. He was among the first of the English clerics to recognize Henry VIII as Supreme Head of the Church of England. His reward for surrendering his monastery to royal control in 1538 was a lifetime interest in the manor of Cumnor and an annual pension of £200.

The abbey was destroyed twice before Henry VIII came along: once in the 9th century by the Danes and then again in 1327 by the people of Abingdon who resented the abbey's power and wealth. Both times, the abbey was rebuilt in grander and more glorious style and managed to continue increasing its dominance, primarily because it always was able to attract royal patronage.

☞ Did you know?

When Abingdon Abbey was turned over to Henry VIII in 1538, it was the sixth richest abbey in England. Its revenues were valued at £1,876, 10s, 9d.

While you're in Abingdon . . .

Take a stroll down Bridge Street to the town's **ancient bridge**. It was built in 1416–1417 to link Abingdon with the main road to London. Next to it, you will find the Tourist Information Centre.

You also may want to peek in at **St. Helen's Church** (open daily) on East St. Helen Street. Once the site of a Saxon nunnery, the current church dates from the 12th century. It's worth your time to stroll through the building and find the Lady Chapel, which has a phenomenal 14th-century painted ceiling consisting of 52 oak panels that outline Jesus' lineage according to the Gospel of St. Matthew. Home to the medieval guilds of Abingdon, St. Helen's was the mustering point for the townspeople's revolt against the abbey in the 14th century.

★★★★★★★★★★★★★★★★★★★★★★★

☞ Did you know?

Abingdon claims to be the oldest town in England, dating from Anglo-Saxon times and deriving its name from an Anglo-Saxon woman of royal birth (Abingdon means "Aebbas Hill" in Anglo-Saxon). However, the town of Abingdon did not receive its first royal charter until 1556, when Queen Mary and her consort, Philip of Spain, granted one.

★★★★★★★★★★★★★★★★★★★★★★★

Also, close by St. Helen's is the 15th-century almshouse known as **Long Alley Almshouse**. Built by the Fraternity of the Holy Cross, the almshouse passed in 1553 to the ownership of Christ's Hospital, which still manages the property today.

〜

✝ Mapledurham House and Watermill
7 Watermill
Reading

>>

PHONE
 01189-723350

E-MAIL
 mtrust1997@aol.com

WEBSITE
 www.mapledurham.co.uk

LOCATED
 4 miles northwest of Reading on the River Thames; follow signs along the A4074

OPEN
2:00–5:30 p.m. Saturday and Sunday,
April–September

ADMISSION
Phone for details

CONVENIENCES
Picnic area, tearoom, gift shops

>>

Grain has been ground at Mapledurham since Saxon times. The present mill building dates from the 15th century and is still grinding flour, which can be purchased in the shops on the property.

Mention of Mapledurham as an estate first appears in the *Domesday Book*, where it is described as two manors—Mapledurham Gurney owned by William de Warenne and Mapledurham Chazey, which belonged to Milo Crispin, lord of Wallingford. Apparently used as a dower property, Mapledurham Gurney (the larger of the two estates) passed through the hands of various noble families until it was purchased in 1490 by Richard Blount of Iver. Blount was a member of a cadet branch of the ancient Le Blond family of Normandy who invaded England along with William the Conqueror. His illustrious relations included the first Lord Mountjoy (d. 1474) and Elizabeth Blount, one of Henry VIII's many mistresses.

Richard's son, also Richard, and his grandson, Michael, both served as Lieutenant of the Tower of London and are buried in the Chapel Royal of St. Peter ad Vincula on the Tower grounds. It was Michael Blount who combined the two estates mentioned in the *Domesday Book*, purchasing the Chazey manor in 1582. He also borrowed £1,500 in 1588 to build the grand mansion seen today. Definitely a fellow with a high opinion of himself, Michael attempted to lay claim to the Mountjoy barony after the Earl of Devonshire, the last man to hold the title, died in 1474. The House of Lords rejected the claim.

The Mapledurham estate fell into decline during the Parliamentarian years. In 1960, it was restored by Blount descendants, who live in the house today.

∿

 Greys Court
Henley-on-Thames

>>>

PHONE
01491-628529

LOCATED
3 miles west of Henley-on-Thames, on the B481

OPEN
2:00–6:00 p.m. Wednesday–Friday, March–September

ADMISSION
£4.80 Adults
£2.40 Children
Family ticket available

CONVENIENCES
Tearoom
>>>

Another ancient estate that can trace its origins to the *Domesday Book*, Greys Court, a.k.a. Rotherfield, is also one of those properties where you have to poke and prod to find the medieval and Tudor traces among the renovations and "improvements" that various owners have made through the centuries — but the effort is worth it. The property boasts a 14th-century Great Tower, and traces of the Tudor origins of the current house can be scouted out. Close by is the medieval **St. Nicholas Church** in Rotherfield Greys with outstanding brass effigies and ancient tombs of the estate's early owners.

From at least the 11th through the first half of the 15th century, Greys Court was among the estates held by the powerful de Grey family, stalwart soldiers and courtiers who also spawned numerous princes of the Church, including several bishops and at least one Archbishop of York. When the de Grey line died out in the mid-15th century, Greys Court passed to the Crown, and Henry VII awarded it to his uncle Jasper Tudor. In 1538, Henry VIII gave the property to Francis Knollys, who became a close councilor to Queen Elizabeth I. Knollys served as Elizabeth's Treasurer of the Royal Household from 1572 to 1596. A staunch Protestant, he was one of the trusted advisors Elizabeth appointed to watch over Mary, Queen of Scots during that unfortunate woman's time as a prisoner of the English Crown.

Knollys died in 1598. He is buried along with his wife, a granddaughter of Thomas Boleyn and thereby a cousin of Queen Elizabeth, in a magnificent tomb in St. Nicholas Church in Rotherfield Greys. In fact, the tomb is adorned on top with a figure of Elizabeth kneeling in prayer. There also is a crowned male mourner that we speculated might be meant to represent Henry VIII (*although it would have been a very flattering portrait of Henry in his later years!*), but we could find no information to confirm or repudiate this idea. It was Knollys who began construction of a Tudor house that was later remodeled in the Jacobean style.

◇◇

KISSING COUSINS: ELIZABETH I AND LETTICE KNOLLYS

Francis Knollys's close relationship with Elizabeth seems not to have suffered from the fact that his daughter, Lettice, was a competitor for the affections of the queen's lifelong favorite, Robert Dudley, Earl of Leicester. Lettice and Leicester had enjoyed an off-and-on dalliance since 1565. The relationship blossomed into a full-fledged affair after Lettice's husband, the Earl of Essex, died in 1576. The couple was secretly married at Kenilworth Castle in the spring of 1578 after Lettice told Leicester she was pregnant.

Elizabeth was infuriated at the marriage and dealt with the situation in true "queenly" style—she simply ignored it, pretended it never happened and kept Leicester close by her side. She did make her displeasure with her cousin Lettice quite plain, however. When Lettice appeared at court, decked to the nines and attended by a host of servants, Elizabeth swooped down and boxed her cousin's ears, saying, "As but one sun lights the East, so I shall have but one queen in England." Lettice got the message and wisely avoided the court until long after Leicester's death in 1588.

In 1597, Lettice's son from her first marriage, the Earl of Essex, was now the chief royal favorite, and he prevailed upon Elizabeth to receive his mother at court again. While Elizabeth yielded to the earl's entreaties, she, as usual, did it in her own way—insisting that the meeting be in private, arranging several encounters and then failing to appear and, finally, giving Lettice a very cool, very brief greeting. Suffice it to say, the relationship between the two women remained strained until Elizabeth's death in 1603.

❖❖

ANCIENT INNS AND EATERIES

~ The George Hotel
High Street
Wallingford
01491-836665

This 16th-century inn claims to have a haunted room, although we don't know who or what is haunting it. The inn also has a restaurant and bar.

~ White Hart Hotel
High Street
Dorchester
01865-340074

There are 19 rooms available in this 15th-century inn, which also boasts a top-notch restaurant with a seasonally changing menu.

~ The George Hotel
High Street
Dorchester
01865-340404

This is a 15th-century inn with a beamed dining room and "en suite" rooms (each room has its own bath).

~ Hill Farm
Newington, Wallingford
01865-891173

Wood beams enhance the ambience of this 16th-century farmhouse.

~ Fyfield Manor
Benson, near Ewelme
01491-825635
Parts of this award-winning manor home date from the 12th century. Dine on organic cuisine in the medieval dining room.

~ North Moreton House
North Moreton, near Abingdon
01235-813282
This historic Tudor B&B was once a vicarage. You can still tour the tithe barn.

~ Stapleton's Chantry
North Moreton, near Abingdon
01235-818900
This is a B&B in a cozy 16th-century family home.

CONTENTS

TRIP 3

Reading

A Royal Mausoleum

 f you're as fascinated as we are by anything and everything connected with the early medieval monarchs,
you'll find it hard to resist a visit to the ruins of Reading Abbey. Easier said than done, we might add. The
town of Reading is exceedingly difficult to maneuver in — a confusing morass of one-way streets and sudden dead ends. To
complicate matters, the Tourist Information Centre, once conveniently located near both the train station and the abbey
ruins, is now located rather *inconveniently* a hearty hike away.
So frustrating did we (and our driver) find our navigation that
we actually considered omitting this trip from our recommendations. But the history is great and the ruins are remarkable,
so here's our caveat. Unless you are a resident of Reading (*in
which case you have both our admiration and our sympathy*), we
strongly urge you to make this trip by train. We do not relish the
thought of our readers wandering the streets of Reading, lost
forever like Charlie on the MTA!

✝ Reading Abbey Ruins
Reading

>>

PHONE
01189-566226 (Reading Tourist Information Centre)

LOCATED
Forbury Gardens, opposite the train station

TRAVEL
42 miles from London. Trains depart Paddington Station for Reading; travel time is approximately 25 minutes.

OPEN
Daylight hours daily, year-round

ADMISSION
Free of charge

>>

Reading Abbey was founded by Henry I (a.k.a. Henry Beauclerc) in 1121. Henry was thinking ahead: 14 years before his death, he envisioned Reading as the final resting spot for himself and his closest kin. This made Reading the first great abbey to be constructed primarily as a royal mausoleum. (King Stephen would continue the trend at Faversham Abbey). Evidently, the idea that Henry might die on one of his many visits to Normandy did not dawn on the aging king, and no adequate plans were made for that very real likelihood. When, in fact, the 77-year-old Henry died at Lyons la Forêt in early December 1135, prolonged ill winds prevented the timely transport of his corpse back to England. For obvious reasons, his escorts eventually were forced to remove his intestines, which were buried in Rouen. On January 4, the rest of his body was finally laid to rest at Reading Abbey.

Although technically a Cluniac abbey (by the end of the 13th century it was considered Benedictine), Reading Abbey had a

◆◆◆◆◆◆◆◆◆◆◆◆◆◆◆◆◆◆◆◆◆◆
☞ Did you know?
Although he was born in Belfast, Northern Ireland, our favorite Shakespearean actor, Kenneth Branagh, spent his youth in Reading. (*We're amazed he ever found his way out!*)
◆◆◆◆◆◆◆◆◆◆◆◆◆◆◆◆◆◆◆◆◆◆

royal charter granting it a high degree of autonomy from the mother house in Cluny. This independence, however, meant the abbey was unusually reliant upon the generosity of its English patrons. Reading was one of the few religious houses to enjoy the munificence of Henry's daughter Matilda. Typically, the former Holy Roman Empress limited her patronage to churches, abbeys and priories close to those castles that supported her struggle to win the English throne from her cousin Stephen. Not only was Reading her father's burial site, but it was close by Wallingford Castle, which was held by one of Matilda's most loyal friends, Brian Fitz Count. Matilda granted the monks of Reading the manor of Blewbury in memory of her ancestors and as a gesture of love and appreciation for the service of Lord Brian. Unfortunately, Fitz Count, often on the brink of starvation during protracted sieges, had been forced to ravage the abbey's lands on several occasions. This did not cast Matilda

❖❖

A MALE TALE

Yes, he sired 21 illegitimate children, but Henry I only fathered two legitimate heirs to the throne. His beloved son and heir apparent, William Audelin, died in the tragic sinking of the *White Ship* off the coast of Normandy in 1120. That left Henry's legitimate daughter, Matilda, next in line for the English throne. Although there was no legal reason preventing Matilda from claiming her father's crown, the English nobility was none too keen about the prospect of being ruled by a woman. Despite the fact that the barons had sworn (on three separate occasions, no less!) to uphold Matilda's accession, most of them wasted no time after Henry's death in throwing their support behind the rival claim made by the late king's nephew Stephen of Blois. Nor did any moss grow under Stephen's feet. Although he was in Normandy when Henry died, he made haste to Winchester, where his brother Henry, Bishop of Winchester, helped him lay claim to the English treasury. With the nation's wealth and baronial support firmly in hand, Stephen then proceeded to London, where he was crowned King of England on December 22, 1135 . . . a mere three weeks after Henry's death. Twelve days later, King Stephen was on hand to officially receive his predecessor's remains at Reading Abbey, while Matilda was still in Normandy, trying to raise an army to advance her rightful claim. It would be another four years before she built the military might necessary to launch an invasion of England . . . and 19 years before the conflict over the crown was resolved.

❖❖

in any worse light, however . . . after all, pillage and plunder were not unknown to Stephen's supporters either (just one more reason for chroniclers to label the 19-year Anarchy as the time "when Christ and His saints slept").

The abbey's wealth was enhanced further by fees it garnered as one of the nation's most popular pilgrim destinations. Its royal status, combined with the ambition and savvy of its earliest abbots, enabled Reading to amass a collection of nearly 250 relics. Twenty-nine of these were "directly" linked with Christ or his blessed mother, although the remains of 79 martyrs and 49 virgins, as well as various and sundry prophets, apostles and "saints-in-waiting" were also part of the collection.

There is an interesting story about one of the abbey's primary relics, the hand of St. James the Apostle, which the widowed Matilda brought back from her years in Germany, seat of the Holy Roman Empire, as a gift for her father. At some point during the Anarchy, the relic fell into the possession of King Stephen's brother, the Bishop of Winchester, but when Matilda's son Henry II succeeded to the throne, he insisted that the hand be returned to Reading. Diplomatically, the bishop agreed. St. James's relic became quite a lucrative pilgrim attraction and was among the abbey's most valuable assets (*apparently Henry I's tomb wasn't much of a draw*) . . . so when Germany began insisting that the relic be returned to the Fatherland, the English royal family was not inclined to agree. Backed by his mother, Henry sent many lovely gifts to the emperor, along with words of praise and admiration. The hand of St. James, however, remained firmly safeguarded be-

• • • • • • • • • • • • • • • • • • • •
☞ Did you know?

Relics that could not be turned into ready cash frequently were destroyed by Henry VIII's henchmen during the Dissolution of the Monasteries. Foreseeing the inevitable, one of the abbey's priests, Father Rugg, replaced the hand of St. James with the "less important" hand of St. Anastasius. The hand of St. James was hidden in an iron chest and buried along the east wall of the abbey. It was discovered during the construction of Reading Gaol in 1786 and put on display in a small, private museum in town before being permanently enshrined in the church of St. Peter in Marlow.
• • • • • • • • • • • • • • • • • • • •

hind the walls of the royal abbey. During his reign, King John formed a particular attachment to the relic and, in an unusually generous gesture, funded a handsome shrine in which the hand could be displayed. John also bestowed upon the abbey another of its most alluring relics: the skull of St. Philip.

Henry I's tomb might not have had a lot of popular appeal, but it did confer "royal" status on the abbey, and the monarch's descendants understood the importance of continuing the dynastic link. In the spring of 1156, when 3-year-old William, eldest son of Henry II and Eleanor of Aquitaine, died at Wallingford Castle, he was buried at the feet of his great-grandfather in Reading Abbey. Nearly 30 years later, as tensions between England and France mounted, Henry took another son, the Young King (and yet another Henry), to the tomb of Henry Beauclerc. There papa made his heir apparent swear "in the presence of holy relics" to obey his father's instructions in all things — particularly the distribution of Continental towns, castles and benefices, as specified in charters housed at the abbey.

Did you know?

Being officially estranged from the Church cannot have been a comfortable position for any medieval Christian, even someone as lacking in conscience as King John apparently was. As a result of a rift with the Vatican, John was excommunicated by Pope Innocent III in 1208, and all of England was placed under a five-year interdict, which essentially barred the citizenry from receiving the sacraments. In an effort to keep himself in God's good graces during his extended religious exile, John borrowed numerous religious manuscripts from Reading Abbey: six bibles, St. Augustine's *City of God*, the teachings of Hugh of St. Victor and Peter Lombard's textbook on theology. John eventually "made nice" and relations with Rome were repaired in 1213. Typical of John, he conveniently "forgot" to return the tomes, which—together with a small but significant collection of histories—formed the nucleus of the future royal library.

Religious matters aside, Reading Abbey played a key role in the politics of the Plantagenet era. By ancient standards, the roads between London and Reading were comparatively "good" and traveled frequently, making Reading a popular stop for the court's annual progress. Because the town had no castle, per se, the royal abbey, spanning 30 acres just on the outskirts of medieval Reading, filled the bill. Nearly every monarch, from Henry III through Edward IV, held important councils or parliaments in the abbey's 79-foot by 42-foot chapter house hall. Its awe-inspiring church was consecrated by Thomas à Becket in 1164. It was here that the Patriarch of Jerusalem presented his country's crown to Henry II. The great soldier and statesman, William Marshall, Protector of England during the minority of Henry III, lay in state in one of the abbey's splendid chapels before being transported to London for burial at the Temple Church. John of Gaunt and Blanche of Lancaster, parents of Henry IV, celebrated their wedding at Reading Abbey. The town was also home to one of England's finest tournament fields; along with Windsor and Eltham, it ranked among the Black Prince's favorite jousting grounds.

Elizabeth Woodville made her official debut at court as the consort of Edward IV at Reading Abbey on Michaelmas Day 1464. She was escorted by her brother-in-law George, Duke of Clarence, and the "Kingmaker," Richard Neville, Earl of Warwick. Although the magnates to a man were stunned by Edward's ill-advised choice of queen (the social-climbing Woodvilles were particularly disliked by the nobility), a veneer of courteous cheer was donned by all assembled. Celebrations in honor of their sovereign lady lasted for a week.

Unfortunately, Reading's royal status did not safeguard it from a particularly wretched fate during the Dissolution of the Monasteries. The harsh suppression of this abbey was fueled by the fact that its last abbot, Hugh Faringdon (a.k.a. Cook), was particularly obstinate about turning the abbey over to the king's authorities. A former friend and hunting companion of the king and one-time Chaplain Royal (he officiated at one of Jane Seymour's funeral masses and, ironically, had preached in favor of Henry's Royal Supremacy), Faringdon was arrested on charges of treason, thrown into the Tower of London and sentenced to death—guilt was conferred upon him, apparently without redress. Together with two priests associated with the abbey, Faringdon was dragged behind a cart through the streets of Reading before being hanged, drawn and quartered on November 15, 1539. His remains were suspended from chains in the abbey's gatehouse as a warning to other theological naysayers. The king's dire point, however, was moot. Faringdon's death, in tandem with the nearly simultaneous fates of the abbots of Colchester and Glastonbury, marked Henry's final triumph over the monastic houses.

Reading's prime location on the traditional royal progress route prompted Henry to convert the abbey buildings into a royal palace, a role it had played in theory through many prior reigns. As an official palace, however, its tenure was relatively short-lived; most of the buildings failed to survive the Cromwellian wars.

◆◆◆◆◆◆◆◆◆◆◆◆◆◆◆◆◆◆◆◆◆◆◆◆◆

🖙 Did you know?

Reading Abbey was yet another religious foundation whose hallowed stones were "recycled" after the Dissolution. Rubble from the abbey has been found in the walls of Reading's schools and shops and is even known to line stretches of the city's sewers.

◆◆◆◆◆◆◆◆◆◆◆◆◆◆◆◆◆◆◆◆◆◆◆◆◆

Today, the remaining bits and pieces of Reading Abbey are owned and maintained by the Reading Corporation and are open for your exploration. We were delighted by how extensive the evocative ruins are and how imaginatively they've been incorporated into a beautiful public park—a welcome retreat after what felt like a circuitous wild goose chase! Portions of the 200-foot dormitory—once Henry VII's grammar school—still exist, as does the inner gatehouse, which was restored in 1861. Your first mission should be to check out the diagram on the gatehouse wall. This will give you a clearer understanding of how the ancient buildings would have related to those currently on-site. Next, stop by the handsome Celtic cross that dominates one quadrant of the park; it was erected in memory of Henry Beauclerc, a.k.a. Henry I.

Continue strolling counterclockwise. The church you are facing looks convincingly medieval, but don't be fooled. This is St. James's Church, built amid the abbey ruins in 1840. To the right of the church school, however, are the extensive remains of the hospitium, which housed medieval pilgrims. As you trace the abbey walls, look for three stone plaques; the first two commemorate Reading's first and last abbots. The third honors the composition of "Sumer is Icumen In," believed to be the earliest English choral work; it was created at Reading Abbey in 1240.

While you're in Reading . . .

There are two medieval churches in Reading, both open at random times to the public. You may phone one central number for schedules of services, concerts and open hours: 01189-571057. We found the more convenient—and interesting—of the two to be **St. Laurence Church**, which can be reached by traversing the abbey parkland and exiting through what was once the abbey's west gate into the churchyard. In the churchyard, you will find an impressive chunk of a tracery from the church's west window. It was dislodged during World War II bombing and now enjoys pride of place as a particularly poignant "sculpture." The other church, **St. Mary-the-Virgin** (a.k.a. St. Mary Butts) is convenient to the Tourist Information Centre, on Change Street at the junction of Broad and Chant Streets. This church dates from 979 CE and is distinguished by the peculiar checkerboard pattern of its belfry.

◆ ◆

☞ Did you know?

Okay—he's not a *medieval* notable, but no one can argue this: Oscar Wilde was a true Renaissance man. As you may have already surmised, Mr. Wilde was imprisoned in Reading Gaol. His experiences there were the "inspiration" for his masterpiece, *The Ballad of Reading Gaol*. The city has commemorated Mr. Wilde with an Oscar Wilde Walk, which winds along the far side of the ruins. (*Apparently the town folk don't hold the observation "The best way to see Reading is going through it on a train" against dear Oscar.*)

◆ ◆

Also while you're in Reading . . .

☩ Museum of Reading
Blagrave Street
Reading

>>

PHONE
01189-399800

OPEN
10:00 a.m.–5:00 p.m. Tuesday–Saturday, year-round
2:00–5:00 p.m. Sunday and Bank Holiday Mondays

ADMISSION
Free of charge

>>

No amateur historian worth his or her salt will want to miss the chance to see England's *only* full-size replica of the Bayeux Tapestry (*Carole had to be physically restrained from swimming across the Atlantic the moment she read about this display*). The Museum traces Reading's history from the Saxon era, with particular attention to the important events of the medieval period. There are several remnants of Reading Abbey on exhibit as well, including a number of 12th-century capitals.

CONTENTS

TRIP 4

Oxford

Town and Gown

nown as the "City of Dreaming Spires," Oxford is a captivating town that retains its medieval aura. Needless to say, Oxford University, its colleges and associated buildings dominate the landscape, sprawling over the city in a rather forbidding manner. Much of what appears to be ancient is not, but let us assure you that persistent poking into lots of different nooks and crannies will yield a treasure trove of medieval and Tudor gems.

There is much to see and do in Oxford. In fact, we recommend that you make this an overnight trip if you are determined to see and do it all. For a thoroughly enjoyable immersion experience in medieval history, you may want to combine Oxford with an overnight stay in the charming village of Minster Lovell, just 14 miles from Oxford (see the next trip in this chapter). Spend the day in Oxford, then travel to Minster Lovell to stay overnight at the 15th-century Old Mill and Swan Inn. Walk the village in the morning, catch the ruins of Minster Lovell castle and then return to Oxford to finish your tour there.

If this plan doesn't fit your schedule, you probably will want to hop onto one of the myriad bus tours that travel around Oxford, particularly one that will allow you to purchase one ticket and then "jump on and jump off" at will when you spy a site you simply must see up close. Trust us; this is the best way to tour Oxford. It will save your feet the bruising numbness that comes from walking miles over cobbled streets and walkways.

CAROLE AND SARAH'S GREATEST HITS

Because there is so much to see and do in Oxford and because the history is so compelling, it can be hard to narrow your choices of sites to visit—particularly if you are pressed for time. We thought you might appreciate some help in prioritizing. Here are "Carole and Sarah's Greatest Hits in Oxford," our opinion of the *not-to-be-missed* attractions in this fair city.

- If you've only got a couple of hours to spare, go see the **cloisters of New College**. There you will find a magnificent collection of 14th-century larger-than-life statues of saints. Follow that up with a visit to **St. Mary the Virgin Church**, where the heresy trial of Archbishop of Canterbury Thomas Cranmer was conducted. Portions of this glorious church date back to the 13th century.

- With another hour or so, you can add visits to the 15th-century **Divinity School at the Old Bodleian Library** and **Christ Church Cathedral**. Christ Church once was part of the 12th-century Norman Priory of St. Frideswide and is now the cathedral of the Diocese of Oxford as well as the chapel for Christ Church College, founded by Cardinal Wolsey.

- If you are quick, you also can stop by **St. Michael at the Northgate Church**. Its Saxon Tower, dating from 1040, is the oldest building in Oxford. The church itself dates primarily from the 13th century.

- Two other lovely **chapels** from our period that you may want to add to your list, time permitting, are those at **Merton College** and **All Souls College**. Both boast original 15th-century stained glass windows and shelter a number of other medieval treasures.

- If you have the whole day available to spend in Oxford, make time for a trip to **Godstow Abbey**, located just four miles from the city center. The ruins are extraordinary, the history inspiring, and the food and beverages at the abbey's former guest house (now called the Trout Inn) provide a welcome respite from a hard day of touring.

Oxford

>>>

LOCATED

M4 to A40

TRAVEL

Trains depart regularly from Victoria Station; bus and coach services also leave the station every 20 minutes. Travel time is about 1½ hours.

Note: Oxford's city center is a very busy place. Tourism officials recommend that visitors rely on public transportation (meaning trains or buses) to get there. However, if you prefer to drive, their recommendation is to park at one of four "park-and-ride" lots located on the outskirts of the city. Regularly scheduled buses provide transport from the parking lots into the city.

CONVENIENCES

Guided bus tours are available at Oxford Railway Station (Guide Friday, 01865-790522) and Gloucester Green Bus Station (Oxford Classic, 01235-819393, with daily tours departing every 15 minutes in the summer and every 30 minutes in the winter).

>>>

History indicates that the town of Oxford began life as a lay community surrounding an Anglo-Saxon priory that housed both monks and nuns. The first prioress of this unusual monastery was a Mercian princess named Frideswide whose father founded it in her honor around 700 CE. The original monastery was constructed on the site where Christ Church College stands today. It was destroyed by fire during the St. Brice's Day massacre of Danes in 1002, but was rebuilt and expanded. In 1122, it was refounded as the Augustinian priory of St. Frideswide.

The town grew in importance when a follower of William the Conqueror, Robert d'Oilly, built a castle here in 1071. A second abbey, Oseney, was founded in 1129 and Henry I built a luxurious palace in 1130. The town gained its charter from Henry II in 1155.

Much of Oxford's history is defined, of course, by the growth of Oxford University. But the relationship between town and gown has not always been smooth. Particularly in medieval and Tudor times, when the scholastic community was dominated by noble clerics, the balance of power was on the side of the university. For example, the university chancellor had legal authority over the townspeople clear up to the 20th century.

Needless to say, this state of affairs caused great resentment

⏵ Did you know?

Legend has it that Frideswide earned her sainthood through the vigor with which she defended her virginity. One determined suitor who tried to capture the abbey and its abbess by force was struck blind. His eyesight was restored after Frideswide forgave him.

among the townspeople. Pitched battles between the scholars and the common folk were regular occurrences. One of the worst occurred on St. Scholastica's Day, February 10, 1354 (or 1355, depending upon the source). Students celebrating at Swyndelstock Tavern took issue with the quality of wine being served. A fight broke out and townspeople rushed to the defense of the innkeeper. The melee lasted for three days with indignant townspeople beating and killing students and looting the colleges. The penalty the town folk paid for their lack of restraint was high. The city was forced to pay for restorations to the colleges. In addition, the mayor and city fathers had to swear allegiance annually to the chancellor of the university and make restitution for damages. The practice continued until 1825.

❖❖❖

PROVISIONS OF OXFORD

Oxford was front and center in the early, heady days of the barons' efforts to force Henry III to accept additional limits on the power of kingship. The barons, led by Henry's brother-in-law Simon de Montfort, Earl of Leicester, sought to build upon and expand the baronial rights and monarchical limitations set forth in Magna Carta. A committee of 24 nobles, 12 appointed by the barons and 12 by the king, met in Oxford in June 1258 and produced the "Provisions of Oxford." This was a set of two dozen recommendations designed to achieve a greater balance of power between the king and his subjects and ensure a voice in government for a broader segment of the population. Needless to say, Henry was not happy with this state of affairs and quickly sought to overturn the provisions. His efforts led to war with his barons that ended with the death of de Montfort in the Battle of Evesham in August 1265. The Provisions of Oxford were then repealed, but they continued to live in men's imaginations and laid the groundwork for the evolution of parliamentary government.

❖❖❖

✝ Oxford Tourist Information Centre
15/16 Broad Street

》》》

PHONE

01865-726871

》》》

The Oxford Tourist Information Centre is the departure point for guided walking tours of the city and university. Each tour takes about two hours. All tours depart daily at 11:00 a.m. and 2:00 p.m., with additional tours scheduled at busy times. The charge for the tours is £6.00 for adults and £3.00 for children. Entrance fees for the colleges are covered by the tour charge. There is also a ghost tour that begins at 8:00 p.m. on Friday and Saturday, July–September. It costs £6.00 for adults and £3.00 for children.

✝ Museum of Oxford
St. Aldate's at the corner of Blue Boar Street

>>

PHONE
01865-815559

E-MAIL
museum@oxford.gov.uk

OPEN
10:00 a.m.–4:00 p.m. Tuesday–Friday, year-round
10:00 a.m.–5:00 p.m. Saturday, year-round
Noon–4:00 p.m. Sunday, year-round

ADMISSION
£2.00 Adults
50p Children
£1.50 Concessions
Family ticket available

CONVENIENCES
Guided tours of the museum and the castle mound; gift shop

>>

Located in the Town Hall, the museum provides a great starting point for anyone who wants to begin a tour of Oxford with a thorough grounding in the history of the town and the university.

✝ The Oxford Story Exhibition
6 Broad Street

>>

PHONE
01865-728822

E-MAIL
info@oxfordstory.co.uk

WEBSITE
www.oxfordstory.co.uk

OPEN
9:30 a.m.–5:00 p.m. daily, July and August
10:00 a.m.–4:30 p.m. daily, January–June and September–December

ADMISSION
£6.50 Adults
£5.00 Children (children under 4 free of charge)
£5.50 Seniors
Family ticket available

CONVENIENCES
Special children's commentary available; gift shop and bookstore

》》》

If you like the Disneyesque approach to history (and if you don't mind absorbing a healthy dose of information about other periods along with your medieval and Tudor fix), you will enjoy the Oxford Story Exhibition, particularly if you are traveling with children. This essentially is an amusement ride through 800 years of Oxford's history. It bills itself as "Europe's longest indoor 'dark' ride." It does give you a good grounding about the medieval roots of the town and university, but it doesn't stop there. One interesting note about the exhibition is that a bastion tower from the original city walls runs through the center of the building. 'Nough said.

᠕

Oxford University
University Offices
Wellington Square

》》》

PHONE
01865-270000

OPEN
Note: Each college that is part of Oxford University posts its own open hours, but all are subject to closure for college functions, exams and other events. If you are desperate to see any particular institution or building, you will be wise to call ahead to the number listed for that specific college.

》》》

One of the best known and most respected institutions of higher education in the world, Oxford University did not spring whole from the ground at a specific point in time. No one waved a magic wand and created a complex of buildings and educational programs that turned out erudite humans overnight. In fact, history does not record a firm date for the establishment of Oxford University.

Historical records indicate that Oxford was a magnet for scholars as early as the 10th century. By the 12th century, the town was firmly established as a training facility for clerics. Its rapid growth as an educational center was helped, no doubt, by Henry II's ban on English students attending the University of Paris, issued in 1167. Generally, however, the practice of learning was a fairly loose affair with students gathering around masters in outdoor settings to soak up knowledge through lectures. There were no formal classrooms, no college dormitories, no collegial facilities for dining, studying or discourse, although some students did live with masters in their homes.

Colleges as we know them today, with designated buildings, a hierarchical administrative structure, tenured professors and rigid achievement standards, did not exist. This system of higher education did not begin evolving until the first buildings specifically intended for academic purposes began to be acquired in the mid-13th century. From that point on, Oxford University grew in a hodgepodge manner as various wealthy medieval and Tudor nobles and churchmen founded institutions of learning, creating memorials to themselves.

• •
☞ Did you know?

The first chancellor of Oxford University was the saintly Robert Grosseteste, who later served as Bishop of Lincoln during the reign of Henry III. A renowned scholar, Grosseteste was a close friend of and advisor to Simon de Montfort, Earl of Leicester and brother-in-law of the king. The bishop was a strong backer of de Montfont's rebellious efforts to reign in the monarchy's powers and guarantee a voice in government for a broader spectrum of people.
• •

As we have done in our other books when we have tackled a complex site with an equally complex history, we are going to take you first on a walk through Oxford, briefly describing the medieval and Tudor features of the university and town in the order you will encounter them. Then (*our favorite part*), we will cover each college in the order it was founded, giving you the highlights of its early history. We encourage you to read the history before taking the walking tour. We assure you it's worth your time; you will have a much better appreciation for the sites you will be seeing if you know their history.*

WALKING TOUR

This self-guided tour of Oxford University, its colleges and related ancient sites starts at the Oxford rail station. Exit the station via the pedestrian bridge to Botley Road and turn right. Botley becomes Park End. Follow Park to Worcester Street and turn left to find the first college you will come across — naturally, **Worcester College**. While Worcester itself is not ancient, its predecessor college, Gloucester, was. The college is not generally open to the public, but if you talk nicely to the porter, he may let you take a peek at a cluster of medieval cottages on the left side of the main quad. These cottages provided lodging for Gloucester College students.

Across from the main gate to Worcester College is Beaumont Street. Just after you cross Walton Street, look to your left for a plaque mounted on a stone pillar that marks the spot where **Beaumont Palace** once stood. Built by Henry I, the palace was the birthplace of Richard the Lionheart and King John.

Continue around Beaumont Street to St. Giles Street. Take your life in your hands and negotiate this very busy traffic square, bearing to your right toward the center of the square. Here you will find an 18th-century **memorial to the Protestant martyrs** who were burned at the stake for heresy in front of Bal-

---

*Although 39 different colleges, plus various halls and supporting facilities, make up Oxford University, we are going to confine ourselves to an exploration of only those colleges that either have firm roots in the Middle and Tudor Ages or occupy buildings that date from those periods.

liol College in the mid-16th century. Across the square, the side wall of **Balliol College**, founded in the 13th century, looms before you. To the left of Balliol is the back of 16th-century **Trinity College**. Farther along St. Giles Street is the entrance to **St. John's College**, also founded in the 16th century. Here, if you have made an appointment, you can visit the college library, built between 1596 and 1598, and gawk at a 15th-century copy of *The Canterbury Tales*. If you're up for a hike, continue down St. Giles Street to the point where it intersects with Woodstock and Banbury roads. In a park in the center of this intersection, you will find the 13th-century **St. Giles Church**. We warn you, however, that this is a substantial walk from St. John's and the church is not always open.

Backtrack down St. Giles Street, crossing Beaumont and Broad streets and walk down Cornmarket Street. Here you will find the **Saxon Tower of St. Michael at the Northgate**, the oldest building in Oxford, and the 14th-century **New Inn**. A little farther down the street on the left is the 11th-century **Carfax Tower**, once St. Martin's Church, which marks the center of the old city. The Swyndelstock Tavern, which provided the fuel that fed the flames of the 1354 riots, was located in

> ••••••••••••••••••••••
> 👉 Did you know?
>
> Next to the New Inn is **Golden Cross Yard**, home to a row of small shops and site of a 12th-century inn. A plaque on the wall relates the ancient history of the site.
> ••••••••••••••••••••••

this area. There is a plaque commemorating the event and the site of the tavern on the Abbey National Bank building on the southwest corner of the intersection.

From Carfax, walk east on High Street to Turl Street and turn left. This is where you will find the entrances to three colleges with medieval and Tudor connections, **Lincoln**, **Jesus** and **Exeter**. Lincoln has the best-preserved medieval buildings at Oxford University. They date from the 15th century.

At the end of Turl Street, cross Broad Street to find the entrance to **Balliol College**, one of the contenders for "oldest college" at Oxford University. Turn right toward the pedestrian walkway and look in the center of the street for the cobble cross that marks the spot where Archbishop of Canterbury Thomas Cranmer and two bishops died for refusing to renounce their faith during the reign of "Bloody" Queen Mary. Opposite the cross, a plaque on the wall of Balliol commemorates the event. It is surrounded by scorch marks from the roaring fires that killed the martyrs.

Next to Balliol (walking east again) is the entrance to **Trinity College**, founded in the 16th century. The oldest structure affiliated with Trinity is the early 15th-century building that now serves as the college library. Unfortunately, it's not open to the public.

A little farther down Broad, on the opposite side of the street, turn right onto Catte Street to find the entrance to the old **Bodleian Library**. (Don't confuse it with the "New" Bodleian Library on Broad Street. Except for its name, it has nothing to do with our period of history.) The library is named for a Tudor noble who spearheaded a drive to rebuild Oxford University's central library. The main attraction here for medieval history buffs is the 15th-century Divinity School, supposedly "the most beautiful medieval building in Oxford."

Just beyond the library, with an entrance on Radcliffe Square, is **Brasenose College**, one of the oddest-named Oxford colleges. The moniker is said to have been derived from a 13th-century brass knocker that may once have graced the door of the medieval Brasenose Hall.

On the far side of Radcliffe Square is **St. Mary the Virgin Church (a.k.a. University Church)**. The tower of this church

---

☞ **Did you know?**

It was to St. Mary's Church that the mayor of Oxford and the city's leading tradesmen reported annually after the riots of 1354. There, they paid tribute to the university chancellor for damage done to university property during the upheaval. Every year until 1825 the townspeople handed over the fine assessed after the riots—a total of 60p, one penny for each of the burgesses who were in business in Oxford in 1354. Another version of the story is that 63 townspeople made the trek to St. Mary's every year to pay a penny each in retribution for each student killed in the rioting.

dates from the 13th century and provides a spectacular view of Oxford. The heresy trials of Archbishop Cranmer and the two bishops were held here. As it has since the earliest days of the university, St. Mary plays a central role in the religious life of Oxford.

Next to St. Mary in High Street is **All Souls College**. Founded as a memorial to Henry V, the college still worships in its original 15th-century chapel.

Across from All Souls is **University College**, probably the oldest college at Oxford, although its founding date is very much in dispute. The best building associated with the college is its 14th-century Great Hall with its original hammerbeam ceiling.

Continue walking east on High Street to Queen's Lane. Here you will find another three colleges with ancient connections. **Queen's College** (entrance on High Street) and **St. Edmund Hall** are located on opposite sides of the street just as you turn left off High Street. **New College** is a little farther north with an entrance on Holywell Street. St. Edmund claims to use the oldest building affiliated with Oxford University and holds out the tantalizing possibility that its hall, once a residential facility for early medieval students, may date from the late 12th century. New College has a 14th-century chapel, dining hall and cloisters.

◆ ◆
☞ Did you know?

Behind the shops and office buildings fronting High Street are more ancient structures. In back of 106–107 High Street, you will find **Tookley Hall**, built in 1324 as a residence hall for students. Number 128 High Street conceals Wheatsheaf Yard. This is where you will find **Gill and Company**, a firm that claims to be the oldest ironmonger in England. It was founded in 1530.

◆ ◆

Retrace your steps back down Queen's Lane to High Street and turn left, passing St. Edmund Hall, till you cross Longwall Street and find the entrance to **Magdalen College**. The most interesting feature here, at least from our perspective, is the college bar, located in what was once the Great Hall of St. John the Baptist Hospital. It dates from the 13th century. (*A twofer! A medieval building and adult beverages. Works for us!*)

From Magdalen College, cross High Street and walk down Merton Street. Here again, you will encounter two more colleges with ties to our favorite period of history, first **Merton College**, then **Corpus Christi College**. Merton is another contender for "oldest college"; its main college hall was built in 1277 and construction of the chapel was started in 1290. You can also find a well-preserved stretch of the old city wall on the grounds of this college.

☞ Did you know?

Thomas Wolsey, future cardinal and power behind the throne of Henry VIII, was a child prodigy. He began his studies at Magdalen College in 1484 at the age of 11. At the time, the usual age for beginning studies at Oxford was 14.

At the end of Merton Street, before turning into Oriel Square, you will find the entrance to **Christ Church Picture Gallery**. In Oriel Square is the entrance to **Oriel College**. Both Corpus Christi and Oriel use ancient buildings, some at Oriel dating from the 14th century and those at Corpus Christi from the 16th.

☞ Did you know?

Across from Christ Church in Brewer Street is a plaque at Number 1 marking the birthplace of Dorothy Sayers (1893), the grand dame of mystery writers (*at least in our opinion*). Many of Sayers's books feature an Oxford theme. Sayers's father was headmaster of Christ Church Cathedral School at the time of her birth and she was a scholarship student at Somerville College at Oxford. Her protagonist, Lord Peter Wimsey, is a graduate of Balliol. (*Okay — not of our period, but we couldn't resist. Dorothy Sayers is the greatest!*)

From Oriel Square, cut down Bear Lane to Blue Boar Street to St. Aldate's Street. There you will find the **Museum of Oxford**. A left turn will take you to the entrance to **Christ Church College**, one of the best known of the Oxford colleges. Founded by Cardinal Thomas Wolsey, the college was claimed by Henry VIII after Wolsey's fall from power. The Great Hall and kitchen constructed by Wolsey in the early 1500s are still in use today. A *not-to-be-missed* attraction here is **Christ Church Cathedral**. The church's nave, crossing and quire once were part of the 12th-century Norman Priory of St. Frideswide.

From Christ Church, turn right and cross the street to find

Brewer Street. Walk down Brewer Street to Littlegate Street; cross the street and look for Turn Again Lane, which will take you to Greyfriars Street. There you will find a plaque, set into a shopping center wall, dedicated to the famous medieval philosopher Roger Bacon (1219–1292), who studied at Oxford.

Follow Greyfriars to Castle Street, where you will find **St. George's Tower**, the remains of Oxford Castle. Most recently used as a prison, the tower is undergoing renovation for conversion into a hotel.

You have now completed a walking tour of medieval and Tudor attractions of Oxford University and are free to meander back to the rail station. In this area, if you are not already overdosed on medieval and Tudor history (*or too footsore even to contemplate taking any more steps than necessary*), you can find the 12th-century church of **St. Thomas the Martyr**, named in honor of Thomas à Becket, on Botley Road.

 University College
High Street

≫≫≫

PHONE
   None

OPEN
   By appointment only; write to:
      The Domestic Bursar
      University College
      High Street
      Oxford OX14BH

ADMISSION
   Free of charge
≫≫≫

University is probably the oldest of all the Oxford colleges. It claims origins in the 9th century and links with Alfred the Great, but this assertion has never been proven. That doesn't stop University from boldly incorporating in its seal emblems said to be representative of King Alfred and the kingdom of Wessex.

However, the exact founding date is hard to pinpoint; it depends upon what one chooses as a marker. If money is your measure, then the founding date is 1249, when William of Durham donated 310 marks to provide for the education of a dozen or so needy scholars. (*And no, don't ask. We don't know if this is the first recorded instance of a scholarship endowment or how elaborate the financial qualification forms to prove need were.*) If you consider the acquisition of land and buildings for use as academic facilities to be the determining factor, then the date is 1253. If the foundation of a college is dated from the granting of official statutes of organization, then University loses the "oldest" title competition; it did not receive its first statutes until 1280.

☞ **Did you know?**

University College was excommunicated in 1411 because the fellows at the time were supporters of John Wycliff. They were followers of the heretical movement known as Lollardism that was sparked by Wycliff's teachings against Roman Catholic Church dogma.

The first buildings constructed for academic use were built on the site where Brasenose College now stands. In 1332, University moved to buildings on High Street, where it has been ever since. The buildings have been extensively expanded and renovated, however. Not a lot of these medieval structures survives, but you won't be disappointed in University's Great Hall with its original hammerbeam roof, if you have written ahead and arranged an appointment to see it.

〜

✝ St. Edmund Hall
Queen's Lane

PHONE
01865-279000

OPEN
Daylight hours daily, year-round

Note: Groups with a maximum of 12 people must report to the college lodge.

ADMISSION
Free of charge

>>

While University may claim to be the oldest college in Oxford, one of the newer colleges actually uses the oldest buildings. St. Edmund Hall, established as a college in 1957, dates from at least the 14th century. The hall itself (located straight back from the college gatehouse) is the only surviving structure that provided residential quarters for medieval Oxford students. Thus, the college claims that it is "the oldest academical society for the education of undergraduates."

The college is named for St. Edmund of Abingdon who served as Archbishop of Canterbury from 1234 to 1240 and was a master in Oxford in the late 12th century. Tradition has it that St. Edmund lived and taught in a house located at the western end of what is the college's front quadrangle today. The college dangles the tantalizing prospect that its hall had its beginnings in this house. What is known is that the property passed to Oseney Abbey in 1272 and that rent roles for 1317–18 include a reference to St. Edmund Hall, establishing it as the oldest structure that is part of Oxford University.

Somewhere around 1531, Oseney Abbey leased the hall to Queen's College. In the mid-1500s, after the suppression of the abbey, the hall had a somewhat muddled ownership history, passing back and forth between private owners and the college. Queen's managed to gain firm control of the hall in 1557 and was charged with responsibility for preserving it. Queen's maintained control of the hall until the 20th century, when it was transformed into the focal point of a new, independent college.

While the history of the medieval hall may make it the most compelling of the college's buildings, it is not the oldest structure associated with St. Edmund Hall. That honor belongs to the 12th-century parish church of St. Peter-in-the-East, which has served as the college library since 1970. Unfortunately, it is not open to the public. A small portion of Oxford's medieval city wall also can be found on the college's grounds, to the left of the gatehouse.

∿

Balliol College
Broad Street

〉〉〉

PHONE
   01865-277777

OPEN
   2:00–5:00 p.m. daily, year-round

   Note: A maximum of 10 people will be escorted on any single tour.

ADMISSION
   £1.00 Adults, children, concessions

TIP!
   You can catch guided tours of the university at Balliol's front gate.

〉〉〉

Another contender for "oldest-college," Balliol was founded sometime around 1260 by John Balliol, a prominent baron and strong supporter of Henry III. As an act of charity, Balliol, at the urging of the Bishop of Durham, rented property in Oxford to provide housing for needy students. However, it was not until after Balliol's death in 1269 that his widow, Dervorguilla, formally established the college. She provided a permanent endowment and created official statutes and a seal the college still uses.

• •
☞ **Did you know?**
In the beginning, just 16 students lived at Balliol. Thanks to the college founder's generosity, they each received 8p per week to support their studies. (*We'd like to see today's college students make do with that kind of pocket change!*)
• •

In the 15th century, Bishop of Ely William Gray, who had

been a member of Balliol, donated his collection of European manuscripts to the college. Today, it is the largest medieval manuscript collection in England.

There is not much to see at Balliol. Most of the buildings postdate our period of history. However, you will want to seek out the memorial that marks the spot where Archbishop of Canterbury Thomas Cranmer and two other martyrs to the Protestant cause were burned at the stake during Mary Tudor's efforts to restore Catholicism in England. It is to the left of the main entrance to Balliol.

☞ Did you know?

Dervorguilla, John Balliol's wife, was a Scottish princess. Through her lineage, their son, also named John, was able to claim the throne of Scotland briefly in 1296. Rival claimants made that seat very insecure and the second John Balliol was soon toppled from it. He fled to England and sought sanctuary from Edward I. Edward, who had his own ambitions for the Scottish crown, gladly provided it. Balliol spent the rest of his life as Edward's prisoner.

BURNED AT THE STAKE

Balliol College was the scene of the gruesome murders of three prominent Protestant martyrs during the reign of "Bloody" Queen Mary. Bishop of Worcester Hugh Latimer and Bishop of London Nicholas Ridley were the first of the three to be tried and convicted of heresy. When they refused to renounce their faith, they were condemned to die and were burned at the stake on October 16, 1555. As the fire was lit, Latimer allegedly turned to Ridley and said, "Be of good comfort, Master Ridley, and play the man. We shall this day light such a candle, by God's grace, in England, as, I trust, shall never be put out." Luckily, Latimer died relatively quickly of smoke inhalation, but Ridley suffered horribly, dying a slow, agonizing death.

Archbishop of Canterbury Thomas Cranmer, who was held in prison until permission could be received from the Pope to execute him, was forced to watch this horrifying spectacle. That may have had something to do with his prison recantation of his Protestantism. But Mary sent him to the stake anyway. No way was she going to forgive one of the men she most blamed for engineering the divorce of her parents, Henry VIII and Katherine of Aragon, and who had played an instrumental role in the establishment of the Anglican church. Cranmer went to the stake on March 21, 1556. In a last act of courage, he refused to repeat his prison recantation in public, repenting his momentary rejection of his faith.

As the flames licked upward, Cranmer held out his right hand and told the assembled crowd that because this hand had signed his recantation, it had offended God and therefore would be the first part of his body to burn.

The site of this martyrdom is marked by a cross in the pavement, and a memorial to the martyrs is located in St. Giles Street. The college wall opposite the cross bears a plaque commemorating the event, surrounded by scorch marks from the fires.

❖❖

✝ Merton College
Merton Street

>>>

PHONE
01865-276310

OPEN
2:00– 4:00 p.m. Monday–Friday, year-round
10:00 a.m.–4:00 p.m. Saturday and Sunday, year-round

ADMISSION
Free of charge for college grounds
£1.00 for the Old Library

>>>

The final candidate for "oldest college" is Merton College, founded in 1264 by Walter de Merton, Bishop of Rochester. The bishop indicated his intention to establish a college in 1262 when he set aside a portion of the revenues from his estates in Surrey for this purpose. Apparently, he was not sure where he wanted that college to be — he bought land in both Oxford and Cambridge. For whatever reason, Oxford won out and students began to be accepted there in 1270.

Merton is located next to a long stretch of the old city wall that runs along the north side of Christ Church Meadow. It also has the most extensive cluster of medieval structures, including the oldest library in England, dating back to 1373–1378. The library shelves were redone in 1623, but they are still equipped with the fittings for chaining books, a common medieval practice to safeguard rare and precious tomes. The main college building, Merton Hall, was built in 1277. Construction of the chapel was begun in 1290; however, Bishop Merton completed only the quire and transepts. The rest of the chapel dates from the 15th century, including the stained glass in the east window. Still, it is one of the loveliest chapels in Oxford. Mob Quad is the oldest university quadrangle, built between 1304 and 1378. At the east end of the hall, the Warden's Lodgings over the archway date from 1497.

❖❖

JOHN WYCLIFF (C. 1330–1384)

One notorious graduate of Merton College was John Wycliff, the man credited with inspiring the Lollard movement, one of the few medieval challenges to the authority of the Catholic Church. A believer in predestination and a rejecter of transubstantiation, Wycliff really gained the ire of Church leaders when he translated the Bible from Latin into English. Wycliff was a fellow at Merton from 1356 to 1360 and went on to serve as Master at Balliol College. He was condemned by the Pope in 1377 for his heretical beliefs and forced to leave Oxford in 1381. Because he was protected by the powerful John of Gaunt, who had his own anticlerical ideas, Wycliff was not sentenced to death for heresy. He retired to his rectory in Lutterworth, Leicestershire, and continued to be a thorn in the Church's side, issuing numerous treatises on his unorthodox views, until his death in 1384.

❖❖

✝ Exeter College
Turl Street

>>>

PHONE
01865-279600

OPEN
2:00–5:00 p.m. daily, year-round

Note: Tours must be scheduled in advance; a maximum of 20 people will be escorted on any single tour.

ADMISSION
Free of charge

>>>

Exeter College was founded in 1314 on the site it still occupies by Walter de Stapeldon, Bishop of Exeter and Treasurer of England for Edward II. The college, first known as Stapeldon Hall, housed about a dozen or so students, mostly drawn from the southwest of England, since the bishop's plan was to educate clerics for his diocese. All that remains of Stapeldon's college is Palmer's Tower, named for a 15th-century rector. You can find the tower east of the college chapel (that dates from the 19th century).

Oriel College
Oriel Square

>>

PHONE
 01865-276555

OPEN
 2:00–5:00 p.m. daily, year-round

 Note: Groups of 20 or more must schedule in advance.

ADMISSION
 Free of charge

>>>

Oriel seems to have no competition for its claim to be the fifth-oldest college at Oxford. It was founded in 1326 by Adam de Brome, a courtier of Edward II. Edward is counted as a co-founder because de Brome convinced the king to endow the college with lands and money.

The original name of the college was the "House of the Blessed Mary the Virgin in Oxford." The current name was drawn from the oriel windows of a tenement building that occu-

• • • • • • • • • • • • • • • • • • • •
☞ Did you know?
Two of Oriel College's more famous fellows (*at least from our perspective*) are Sir Thomas More and Sir Walter Raleigh.
• • • • • • • • • • • • • • • • • • • •

pied this site before construction of the college buildings. Most of the ancient buildings were rebuilt in the 17th century, but the hall and chapel of the 14th-century St. Mary's Hall still exist. The chapel now serves as the Junior Library and the hall is the Junior Common Room.

⌁

Queen's College
High Street

>>>

PHONE
  01865-279120

OPEN
  Afternoons by prior appointment only for groups who must be accompanied by an official guide; contact the Tourist Information Centre to make arrangements.

ADMISSION
  Free of charge

>>>

Although it is named for one, Queen's College was not actually established by one of England's medieval queens. It was started in 1341 by Robert de Eglesfield, chaplain to Edward III's consort Queen Philippa. Eglesfield named the college in honor of his mistress. Philippa eventually did become a benefactress of the college, endowing it with the lands and revenues of a Southampton hospital in 1343.

The original buildings of Queen's College were replaced in the 17th and 18th centuries. About the only physical connection you will find with the college's medieval roots is in the library, which has an extremely valuable collection of medieval manuscripts and documents. (*We didn't say you could see them; we're just telling you they are there.*)

✝ New College
New College Lane

>>>

PHONE

01865-279555

OPEN

11:00 a.m.–5:00 p.m. daily, April–October

2:00–4:00 p.m. daily, November–March

Note: A maximum of 10 people will be escorted on any single tour.

ADMISSION

£2.00 Adults, April–October

£1.00 Children, April–October

Free of charge, November–March

>>>

Although Christ Church College and its cathedral are the best known and most visited parts of Oxford University, we actually found New College to be the most intriguing—at least from the perspective of a medieval history enthusiast. In fact, if you only have time to take in the sites of a single college during your trip to Oxford, we recommend you visit this one.

Founded in 1379 by William Wykeham, Bishop of Winchester and Chancellor of England, this college originally was dubbed "St. Mary's." Unfortunately, there was already a St. Mary's college in Oxford—the aforementioned Oriel College. So Wykeham's institution became known as the "New St. Mary's College" which, of course, was shortened over time to simply "New College."

Wykeham's plan for the new school was to serve as a training ground for priests needed to replace the hundreds who had died during the Black Plague. He made sure the college would have a steady supply of students by establishing a feeder grammar school at Winchester—a revolutionary concept for the time. It was not until 1854 that New College began accepting students from any other place.

The bishop also intended for his college to contain a chantry chapel where priests could pray daily for his soul. Therefore, he devoted a great deal of attention to construction of the college chapel, still a spiritually inspiring space. One amusing feature in the chapel is a 14th-century carved misericord representing a book carrier (*a slightly different style from the hefty book bags students lug around today*). The chapel also contains original stained glass windows in the antechamber. Wykeham's crozier can be found behind glass to the left of the altar.

• •

☞ Did you know?

The original charter for New College required it to assume responsibility for maintaining the section of the city wall that formed one of its boundaries. That may be why that section of the medieval wall is so well preserved.

• •

One of the most outstanding features of New College—and a reason why we rank it as a *must-see*—is the collection of 14th-century larger-than-life stone figures that dominate the cloisters in front of the chapel. These are magnificent renderings of saints, including Jesus himself. To our amazement, we could find no information anywhere at the college or in Oxford itself that revealed more about the history of these remarkable statues.

New College set the pattern for the architectural design of colleges to come with its cloistered quadrangles. The boundary of the college garden is marked by the original city wall, which still has its medieval bastions. The college's Muniment Tower was constructed to be a giant safe and is used today to store college records. Other 14th-century structures include the dining hall (the linenfold paneling dates from the 16th century) and the Bell Tower that rises above the cloisters.

ᴧᴧ

✝ Lincoln College
Turl Street

>>

PHONE
    01865-279800

OPEN
    2:00–5:00 p.m. Monday–Friday, year-round

11:00 a.m.–5:00 p.m. Sunday, year-round
Closed Saturday

Note: Tour groups are admitted by appointment only.

ADMISSION
Free of charge

>>

Probably the best-preserved medieval buildings at Oxford University can be found at Lincoln College, established in 1427 by Richard Fleming, Bishop of Lincoln, one of the persecutors of John Wycliff. Most likely because of Wycliff's deleterious effect on Oxford, Fleming felt the need to found a college that would "defend the mysteries of scripture against those ignorant laymen who profaned with swinish snouts its most holy pearls." (*Guess it's pretty clear what Fleming thought about the common man and Wycliff's English translation of the Bible.*) The buildings around Front Quad along the west range were constructed c. 1430. The hall and kitchen in the north range were built around 1437. Don't be fooled by the buildings in Chapel Quad, including the chapel itself. They may look 15th century, but they actually date from the 17th.

~

All Souls College
High Street

>>
PHONE
01865-279379
OPEN
2:00–4:00 p.m. Monday–Friday, year-round

Note: Groups of six or more must schedule in advance.

ADMISSION
Free of charge

>>

The College of All Souls of the Faithful Departed was established in 1437 by Henry Chichele, Archbishop of Canterbury, with Henry VI as a co-founder. The college began life as a memorial to Henry V and all the Englishmen who died during the Hundred Years War with France. Its purpose was to produce a superior group of highly educated clergy to serve Church and State.

With this goal in mind, Chichele, who had been a member of New College, spent lavishly on the construction and endowment of the college to ensure its future prosperity. Records indicate he invested a total of £9,500 (equivalent to about £3 million today): £4,500 to construct the buildings and £5,000 to endow it with estates spread all over England. In addition, Chichele created a set of statutes for the college that guaranteed (*at least in his opinion*) that only the best and brightest students would be accepted as members. First, he limited enrollment to just 40 fellows. Then he decreed that, to be accepted, students had to be between the ages of 18 and 25 and had to have been born legitimately in the Province of Canterbury. No novices were to be admitted either; students would not be considered unless they already had studied at the university for three years. In return, students would receive living quarters and a new set of clothes every year.

The Front Quad looks very much like it did when it was first built in 1438–1443, thanks to a careful Victorian restoration that preserved the 15th-century facade of the buildings and protected the statues of Archbishop Chichele and Henry VI that adorn the gatehouse entrance. The chapel, which was consecrated in June 1442, is the real thing, with a hammerbeam roof, several original stalls and original stained glass windows. Of particularly high quality is the glass in the east window, which depicts the Apostles and the Holy Women, and that in the southwest window, which has representations of several English kings, including Alfred the Great, Edward II and Henry V. Traces of the original medieval paint also can be seen in the reredos (c. 1447), although the statues in it are of a later period. The Old Library boasts a heraldic ceiling that was installed in 1598.

While you're in the neighborhood . . .

✝ **St. Mary the Virgin Church (a.k.a. University Church)**

High Street

>>

PHONE
None

OPEN
Church tower & shop
9:00 a.m.–7:00 p.m. Monday–Friday, April–October
Noon–5:30 p.m. Sunday, April–October
9:00 a.m.–5:00 p.m. Monday–Friday, November–March
Noon–dusk Sunday, November–March

ADMISSION
Church
Free of charge
Tower
£1.60 Adults
80p Children

CONVENIENCES
Coffee shop

>>

Close by All Souls College in High Street is the magnificent St. Mary the Virgin Church. It was here during the reign of Mary Tudor that Archbishop of Canterbury Thomas Cranmer and the Bishops Latimer and Ridley were tried and convicted of treason and heresy because of their refusal to recant their Protestant faith. They were subsequently burned at the stake in front of Balliol College.

There has been a church on the site of St. Mary since Anglo-Saxon times. The oldest parts of the present church are the tower, built in 1280, and its spire, added in 1315–1325. The Gothic tower and steeple, considered to be among the finest in England, provide a spectacular view of Oxford, if one is inclined to climb to the top. The north chapel was constructed in 1328 by Adam de Brome, the church rector and founder of Oriel

College. He also is buried here. The chancel was rebuilt in 1453 and the nave renovated in 1510.

At the physical center of the walled city, St. Mary was a focal point of university life for many years, even providing space for the university's first library in the Old Congregation House (c. 1320), on the northeast side of the church. The Adam de Brome Chapel served as a courtroom from which the university chancellor dispensed justice over students and townspeople alike. The church remains a primary center of university religious life. Most Sundays when the university is in session, the vice chancellor and college provosts come in ceremonial order and garb, assembling themselves in throne-like seats in the back of the nave, to hear the official university sermon.

◆◆◆◆◆◆◆◆◆◆◆◆◆◆◆◆◆◆◆◆◆◆

🖙 Did you know?

Legend has it that Amy Robsart, the first wife of Robert Dudley, Earl of Leicester, was buried in St. Mary. Leicester, as you will recall, was Queen Elizabeth's very special favorite and for years harbored ambitions of becoming her consort. Therefore, Amy's death in 1560 caused a major scandal. She was found at the bottom of a flight of stairs in a house near Oxford and rumors rapidly spread that Robert was responsible for her death. Allegedly, he was removing an impediment to his pursuit of Elizabeth. The jury for the inquest into Amy's death judged it to be accidental, but that verdict did not erase the suspicion surrounding Dudley. Nor did becoming a widower get him closer to the altar with Elizabeth. The Virgin Queen continued to play the coy seductress, keeping Robert close by her side and showering him with honors, but never the one he really wanted—to be her royal mate.

◆◆◆

Magdalen College
High Street

>>

PHONE

01865-276000

OPEN

Noon–6:00 p.m. daily, June 25–September 30

2:00–6:00 p.m. daily, October 1–June 20

Note: A maximum of 20 people will be escorted on any single tour.

ADMISSION

£2.00 Adults, April 13–September 30

£1.00 Children, April 13–September 30

£1.00 Concessions, April 13–September 30

Free of charge October 1–April 12

>>

If you are a Yank reading this book, you can forget any preconceived notions you may have about the way the name of this college is pronounced. This is another of those quirky British pronunciations that has nothing to do with the actual spelling of the name. The correct pronunciation is "maudlin," as in overly sentimental. According to the college's literature, the pronunciation is derived from the way the name is spelled in the founding charter—"Maudelayne." (*To avoid confusion, maybe they should have retained the original spelling, but that would make it all way too easy, wouldn't it?*)

☞ **Did you know?**

One college with roots in the 13th century (but that is not a contender for the "oldest" title) is Hertford College. Perhaps that is because the college has been dissolved and re-established several times since it was created by Elias de Hertford in 1282. Today, the college counts its date of birth as 1874, when it was given new life by an Act of Parliament. Some of the college's buildings, particularly those in the Old Quad, date from the 15th century, but we are at a loss to tell you which ones.

Magdalen was founded as Magdalen Hall on High Street in 1458 by William of Waynflete, Bishop of Winchester and one-time Chancellor of England under Henry VI. Not content with a simple academic hall, Waynflete was ambitious and planned ahead for expansion. He bought land beyond the city walls and established a college dedicated to St. Mary Magdalen. The old hall later became part of Hertford College. The current college grounds spread over 100 acres of land beside the river. This is where you can find Deer Park, which shelters the college's 300-year-old herd of deer.

Magdalen was one of the first colleges at Oxford to add science to its curriculum. The school is also well known for its arts program. Every year on May 1, the Magdalen Choir welcomes the dawn in a chorus of song from the college's medieval Great Tower, a tradition dating back to the college's founding.

When Waynflete began construction of Magdalen College, he petitioned Henry VI to grant him ownership of the decrepit St. John the Baptist Hospital. While the new college was being built, the bishop used some of the hospital's 13th-century structures as educational quarters, a "temporary" solution that has lasted for eight centuries. The old chapel of the hospital became part of the Chaplain's Quadrangle, and the hospital's Great Hall served as the college's kitchen until 1980. Today it is the college bar (open to the public only out of term). Most of the buildings surrounding the Cloister Quadrangle date from the 15th century, although a third story was added in the 16th century and the roofs of the chapel and hall were raised in the 18th. The statues of St. John the Baptist and St. Mary Magdalen that decorate the niches at the top of the Great Tower are also 15th century. Those that are in the central quad date from the early 16th century and represent the seven deadly sins as well as heraldic and biblical figures.

••••••••••••••••••••••
☞ Did you know?
Both Oscar Wilde and C. S. Lewis were graduates of Magdalen College. (*Okay, they're not of our period— something about which we are generally sticklers—but we like their work.*)
••••••••••••••••••••••

✝ Brasenose College
Radcliffe Square

>>

PHONE

01865-277830

OPEN

10:00–11:30 a.m. daily, year-round (prescheduled tour groups only)
2:00–4:30 p.m. daily, year-round

ADMISSION

£1.00 Adults, children, concessions

>>

The official date for the founding of Brasenose College is 1509, although a Brasenose Hall existed on this site in the 13th century. A lawyer, Sir Richard Sutton, and William Smith, Bishop of Lincoln, teamed to establish the college. Oxford was then part of the Lincoln diocese (the Oxford diocese was not established until 1542), so the bishop's motivation for founding the institution is relatively clear. We don't know why Sir Richard helped him.

Originally called "The King's Hall and College of Brasenose," the unusual college name comes from the knocker that adorned the door of the 13th-century hall. The knocker was made of brass and shaped like a nose—hence, "Brasenose." It was stolen in the 14th century and eventually turned up on the door of a house in Stamford Street. The college retrieved its knocker during the reign of Queen Victoria by buying the house. The knocker now resides in a place of honor over the high table in the college dining room.

• •
☞ **Did you know?**
Linacre is another Oxford University college with no medieval roots other than its name, which is in honor of Thomas Linacre (c. 1460–1524), a prominent Tudor scholar and diplomat. Born in Canterbury, Linacre studied medicine at Oxford, became a diplomat for Henry VII and served as court physician for Henry VIII.
• •

Corpus Christi College

Merton Street

>>

PHONE
01865-276700

OPEN
1:30–4:30 p.m. daily, year-round

Note: Groups are limited to a maximum of 20 people and must check in with the college lodge before entering.

ADMISSION
Free of charge

>>

Corpus Christi College was founded in 1517 by Richard Fox, Bishop of Winchester, to promote classical studies. To achieve this, Fox established an extensive library that even Erasmus, during a late 15th-century visit to Oxford, said would rival that of the Vatican.

The buildings of the main quad of Corpus Christi College are those that were constructed by Fox. In the center of the quad is a sundial decorated with a pelican, a symbol of the Eucharist that Fox had adopted. Behind the sundial, in a niche at the top of one of the main quad buildings, is a statue of Fox. The college chapel dates from the mid-16th century.

Christ Church College
St. Aldate's

>>

PHONE
01865-286573

E-MAIL
custodian@chch.ox.ac.uk

OPEN
9:30 a.m.–5:30 p.m. Monday–Saturday, year-round
Noon–5:30 p.m. Sunday, year-round

ADMISSION
  £4.00 Adults
  £3.00 Children
  £3.00 Concessions

TIP!

On Saturday at 11:00 a.m. and 2:00 p.m., there is a special tour of
Christ Church Cathedral that leaves from Carfax Tower (located at
the corner of Queen and Cornmarket streets). This tour costs £7.00
for adults and £3.50 for children.

>>

Christ Church College actually started as Cardinal College.
Founded in 1525 by Cardinal Thomas Wolsey, the college was
suppressed by Henry VIII after Wolsey's fall from power in 1529.
Henry soon reversed himself and refounded the college in his
own name, only to refound it again in 1546 as Christ Church
College.

The beautiful architecture of the college bears the mark of
Wolsey's grand eye for design. Just as he did when he built York
Palace (a.k.a. Whitehall Palace) in London and Hampton
Court Palace, Wolsey set out at Cardinal College to create a
complex that would awe and inspire. Employing the architect
Henry Redman, who was responsible for York and Hampton
Court palaces, Wolsey succeeded in his initial efforts to establish a fantastical educational monument to himself. The Great
Hall he constructed, with its hammerbeam ceiling and marvelous fan-vaulted staircase, and its associated kitchen—all completed by 1529—are still in use today. The Great Quadrangle,
a.k.a. Tom Quad, that he designed remains the largest at the
university. (Don't be fooled, though; the tower in the quad,
called Tom Tower, actually is a 17th-century Christopher Wren
creation, although its Great
Tom Bell came from Oseney
Abbey.)

Wolsey financed this grand
construction scheme with revenues from the suppression of

••••••••••••••••••••••••
☞ Did you know?
Altogether, Wolsey used the revenues
of 22 suppressed monasteries to fund
the construction and endowment of
his college.
••••••••••••••••••••••••

other religious institutions in the area, including the priory of St. Frideswide. In fact, he chose to build his college on the grounds previously owned by the priory and incorporated some of the monastic buildings into his construction plans. The abbey cathedral was converted into a chapel for the college, and the former refectory, dating from the 15th century, was pressed into use as the library. In the library, you will find the original of Wolsey's cardinal hat that is used in the college crest.

* *

☞ Did you know?

In the early Middle Ages, Oxford was home to a large community of wealthy Jewish merchants. The remains of their synagogue can be found on the grounds of Christ Church.

* *

In refounding Christ Church College, Henry VIII took a major step to reinforce his reform of the Church in England. He abolished the study of canon law at the college; establishing instead chairs for the study of medicine, law, Greek, theology and Hebrew. This action set the precedent for transforming Oxford University from a training ground for church officials into a more secularly oriented institution of higher learning.

✚ A lost treasure . . .
Oseney Abbey

≫≫

Founded in 1129, Oseney Abbey once was one of the most glorious abbeys in Europe and had one of the largest churches in England, measuring 332 feet in length, with 24 altars. It began life as an Augustinian abbey dedicated to the Virgin Mary and played a major role in the growth and development of Oxford as an educational center, until it was dissolved by Henry VIII. During the construction of Christ Church College, many of the abbey's structures were demolished and the components were recycled into the new college's buildings.

All that remains of Oseney Abbey today are outlines of building foundations on the original site and a small 15th-century building, located in Botley Road. You can find a depiction of the abbey in the Bishop King Window in the Military Chapel of Christ Church Cathedral.

 # Cathedral Church of Christ
St. Aldate's

>>

PHONE
01865-276150

OPEN
9:30 a.m.–5:30 p.m. Monday–Saturday, year-round
Noon–5:30 p.m. Sunday, year-round

WORSHIP
Holy Communion: 8:00 a.m. Sunday
   7:35 a.m. Monday–Saturday
   1:00 p.m. Wednesday
College Communion: 9:00 a.m. Sunday
Matins: 10:00 a.m. Sunday
   7:15 a.m. Monday–Saturday
Sung Eucharist: 11:15 a.m. Sunday
Evensong: 6:00 p.m. daily

ADMISSION
Donation suggested

CONVENIENCES
Gift shop

>>

This is a *not-to-be-missed* stop on your tour of Oxford. The main portions of this beautiful church—the nave, crossing and quire—were once part of the 12th-century Norman Priory of St. Frideswide. The shrine of St. Frideswide is located in the Lady Chapel. Built in 1289, it was destroyed during the Dissolution of the Monasteries in 1538 and rebuilt in 1889. The cathedral also boasts a beautiful 14th-century stained glass window with a panel depicting the martyrdom of St. Thomas à Becket. Among the medieval tombs and effigies in the cathedral are those of Robert King, the last abbot of Oseney and the first bishop of Oxford, and Alexander de Sutton, a 14th-century prior of St. Frideswide's.

The gift shop for Christ Church College and Cathedral is located in the beautifully preserved Chapter House of the medieval monastery. On display there is a fabulous collection of ancient mass chalices, cups and patens.

◆◆◆◆◆◆◆◆◆◆◆◆◆◆◆◆◆◆◆◆◆

☞ Did you know?

Christ Church Cathedral bears the distinction of being the only church in the world that does double duty as a college chapel and a cathedral. It serves as the cathedral for the Diocese of Oxford.

◆◆◆◆◆◆◆◆◆◆◆◆◆◆◆◆◆◆◆◆◆

✝ Christ Church Picture Gallery
Canterbury Gate

PHONE
01865-276172

LOCATED
The entrance to the gallery is somewhat difficult to find; it is located beside Canterbury Gate between Oriel Square and Merton Street.

OPEN
10:30 a.m.–1:00 p.m., 2:30–5:30 p.m. Monday–Saturday, April–September
2:30–4:30 p.m. Sunday, year-round
10:30 a.m.–1:00 p.m., 2:30–4:30 p.m. Monday–Saturday, October–March

ADMISSION
£2.00 Adults
Children under 12 free of charge
£1.00 Concessions

The gallery features a collection of continental Renaissance artists, including works by Leonardo da Vinci. It's worth a drop-by if you are intrigued by works of art from the 15th and 16th centuries, although you should not expect to find portraits of the English heroes and heroines who populate the pages of this book.

✝ St. John's College
St. Giles

>>>

PHONE
  01865-277300

OPEN
  1:00–5:00 p.m. daily, year-round

  Note: A maximum of 15 people will be included in any single tour.

ADMISSION
  Free of charge

>>>

Founded in 1555 by Sir Thomas White, a former Lord Mayor of London, St. John's is the second college to occupy this site. Its predecessor, founded by Bishop Chichele in 1437, was dedicated to St. Bernard and trained Cistercian monks. That college was abolished during the Dissolution of the Monasteries. However, the spirit of the first school lives on in the 15th-century statue of St. Bernard that graces the gateway to the college. On either side of St. Bernard are statues of both colleges' founders.

The buildings in the front quad of St. John's are heavily restored remnants of the 16th-century college. The library, built in 1596–1598, was the first in Oxford to have seats rather than stalls. It has on display a copy of an illustrated version of *The Canterbury Tales* printed in 1482 by William Caxton, England's first printer.

While you're in the neighborhood . . .

✝ St. Giles Church
10 Woodstock Road

>>

PHONE
01865-311198

E-MAIL
admin@st-giles-church.org

OPEN
Noon–2:00 p.m. Monday–Friday, year-round

ADMISSION
Free of charge

>>

Consecrated in 1200 by Hugh, Bishop of Lincoln (a cross of interlaced circles on the western column of the church tower supposedly commemorates the event), St. Giles became linked with St. John's College in the 16th century. In 1535, during the Dissolution of the Monasteries, St. Giles was given to Henry VIII's physician, Dr. George Owen of Godstow. Dr. Owen's son sold the church in 1573 to Sir Thomas White, Lord Mayor of London and founder of St. John's College. White then gave the church to the college. St. John's has provided vicars for St. Giles ever since.

👉 **Did you know?**

Although not medieval in origin, St. Hugh's College does have connections with Oxford University's earliest roots. It was named for Bishop Hugh, who was canonized in 1220. Oxford was part of the Diocese of Lincoln in the Middle Ages.

✝ Trinity College
Broad Street

>>

PHONE
    01865-279900

OPEN
    10:00 a.m.–noon, 2:00–4:00 p.m. daily, year-round

ADMISSION
    £1.50 Adults
    75p Children
    75p Concessions

>>

Trinity is another college founded in the 16th century that replaced an older institution. Durham College, founded in 1286, was dedicated to the education of monks from the Cathedral Church of Durham. Trinity was created in 1555 by Sir Thomas Pope, Treasurer of the Court of Augmentation, the bureaucracy with responsibility for dissolving the monasteries for Henry VIII. Pope also was a counselor to Mary I and it was she who gave him approval to establish Trinity. Despite his role in the Dissolution of the Monasteries, Pope was a devout Catholic who demanded in the college's charter that all students take holy orders and not marry. Trinity's oldest structure is the library; it dates from 1421. It is not open to the public, however.

☞ Did you know?

So trusted by Mary was Sir Thomas Pope that the queen appointed him "governor" of her sister Elizabeth in 1556. This was at a time when Elizabeth was tainted by a treasonous plot to overthrow Mary and install Elizabeth on the throne. Dubbed the "Dudley conspiracy" after its leader, Sir Henry Dudley, the plot was foiled and no evidence that Elizabeth was involved or even knew of the scheming was ever found. Still, Mary thought it prudent to place a watchdog in Elizabeth's household. Therefore, Sir Thomas was dispatched to join Elizabeth at Hatfield. Their common intellectual interests created a bond between them and Pope was to become an advocate for Elizabeth in future confrontations with Mary.

✝ Jesus College
Turl Street

>>

PHONE
01865-279700

OPEN
Not open to the public

>>

Jesus is the only college established during the reign of Elizabeth I. In the charter granted the college on June 27, 1571, the name was recorded as "Jesus College in the University of Oxford of Queen Elizabeth's Foundation." It was founded by a group of lawyers and clergymen whose intent was to produce a learned crop of Protestant ministers. Although it was built on the site of a 13th-century academic facility called White Hall, Jesus College has no buildings of ancient origin. Most of its structures date from the 17th century.

• •
 Did you know?
Robert Dudley, Earl of Leicester and Queen Elizabeth's very favorite courtier, served as Chancellor of Oxford University during Elizabeth's reign.
• •

✝ Worcester College
Worcester Street

>>

PHONE
01865-278300

OPEN
2:00–5:00 p.m. daily, year-round

Note: A maximum of eight people will be included on any single tour; groups must schedule in advance.

ADMISSION
Free of charge

>>

Although Worcester College, founded in 1714, is not rooted in medieval or Tudor history, the site it occupies is. Gloucester College, an institution for Benedictine monks, was created here in 1283. It was dissolved by Henry VIII in 1541. About the only part of Gloucester College surviving today is a cluster of medieval cottages on the left side of the main quad that serve as lodgings.

Bodleian Library
Broad Street

>>

PHONE

01865-277224

OPEN

9:00 a.m.–5:00 p.m. Monday–Friday, year-round
9:00 a.m.–12:30 p.m. Saturday, year-round
Closed Sunday

ADMISSION

£3.50 for guided tour

TIP!

There are four guided tours daily Monday through Friday of the old Bodleian Library, at 10:30 and 11:30 a.m. and at 2:00 and 4:00 p.m. On Saturdays, there are only morning tours at 10:30 and 11:30. However, if you are not interested in the full library tour and are willing to skip a glimpse of Duke Humphrey's Library, you can get a good peek at the Divinity School just by stepping into the room. The entrance is straight through the library gift shop. This is where the tours start and tickets are purchased so the room is not blocked from public view. It is definitely worth a once-over.

>>

One of the oldest libraries in Europe, Bodleian is a descendant of Oxford University's first library, established c. 1320 in the Congregation House of St. Mary the Virgin Church. This first library was founded by Thomas Cobham, Bishop of Worcester, but it also benefited from the generosity of the House of Lancaster in building its stock of books. Henry IV and all his sons—the future Henry V, Thomas, John and Humphrey, Duke of Gloucester—all helped add to the furnishing of the library and the increase of its collection.

Humphrey, in particular, was a generous benefactor of the library. From 1435 to 1447, he donated an enormous collection of rare manuscripts. In fact, his donations so expanded the library's collection that the university determined it needed a larger room to house its precious volumes. A room of the Divinity School, then under construction, was specially equipped as a new library and the collection was moved there in 1488. The room, called Duke Humphrey's Library, still exists in the heart of the Bodleian, as does the Divinity School, described as "the most beautiful medieval building in Oxford." You can reach the Divinity School through a door on the west side of the School's Quadrangle in Radcliffe Square.

The mid-16th century brought about a decline in the university library's fortune. Political and religious upheaval, a general decline in the university's prosperity and competition from individual college libraries resulted in the dispersal of the university library in 1556, and it was not revived until 1598. In that year, Sir Thomas Bodley set himself a mission of rebuilding the university library. He started by restoring Duke Humphrey's Library and stocking it with books he donated or solicited from others. It

☞ Did you know?

Sir Thomas Bodley scored a major coup on behalf of his library when he reached an agreement with the Stationer's Company in London to give the library a copy of every book it published. That valuable entitlement is still in place today.

took two years to get this project off the ground; the new library was not formally opened until November 8, 1602. But once it was up and running, the university library began expanding rapidly. The first extension, Arts End, was added to Duke Humphrey's Library in 1612.

Today, Duke Humphrey's Library is still furnished with the

book presses and benches supplied by Sir Thomas. The painted ceiling, also dating from his restoration, is decorated with the coat of arms of the university and those of Sir Thomas.

❖❖❖

SIR THOMAS BODLEY (1545–1613)

Although best known to history as a bibliophile, Sir Thomas Bodley actually had made his mark on the world long before he conceived of the restoration of the Oxford University library. A diplomat and a scholar, Sir Thomas was an active force during the reign of Queen Elizabeth.

Born in England to devoutly Protestant parents, Sir Thomas and his family fled their country for Geneva during the tumultuous reign of Queen Mary. After Elizabeth gained the throne in 1558, the family returned to England and Bodley joined the Oxford community. He remained a part of the academic world for the next 20 years. He was then elected to Parliament and joined Elizabeth's diplomatic corps in 1585. Sometime around 1584 to 1596, Bodley served as ambassador to the United Dutch provinces. This lucrative post allowed him to amass the fortune he later used to reconstruct the Oxford University library.

❖❖❖

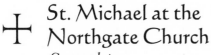

✝ St. Michael at the Northgate Church
Cornmarket

>>

PHONE
01865-240940

OPEN
10:00 a.m.–5:00 p.m. daily, April–October
10:00 a.m.–4:00 p.m. daily, November–March

ADMISSION
£1.50 Adults
80p Children
£1.00 Concessions

CONVENIENCES
Gift shop and café

>>

The Saxon Tower of St. Michael is the oldest building in Oxford. It dates from 1040 and marks the location of the old North Gate to the walled city. The church was built in the 13th century. The window above the altar contains medallions dating from c. 1290, the oldest pieces of stained glass in Oxford. There also is a 15th-century stained glass window in the Lady Chapel depicting a crucified Christ on a lily. The Lady Chapel also has a 14th-century reredos. Other medieval features include a 14th-century font and a 15th-century pulpit and sedilia. On display in the tower are financial accounts from the 15th century, chalices from the 16th and the door of the cell in which Archbishop Cranmer and Bishops Latimer and Ridley were confined before their executions.

Next to the church is the **New Inn**, built between 1386 and 1396. It claims to be the oldest surviving three-story building in Oxford. (*Have you noticed there are lots of contenders for "oldest" of just about everything in Oxford?*)

✝ St. Martin's Church (a.k.a. Carfax Tower)
Carfax, at the corner of Queen and Cornmarket Streets

»»»

PHONE
01865-792653

OPEN
10:00 a.m.–5:15 p.m. daily, April–October
10:00 a.m.–3:30 p.m. daily, November–March

ADMISSION
£1.20 Adults
60p Children

»»»

Built in the 11th century, St. Martin's once served as the main church for Oxford. All that remains today is its tower, now known as the Carfax Tower. The 72-foot-high tower marks the center of the old Saxon town where four roads once crossed. The name actually is derived from the Latin phrase, *quadri furcus*, meaning "four-forked." If you have the stamina to climb the 99 steps to the top of the tower, your reward will be a spectacular view of Oxford.

Carfax Tower is also a symbol of the trying relationship that once existed between town and gown. When the fight between students and the owner of Swyndelstock Tavern broke out on St. Scholastica's Day 1354, townspeople rushed to ring St. Martin's bell and summon aid. In retaliation, the chancellor of Oxford University had the bells of St. Mary rung. In response, students and masters rushed to the aid of their beleaguered colleagues. The resulting battle lasted for three days, leaving 63 students dead.

St. Thomas the Martyr Church
Botley Road

>>

PHONE
01865-251403

OPEN
Not generally open other than for worship

ADMISSION
Donation suggested

>>

We're not sure what to say about this church, other than it has posed one of the most challenging research tasks we've encountered so far. And, despite our most diligent efforts, we're still not absolutely positive we got it right. If you can do any better, we'd like to hear about it. (*On the other hand, maybe we'll just bask in ignorance on this one.*)

Our first challenge was to discover whether the church actually still existed (*no mean feat, believe us!*). Then we never could pin down the story of its founding, how it came to be named for

Thomas à Becket and whether it had any affiliation with Oseney Abbey. For what it's worth, here's what we did find.

According to an entry in the records of Oseney Abbey, the monks built the church during King Stephen's 1142 siege of Oxford Castle. They did so to provide a place of worship for townspeople who no longer had access to St. George's church, located within the castle precincts. The reliability of this report, written in 1284, is somewhat doubtful, however. The land on which the church is located was not deeded to the abbey until 1172.

The truth is that no one knows when or how the church was established and named (*not that we could find, anyway*). Even its later history is somewhat murky. At various times, it has been know as St. Nicolas's church and was affiliated for a while with Christ Church College following the Dissolution of the Monasteries. Today, it is a historic property managed by the City of Oxford.

∿

† Lost treasures ...
# Oxford Castle and Beaumont Palace
>>>

The once mighty royal castle of Oxford—scene of bloody battles, devastating sieges and dramatic escapes—has all but disappeared from the Oxford landscape. It once stood on Castle Street; all that is left is the castle mound and St. George's Tower, once the tower of the castle church, most recently a prison and now being renovated as a hotel.

The castle was built in 1071 by Robert d'Oilly, a veteran of the Battle of Hastings. D'Oilly positioned his castle to the west of the old Anglo-Saxon town and realigned the town walls. He also constructed a major new road, the Grandpont, which improved access to the town and helped establish Oxford as a major trade center. One of the founders of the castle chapel of St. George, d'Oilly was a close confidant of William the Conqueror. He held the posts of constable of the royal household, constable of the castle of Oxford and sheriff of Oxfordshire and Warwickshire.

Henry I must not have appreciated d'Oilly's architectural design because in 1130 he built a castle north of the city that he dubbed Beaumont Palace. That residence also has long since disappeared, but it must have been more a comfortable manor house than a fortress; future royals continued to occupy Oxford Castle when security was a concern, while Beaumont Palace was associated more with happy family occasions.

◆◆◆◆◆◆◆◆◆◆◆◆◆◆◆◆◆◆◆◆◆◆◆

☞ Did you know?

D'Oilly's heirs found unique and interesting ways to retain the family's influence with the reigning monarch. The second Robert d'Oilly, a nephew of the first, stayed close to Henry I through his wife, Edith Forne, who had been one of the king's many mistresses. After Edith bore Henry a son, named Robert Fitz Roy, the king provided her with a generous dowry that no doubt added substantially to her appeal on the marriage market and helped d'Oilly expand the family fortunes.

◆◆◆◆◆◆◆◆◆◆◆◆◆◆◆◆◆◆◆◆◆◆◆

For example, Oxford Castle provided the backdrop for one of the most dramatic events of the struggle for the English crown between Henry I's heir and daughter Empress Matilda and the usurper king Stephen of Blois. In the winter of 1142, Matilda was trapped in the castle, besieged by Stephen's forces. Exhausted, starving and broken in spirit after three months of siege, Matilda's meager force defending the castle could not hold out much longer. Rather than surrender to Stephen, Matilda decided upon a risky course of action. In the height of a snowstorm, she and three or four guards, all dressed in white, escaped from the castle. Some accounts claim Matilda and her cohorts climbed out of a tower by means of a rope; others say Matilda was lowered to the ground in a basket made of sheets. The least compelling portrayal has it that they fled through a postern gate. Fighting the blizzard, they slipped past Stephen's army and made it to the Thames. Matilda and her companions walked six miles down the frozen river to Abingdon Abbey, where they obtained horses and galloped the 10 miles to Wallingford Castle, safe in the hands of Matilda's supporters.

One version of Matilda's theatrical escape was told by the medieval chronicler John of Marmoutier, who wrote a biography of the empress's husband Geoffrey Plantagenet sometime around 1170. About Matilda's adventure, John wrote, "In the seventh year of his reign, the king besieged Empress Matilda at Oxford, from after Michaelmas till Advent. Not long before Christmas the empress escaped across the frozen Thames wrapped in white clothes, deceiving the besiegers by appearing so like the dazzling snow. She fled to the castle of Wallingford, and Oxford was surrendered to the king."

Oxford Castle also played a dramatic role in the life of Matilda and Geoffrey's son Henry. After 19 years of bloody civil war, the English barons finally forced a peace between Matilda and Stephen. The key provision of the agreement was that Stephen would hold the crown for the rest of his life and Henry would inherit it upon the king's death. The barons met Henry at Oxford Castle on January 13, 1154, to swear their allegiance to him and pledge to support his claim to the throne after Stephen's death.

Henry's queen, Eleanor of Aquitaine, appeared to have more of an affinity with Beaumont Palace. She chose it for her confinement for the births of two sons; both the future Richard the Lionheart and King John were born there. Beaumont Palace eventually became one of John's favorite palaces as well.

John's successors seemed not so fond of either Beaumont Palace or Oxford Castle. Both structures gradually fell into disrepair. In 1331, Edward III ordered a massive renovation of the castle, but the work didn't seem to make the fortress any more appealing to future monarchs. So little regard did Edward VI have for the ancient castle that he gave it and its mill to the See of Oxford. Ultimately, Elizabeth I reclaimed the property, but Oxford Castle never regained its stature as a major royal stronghold. James I sold it early in the 17th century and, once again, the castle was allowed to decay. We couldn't find any records of the demise of Beaumont Palace, but the only trace of it you will find is a plaque in Beaumont Street marking the site where it once stood.

While you're in Oxford ...

✝ Godstow Abbey

Godstow Road
Lower Wolvercote, Oxford

≫≫

LOCATED
About 4 miles from the center of Oxford

OPEN
Daylight hours daily, year-round

ADMISSION
Free of charge

≫≫

We cannot begin to tell you how excited we were to stumble across this site (*or, rather, have our driver do it for us! Way to go, Roy!*). Nowhere in our diligent research had it popped up on our radar screen as an existing site. We thought it was a lost treasure. You can imagine our delight, then, when we realized, while we were reading menus in a restaurant, that we were actually sitting in the former guest house of Godstow Abbey with extensive ruins of the abbey itself right next door! We're sure we don't have to tell you why we were so thrilled by this discovery, but just in case you are one of the few people in the world who are not familiar with the romantic story of Henry II and Rosamund the Fair, we'll tell it quickly.

Godstow Abbey was founded in 1133 as a Benedictine nunnery. An aristocratic institution, Godstow, as many other nunneries of the time, served as a boarding school for the daughters of England's nobility. Among those educated there, at least according to legend, was Rosamund, the daughter of the Marcher lord Walter de Clifford.

No one knows when or how Rosamund met Henry II, but there is no doubt that she became the great love of his life and probably played some role in the volcanic breakup of his marriage to Eleanor of Aquitaine. Rosamund and Henry's affair most likely began sometime in the 1160s, but remained somewhat discreet until Eleanor joined her sons in rebellion against their father in 1173–1174. After that, when Henry had captured and imprisoned Eleanor, he flaunted his relationship with Rosamund, letting her live publicly at Woodstock Palace until she grew deathly ill sometime in 1176–1177.

Rosamund then retired to Godstow Abbey. Ironically, she — who at this point had been involved for at least a decade in an adulterous liaison — took vows as a nun. No one knows the cause of her death or whether knowledge that she was dying was the motivating factor for her sudden burst of piety. (*Passionate fans of Eleanor of Aquitaine, we do not for one moment believe any of the nasty tales that attribute Rosamund's demise to that great lady.*) Rosamund was buried at Godstow in an elaborate shrine paid for by a grief-stricken Henry.

After the death of Henry II and the dismantling of Rosamund's tomb, Godstow Abbey receded from the forefront of history until the Dissolution of the Monasteries. Henry VIII gave Godstow to his physician, Dr. George Owen, who lived on the property for a time. A fire in 1645 destroyed most of the structures once associated with the abbey, leaving only the evocative ruins you see today and the guest house located across the small river dividing the properties. That guest house, now called **The Trout Inn**, is well worth a visit, both for the history and the food — they are equally excellent. (See the listing in Ancient Inns and Eateries for the address and telephone number.) We hope you enjoy yourself as much as we did.

• •

☞ Did you know?

In 1191, four years after Henry's death, the saintly Bishop Hugh of London, deeming Rosamund a "harlot," had her tomb moved from the high altar of Godstow Abbey and ordered her re-burial in the adjacent cemetery with the common folk.

• •

ANCIENT INNS AND EATERIES

~ The Trout Inn
   195 Godstow Road
   Lower Wolvercote, Oxford
   01865-302071
The 12th-century former guest house of Godstow Abbey.

~ Four Pillars Hotel
Henley Road
Sandford on Thames
01865-334444
Located about 4 miles outside of Oxford, this hotel actually is a complex of buildings that incorporates two medieval barns and a manor house in its hospitality facilities.

~ Jersey Arms
Middleton Stoney
01869-343234
Fifteenth-century inn with 16 bedrooms around a walled court-yard and restaurants.

~ Mitre Inn
High Street
Oxford
This coaching inn was built in 1600 atop 13th-century cellars.

~ Old Parsonage Hotel
Oxford
This is a 16th-century hotel that once served as home to Oscar Wilde (*once again, we do know he is not of our favorite period of history, but we do admire his wit!*).

~ Restaurant Elizabeth
82 St. Aldate's
Oxford
01865-242230
The building that houses this restaurant dates from the 15th century.

~ Turf Tavern
St. Helen's Passage
Oxford
This is a highly rated pub resting against the remnants of the city wall. It dates from the 13th century, although most of the current building is 16th-century.

CONTENTS

Minster Lovell/Banbury

Riding Cock Horses

his is one for those of you who like to amble around the English countryside and take in a variety of medieval and Tudor sites. There is a great collection on this trip that starts in Minster Lovell, meanders throughout Oxfordshire and Berkshire (picking up all the fascinating ancient places that didn't fit into other trips) and winds up with the medieval market town of Banbury as an anchor point for surrounding attractions. It's also an unusual collection of sites, including a couple of medieval barns and a very special ancient inn. We think you will enjoy this trip. We certainly did.

✠ Minster Lovell

>>>

LOCATED

Approximately 14 miles west of Oxford, just off the A40 about 3 miles west of Witney, off the B4047

TRAVEL

About 1 hour travel time from London by car, or frequent train service to Oxford; Stagecoach bus service from Gloucester Green to Witney; taxi or rental car to Minster Lovell

>>>

Minster Lovell is a charming medieval village drenched in atmosphere and compelling history. In particular, it holds won-

derful surprises for amateur historians who are especially interested in the Wars of the Roses and partial to Richard III. It is a
great place for those of you who are looking to immerse your-
selves in an overnight experience of life in the Middle Ages.

Minster Lovell Hall
Minster Lovell

>>
OPEN
Daylight hours daily, year-round
ADMISSION
Free of charge
>>

The ancestral home of the Lords Lovell since the 12th century,
Minster Lovell Hall today is a ruin. The remains are those of the
second house to be constructed on the site; a 15th-century fortified manor house built by William, the seventh Baron Lovell of
Tichmarsh. The house was dismantled in the 18th century and
all that is left are the walls of the entrance porch and Great Hall
and the foundations of other buildings. A short, easy walk will
gain you access to a medieval dovecote as well.

Following the Battle of Bosworth, Francis Lovell was attainted and his manor confiscated by Henry VII. Henry then
gave the lands to his most favored uncle Jasper Tudor, Duke of
Bedford, and visited there in 1493, 1497 and 1503. After Jasper's
death, Henry bestowed Minster Lovell on his 4-year-old son,
the Duke of York and the future Henry VIII. That Henry, who
did love to renovate, invested in substantial repairs and expansion of the house.

From 1536 until 1602, Minster Lovell experienced a rather
convoluted ownership history, with leases and titles moving
back and forth between the Crown and preferred courtiers. In
1602, the house was purchased by Sir Edward Coke, Elizabeth's
attorney-general. It remained in Coke family hands for another
200 years, although the house was abandoned in the mid-18th
century and many of the buildings were demolished.

Near by Minster Lovell Hall is **St. Kenelm's Parish Church**, built along with the manor house by William Lovell in about 1450. Among its other medieval treasures, the church has a fine effigy of a medieval knight. Although the tomb bears no inscription, the effigy is thought to be that of Lord William (d. 1455).

Ghost Alert!

The last Lord Lovell, Francis, was a childhood friend and staunch supporter of Richard III. In fact, Richard visited his friend at Minster Lovell Hall in 1483. Although he fought at the Battle of Bosworth, Lovell was one of the lucky few of Richard's battle companions who escaped the carnage. His end is uncertain. One story has it that he was banished from England by Henry VII and then killed at the Battle of Stoke when the remnants of the Plantagenet forces tried to force Henry from the throne. Another story is that he went into hiding after the rebellion failed. Support for this tale grew in 1708 when the skeleton of a man was found walled up in a secret chamber at Minster Lovell. Needless to say, that counts as a Ghost Alert!

The Mill and Old Swan Hotel
Minster Lovell

PHONE

01993-774441

E-MAIL

themill@initialstyle.co.uk

This complex is so special it deserves much more than a listing in Ancient Inns and Eateries. Two of the three mills at Minster Lovell recorded in the *Domesday Book* are now this retreat's hotel and conference center. The original weir that powered the mill is still on the grounds. The 15th-century inn features oak beams, medieval fireplaces and original flagstone floors.

The *pièce de résistance*, however, is a room with ancient graffiti. During Richard III's 1483 visit to Minster Lovell, the overflow of his retinue was housed in the Old Swan. One enthusiastic follower carved Richard's "Sun in Splendor" crest into the wall, where it is now protected behind glass. (*It is so splendid that Sarah nearly fainted from excitement when she saw it.*) The room, with its precious ornamentation is, needless to say, called "The Richard III Room" and the furniture in it is adorned with more modern renditions of "The Sun in Splendor." Ask for it if you decide to stay overnight here.

 ## Bishop's Palace Witney
Cogges Manor Farm Museum
Church Lane
Cogges, Witney

>>

PHONE
01993-772602

LOCATED
A40 to A4095

TRAVEL
Frequent train service to Oxford; Stagecoach bus service from Gloucester Green with a Cogges Manor Farm stop in Witney

OPEN
2:00–4:00 p.m. Saturday and Sunday, April–mid-September

ADMISSION
Free of charge

>>

On the grounds of a working farm museum of Victoriana you will find the ruins of one of the 24 palaces once owned by the bishops of Winchester. The property first passed into the hands of the bishops of Winchester when Emma, mother of Edward the Confessor, gave it to the diocese in 1044. Most likely, the bishops had a house there they used as a hunting lodge until William Gifford, who became bishop in 1110, decided to build a stone house. Bishop Henry of Blois, brother of King Stephen, transformed the simple house into a grand palace in the 1130s. It is the footprint of Bishop Henry's palace that you see in the current excavations of the site.

While you're in Witney . . .

A central feature of Witney's Market Square is the **Buttercross**, a covered medieval market where women sold butter and eggs. The clock turret was added in 1683. Just off Market Square in **Church Green**, is the 13th-century church of **St. Mary**. In nearby **South Leigh** is another church, **St. James**, that has good-quality medieval wall paintings.

 ## Tolsey Museum
126 High Street
Burford

>>

PHONE
01367-810294

LOCATED
On the A40 about 20 miles west of Oxford

TRAVEL
Frequent train service to Oxford; Stagecoach bus service from Gloucester Green to Burford

OPEN
2:00–5:00 p.m. Monday–Friday, March 25–October
11:00 a.m.–5:00 p.m. Saturday and Sunday, March 25–October

ADMISSION
50p Adults
10p Children

>>

Once a center for collecting tolls from traders, this Tudor structure has been transformed into an eclectic museum that contains an oddment of relics from Burford's past, including town charters dating back to 1350.

While you're in Burford . . .

The church of **St. John** in Burford is a hodgepodge of architecture and memorials from the Middle and Tudor Ages. The tower and west door are Norman. The Guild of Merchants Chapel was built c. 1200 as a separate building and then was joined with the main church in the late 15th century. Inside is the tomb of Henry VIII's barber Edmund Harman (d. 1569), a beneficiary of the king's generosity to his friends during the Dissolution of the Monasteries. The barber received as a gift the Burford Hospital of St. John. As a newfound property owner, Harman was able to marry into the ranks of the wealthiest town merchants, the Sylvester family, thus earning himself a spot in the family's favorite burial place—the church of St. John. Harman's tomb is decorated with one of the earliest depictions in England of New World natives. No one knows why.

Great Coxwell Barn
Faringdon

>>

PHONE
    01793-762209 (Coleshill Estate Office)

E-MAIL
    greatcoxwellbarn@ntrust.org.uk

LOCATED
    2 miles southwest of Faringdon between the A420 and B4019

TRAVEL
    Frequent train service to Oxford; Stagecoach bus service from Gloucester Green to Swindon; the barn is located three quarters of a mile from the Great Coxwell Turn stop.

OPEN
    Daylight hours daily, year-round

ADMISSION
    50p Adults, children, concessions

>>

A National Trust property, Great Coxwell is probably the most well-known and well-preserved barn in England. Built of stone in the mid-13th century by Cistercian monks, the barn is 152 feet long by 44 feet wide and 48 feet high. The walls are 4 feet thick.

While you're in the area . . .

If you are ready for a break from medieval and Tudor history and want to go in search of *really* ancient stuff, Oxfordshire boasts some of the best prehistoric sites in England. They are the **Rollright Stones**, one of the country's smaller stone circles and a burial chamber that date back to about 2000 BCE; the **Uffington White Horse**, a chalk circle, probably Celtic in origin, that again dates to about 2000 BCE; and **Wayland's Smithy**, a burial chamber dating from around 2800 BCE.

⊥ Banbury

>>>

LOCATED
> Off M40

TRAVEL
> Frequent train service from London Marylebone Station or from Paddington Station through Oxford; from Marylebone, travel time is just over 1 hour.

>>>

Ride a cock horse
to Banbury Cross
To see a fine lady
Upon a white horse
With rings on her fingers
and bells on her toes
She shall have music
Wherever she goes.

"Ah ha!" you say! You just *knew* you had heard of Banbury somewhere. Now you know. It's in the nursery rhyme we all pranced to as children. The big question is—who was the "fine lady"? Some legends have it that she was Lady Godiva and the "rings on her fingers and bells on her toes" were her only adornment on her famous ride through Coventry (*what Banbury Cross has to do with that we haven't a clue*). Other tales suggest that the "fine lady" was a reference to Queen Elizabeth and a visit she paid to Banbury. But the locals seem to prefer the mundane story that the rhyme simply refers to a medieval Banbury maiden riding in a May Day procession.

Regardless of the basis of the tale, the really disappointing fact about Banbury is that the original medieval cross no longer exists. It was pulled down in the late 1600s in a wave of Protestant fervor that swept through Banbury. The current cross is 19th-century.

Although Banbury is an ancient town dating back to Saxon times, there is little left to see of its medieval and Tudor history—not even the ruins of Banbury Castle or its motte. We arbitrarily decided to partially name this trip "Banbury" not because Banbury itself is such a great place to visit for medieval and Tudor fans, but because it

☞ Did you know?

Ever wonder what a "cock horse" actually was? In medieval times, it was a two-person means of transportation —a knight riding a horse with a lady behind him.

is a central location for several fascinating sites that all bear a Banbury address. (*Besides, we wanted to use the nursery rhyme.*) So you can waltz right through the town of Banbury and move on to more interesting places, if you are so inclined.

"COCK HORSES" OR COCK-AND-BULL?

In recent years, the "interpretation" of children's nursery rhymes has become a vigorous competition, testing the imaginations of linguists, folklorists, historians, theologians, even child psychologists. Although few actually agree on the exact roots or specific meanings of the most ancient rhymes, most agree that when it comes to these playful ditties all is not what it seems.

For instance, a briefly popular theory linked "Ring Around the Rosie" to the 14th century's Black Death, with its round, rose-colored sores, pockets of medicinal posies and ashes from the mass elimination of corpses. In fact, cremation was not acceptable in Catholic medieval society and any connection between the plague and this children's song appears to have been debunked.

Other rhymes have been ascribed political overtones. "The Noble Duke of York" with his 10,000 men is assumed by some to portray Richard, Duke of York as he prepared for a pivotal 1455 battle in the Wars of the Roses. The character of "Old Mother Hubbard" is widely believed to symbolize Cardinal Wolsey, who found the Church's "cupboard" bare when he went to fetch his poor "doggie" (Henry VIII) a bone/divorce. "Mistress Mary Quite Contrary" could conceivably be a veiled allusion to Bloody Mary, her gardens (cemeteries) growing with Protestants who have succumbed to the Tudor torture devices known as "silver bells, cockleshells and pretty maids."

Interesting as these theories may be, we tend to be skeptical. Trolling ancient nursery rhymes for significant symbolism reminds us too much of the hours wasted hoping to glean deeper meanings from the Beatles' "Lucy in the Sky, With Diamonds" and "I Am the Walrus"—pleasant pastimes, largely dependent on the ear of the listener.

◇ ◇

✝ Sulgrave Manor
Sulgrave, Banbury

>>

PHONE
01295-760205

E-MAIL
sulgrave-manor@talk21.com

LOCATED
M40, junction 11, 7 miles northeast of Banbury, off the B4525

TRAVEL
About 70 miles from London; frequent train service from London's Marylebone Station to Banbury; taxi or rental car to Sulgrave Manor

OPEN
2:00–5:30 p.m. Saturday, Sunday, Tuesday–Thursday, April–October

Note: Group tours can be prebooked throughout the year.

ADMISSION
£5.00 Adults
£2.50 Children

CONVENIENCES
Café and light refreshments

>>

Sulgrave Manor is a *must-see* for Americans who like their history seasoned with a medieval and Tudor flavor. The ancestral home of George Washington, the property was purchased in 1539 from Henry VIII by George's great-great-great (*we think we counted right*) grandfather, Lawrence Washington. Lawrence, a rich wool merchant and the mayor of Northampton, finished building the house you see today in 1600. His descendants lived there until 1659.

◆◆◆◆◆◆◆◆◆◆◆◆◆◆◆◆◆◆◆◆◆◆

☞ Did you know?

In another "George Washington slept here" analogy (*sorry, we couldn't resist*), Queen Elizabeth supposedly visited Sulgrave Manor as a child and hid from her keepers in the rafters.

◆◆◆◆◆◆◆◆◆◆◆◆◆◆◆◆◆◆◆◆◆◆

Tip!

In addition to its regular open hours from April through October, Sulgrave Manor hosts a Tudor Christmas celebration the first three weekends of December as well as December 27 and 30. A period event showcasing the traditions of a Tudor Christmas, activities run from 10:30 a.m. to 4:30 p.m. each Saturday and Sunday.

〰

✝ Broughton Castle
   Banbury

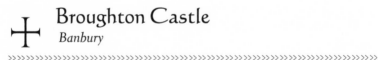

PHONE
   01295-276070

E-MAIL
   admin@broughtoncastle.demon.co.uk

LOCATED
   2 miles west of Banbury, M40, junction 11, to the B4035

TRAVEL
   Frequent train service from London's Marylebone Station to Banbury; taxi or rental car to Broughton Castle

OPEN
2:00–5:00 p.m. Wednesday, Thursday, Sunday, Bank Holiday
Mondays, July and August
2:00–5:00 p.m. Wednesday and Sunday, May, June and September
Closed October–April

ADMISSION
£5.00 Adults
£2.00 Children
£4.00 Groups & seniors

CONVENIENCES
Tearoom & gift shop
>>

This is a fun one for movie fans dedicated to tracking down locations featured in their favorite flicks. Broughton Castle was one of the main locations for two of our most adored films — *Shakespeare in Love* and *The Madness of King George III*. Even better, the castle has a direct connection with the star of *Shakespeare in Love*, Joseph Fiennes, and his brother Ralph; it is owned by their cousins. (*We were mightily disappointed that we didn't catch a glimpse of either one during our visit. We also must warn you that you have to weave your way through a very large flock of sheep, dodging droppings on the way, to get to the house.*)

More fortified manor house than castle, Broughton was built c. 1300 by Sir John de Broughton. It was bought in 1377 by William of Wykeham, Bishop of Winchester, Chancellor of England and founder of New College, Oxford. Eventually, the property passed to the bishop's sister Margaret Wykeham. It was later inherited by her granddaughter, who married Sir William Fiennes, Lord Saye and Sele, in 1451. The property has stayed in the family ever since.

Like most castles built in the Middle Ages, Broughton has been added to and renovated many times. Still, it maintains its medieval aura and many original features. The Great Hall, vaulted dining room, chapel and moat are all 14th-century. A copy of a portrait of William of Wykeham hangs above the fireplace in the Great Hall. The two floors above the Great Hall and the west wing were added in Tudor times. The west wing consists of two rooms—the magnificent paneled Oak Drawing Room and the Great Parlor, which has a plaster ceiling bearing the date 1599. The King's Chamber, so-called because King James I stayed here in 1604, contains a mid-16th-century stone and stucco chimneypiece built by French workmen. Queen Anne's Room, named for James's wife, also contains a stone chimneypiece carved in 1551 by English masons.

Across from the 14th-century gatehouse built by William of Wykeham, outside the castle wall, is the 14th-century church of **St. Mary**. In addition to some decently preserved fragments of medieval wall paintings, believed to date from 1340, the church contains a number of medieval and Tudor tombs and effigies. One of the most colorful is that of Sir John de Broughton (d. 1315), who built the church c. 1306. There also is one of a knight wearing a collar of the suns and roses of the House of York and dressed in armor of the style worn around 1470. Speculation is that the effigy is that of the second Lord Saye & Sele, who died fighting in the Battle of Barnet in 1471.

◆◆

WILLIAM OF WYKEHAM (C. 1324–1404)

A man of many talents, William of Wykeham rose from humble birth to twice become chancellor of England, once under Edward III (1367–1371) and again under Richard II (1389–1391). Although Wykeham clearly was a wily and astute politician, it was his architectural abilities that first brought him to the notice of Edward III.

Born in Hampshire and educated at Winchester, Wykeham entered royal service sometime around 1347. He was first employed to supervise building projects. Edward III was so pleased with Wykeham's results, especially at Windsor and Queenborough castles, that the king soon promoted his new favorite to Clerk of Works and then Keeper of the Privy Seal in 1363. The titles were nice, but Wykeham also needed an income to support him in royal service. Edward named him Bishop of Winchester in 1367, despite opposition from the Pope, who thought Wykeham's lack of a university education made him less than qualified for the position. Edward prevailed, however, and the appointment made Wykeham one of the richest men in England. From there, Wykeham was off and running on a career that would keep him in the forefront of court politics and intrigues for nearly 40 years.

Wykeham left his mark in England not just in the many architectural projects that survive today. He also was a great patron of education (*perhaps making up for that lack of a university education?*). His establishment of Winchester College, a free grammar school for 70 scholars, earned him a historical tip of the hat as the founder of England's public education system. Winchester served as a feeder school for Wykeham's other major educational endeavor, New College, Oxford, founded in 1379. This pioneering system was not duplicated until Henry VI adopted a similar plan for Eton and King's College, Cambridge.

❖❖

Swalcliffe Barn
Shipston Road
Banbury

>>>

PHONE
01295-788278

LOCATED
West of Broughton Castle on the B4035

TRAVEL
Frequent train service from London's Marylebone Station to Banbury; taxi or rental car to Swalcliffe Barn

OPEN
2:00–5:00 p.m. Easter Sunday and Monday
2:00–5:00 p.m. Sunday, May and September
2:00–5:00 p.m. Saturday and Sunday, June–August

ADMISSION
Free of charge

>>>

Built between 1400 and 1409, Swalcliffe Barn, a.k.a. the Tythe Barn, is considered to be one of the best medieval barns in England. It was constructed by New College of Oxford for the college-owned Rectorial Manor of Swalcliffe. Today, the barn houses a museum of agricultural tools and equipment, some dating back to Roman times.

While you're in the area . . .

✝ St. Peter ad Vincula
South Newington

>>>

LOCATED
About 6 miles south of Banbury on the A361

TRAVEL
Frequent train service from London's Marylebone Station to
Banbury; taxi or rental car to the church

OPEN
10:00 a.m.–5:00 p.m. daily, April–September

ADMISSION
Donation suggested

>>>

You're going to need a good map to find it, but the feature that
makes this little church worth a drop-by is its outstanding medieval wall paintings. With the earliest dating from the 1340s,
these paintings are among the very best in England. A particularly striking one is of the murder of Thomas à Becket. There
also is one of the murder of Thomas of Lancaster, a grandson of
Henry III, who was a perpetual thorn in the side of his nephew
Edward II. The most outstanding painting, with its delicate
figures and strong coloring, is of the Virgin and Child.

◆◆◆

MEDIEVAL WALL PAINTINGS: SUBLIME OR SUBLIMINAL?

The rare and evocative wall paintings found in some of England's ancient
churches are among the amateur historian's favorite medieval treasures. We
look upon them as masterpieces—and indeed they are. But at the time, these
colorful murals were much akin to advertising billboards . . . temporary visuals
geared to drive home a particular message in an agreeable, accessible and memorable manner. Church murals were updated fairly regularly; the themes would
change depending upon the moral challenges facing a congregation. During
the Reformation, most of the medieval wall paintings in parish churches were
defaced—gilt was scraped off and the remaining images scorched or slashed beyond repair. In extreme instances, the paintings were literally "erased" with a

layer of lime-based whitewash. Ironically, the wash served as a preservative. The flurry of church renovation during the Victorian era uncovered many of these "erased" murals, their colors as vibrant as on the day Henry's zealots staged their attack. (*We bet a few of Hal's henchmen would froth at the mouth to know they had served as Papist preservationists!*).

◇◇◇

✝ Also while you're in the area . . .
Churchill and Sarsden Heritage Centre
Churchill

>>

LOCATED
Southwest of Banbury, A361 through Chipping Norton to B4450 or A44 through Chipping Norton to B4450

TRAVEL
Frequent train service from London's Marylebone Station to Banbury; Stagecoach Bus service to Chipping Norton

OPEN
1:30–4:30 p.m. Saturday, April to September

ADMISSION
Donation suggested

>>

Even though it's off the beaten path and the history is not particularly compelling, we've included this former medieval church in this trip because we love the modern tale of its survival. We are always thrilled to discover other people who are as passionate about this period of history as we are and the 500 or so

● ●
☞ **Did you know?**
The name Churchill dates back to the 9th century and the Saxon word *cercehil*.
● ●

villagers of Churchill certainly fall into this category. They rallied at a critical time to save this 14th-century church from demolition. The Church of England had written it off because it wasn't being used and the building was in disrepair. The villagers said, "No way!," got together and organized themselves as the Churchill Old Church Preservation Society. They raised £20,000 through various public-spirited events and converted the church into a village museum. It's worth a drop-by if only to applaud the villagers for saving another precious bit of ancient history. Three cheers for them!

<h1>✝ A lost treasure ...
Woodstock Palace</h1>

>>>

More hunting lodge than royal palace, Woodstock was a favored retreat of medieval and Tudor monarchs from Henry I through Elizabeth. It gained its fame, though, as the home of "Fair" Rosamund Clifford, allegedly the love of Henry II's life.

No one knows exactly when the liaison between Henry and Rosamund, the daughter of Marcher lord Walter de Clifford, began, although it is commonly assumed to have started sometime in the 1160s. What is fact is that Henry publicly acknowledged Rosamund after capturing and imprisoning his queen, Eleanor of Aquitaine, when she incited their sons into rebellion in 1173–1174. Rosamund then lived at Woodstock for about two years until her death, sometime around 1176–1177.

Many legends grew up to embellish the love affair between Rosamund and Henry. One such was that Henry created a special bower for her at Woodstock. Consisting of a tower, maze and spring, the design of this hideaway on the grounds of the lodge was based on the romantic story of Tristan and Yseult in which the lovers communicated by dropping twigs into a stream that flowed through Yseult's chamber. The truth is that Henry most likely had the haven built to please the literature-loving Eleanor of Aquitaine. Another pivotal point of the tall tales told is of Eleanor's supposed jealousy, which induced her to plot Rosamund's death, either by poison or dagger. Since Eleanor was tightly caged by Henry at the time of Rosamund's death, it is hardly likely that the queen played any role in the concubine's demise. (*Regardless of how "fair" Rosamund was, our sympathies are firmly with Eleanor.*)

Woodstock also proved to be popular with Edward III and his queen Philippa. The eldest and youngest of their 12 children were born here — the Black Prince Edward on June 15, 1330, and Thomas, the future Earl of Buckingham and Duke of Gloucester, in 1355. Thomas's birth and the queen's subsequent "churching" were celebrated with a grand tournament at Woodstock in which Prince Edward participated.

Henry VII rebuilt Woodstock between 1495 and 1501, but his son Henry VIII apparently didn't care much for the place and allowed it to fall into disrepair. The dilapidated condition of the property didn't stop Mary Tudor, however, from using the manor as a prison for her sister Elizabeth in 1554. Elizabeth had been implicated in a rebellion against Mary and first imprisoned in the Tower of London. No evidence of the princess's involvement in the plot could be found, so Mary had no reason to continue holding Elizabeth in the Tower. Still, Mary did not trust her sister and wanted her closely watched. The queen ordered that Elizabeth be taken to Woodstock in the care of a trusted courtier. Elizabeth complained bitterly about the conditions at Woodstock; there was not enough room for all her attendants, the rooms were in disrepair and the

☞ Did you know?

Woodstock Palace had less pleasant associations for the rulers of England's neighboring principality of Wales. It was here that Welsh princes, along with King Malcolm of Scotland, were forced to give an oath of allegiance to Henry II, acknowledging him as their overlord, in July 1163. And in 1247, the feuding grandsons of the great Welsh leader Llewelyn Fawr, Owain and another Llewelyn, were compelled to pay homage to Henry III in a humiliating ceremony at Woodstock.

furnishings were shabby. Nevertheless, Elizabeth spent a year here until Mary relented and summoned her sister back to court. Needless to say, this experience dampened Elizabeth's enthusiasm for Woodstock, although she did stay there occasionally when she was on progress as queen.

Despite its illustrious history, the Parliamentarians had little regard for Woodstock Palace and it was seriously damaged during the Civil War. The remaining structures finally were demolished at the beginning of the 18th century so that Blenheim Palace, birthplace of Winston Churchill, could be built on the site for the Duke of Marlborough. You can visit Blenheim Palace today, but there is nothing left of the medieval and Tudor retreat.

ANCIENT INNS AND EATERIES

~ The Cartwright Arms Hotel
Aynho, Banbury
01869-811111
A 16th-century coaching inn, the hotel has 20 rooms.

~ Golden Pheasant Hotel
91 High Street
Burford
01993-823223
This 12-room inn has features that date back to the 16th century.

~ Heritage Hotel/The Bear
Park Street
Woodstock
This is a former coaching inn dating back to the 13th century.

~ The Hotel & Hopcroft's Holt
Steeple Aston
Oxford
01869-340259
Another former coaching inn, this one built in 1475, the hotel has 86 rooms, a restaurant and bar and serves afternoon tea.

WARWICKSHIR

STAFFORDSHIRE

LEICESTERSHIRE

● Wolverhampton

Birmingham
●

HEREFORD & WORCESTER

⌂ Packwood House

● Coventry

Kenilworth
Castle
🏰 Stoneleigh Abbey

● Baddesley
Clinton

● Warwick
🏰 Warwick Castle

● Charlecote Park
● Stratford-upon-Avon

NORTHAMPTONSHI

0 Miles   10
0 Kilometers   16

Key

🏰 Cathedral
🏰 Abbey or Priory
🏰 Castle
⌂ Notable building or structure

This map provided for orientation purposes only.
You will need to acquire a detailed roadmap of
The Heart of England if you plan to drive.

GLOUCESTERSHIRE

OXFORDSHIRE

Warwickshire

◇   ◇   ◇

CONTENTS

Warwick

Movers, Shakers and King Makers

hen you envision the seat of power during the Middle Ages, what comes to mind? Do you imagine monarchs issuing ultimatums from the halls of Windsor and Westminster? Privy Councils huddled in consultation in the temporary court at York? When we think of medieval might, we think of Warwickshire. At the time, this remote county was a true contender in the game of political King of the Mountain. Throughout the Norman and Plantagenet eras, Warwickshire was shored up by some of the most significant power players—and power *plays*—in English history. The roster of Warwickshire worthies is peppered with heavyweight champions: Robert de Beaumont, Simon de Montfort, Piers Gaveston, John of Gaunt, Richard Beauchamp, Richard Neville, Robert Dudley . . . as well as the requisite number of royal landowners attempting to keep the nobility's power in check. From the ruins of Kenilworth to the ramparts of Warwick, you'll be walking in the footsteps of those who made kings, feted queens and felled more than a few princes of the realm. If you note an extra swagger in your walk, don't be surprised: there's something about this trip that makes you want to flex your muscles!

✝ Warwick Castle
Warwick

>>

PHONE

01926-406600

LOCATED

94 miles northwest of London, 2 miles from the M40, junction 15. Cars should approach by way of the A429, ½ mile from the town center of Warwick.

TRAVEL

Trains depart Marylebone and Paddington stations for Warwick. Travel time is approximately 2 hours. The castle is a 10-minute walk from the train station.

OPEN

10:00 a.m.–6:00 p.m. daily, April–October
10:00 a.m.–5:00 p.m. daily, November–March

ADMISSION

£12.50 Adults
£ 7.40 Children
£ 9.00 Seniors
Family ticket available

CONVENIENCES

Two restaurants, several snack bars and *many* gift shops; medieval banquets may be attended, by reservation; phone 01926-495421 for further information.

TIP!

During our first several trips to England, Warwick Castle ranked among our very favorite ancient sites. It is, indeed, a remarkable structure. However, over the years the castle has evolved (*in our opinion "devolved"*) from one of the best-preserved medieval castles in the country to one of the most expensive and commercial enterprises we've encountered in our travels. Owned and operated by Madame Tussaud's—of Wax Museum fame—Warwick now suffers from an overdose of "merrie olde" preciousness. With its perpetual on-site Renaissance Faire, a prescribed tour that forces you to navigate innumerable gift shops, and its melodramatic "Day in the Life" of Richard Neville, Warwick is no longer a castle for connoisseurs. It *is*, however, England's most-visited tourist attraction, having surpassed the Tower of London in popularity, so clearly not *everyone* agrees with our opinion. Here's our bottom line: if you're a first-time castle-goer or are traveling with school-age children, Warwick can lend an entertaining—but costly—insight into the architecture, role and lifestyle of a medieval castle and its residents. If you're a castle veteran, or are particularly averse to hordes of kids on field trips, we recommend you tour the town of Warwick—by all means!—but satisfy your castle craving at nearby Kenilworth Castle.

>>>

Considered by many to be England's finest castle, Warwick is truly thrilling to behold. Even before you stop to reflect on the rich history that unfolded inside these mighty walls, the mere vision of turrets, towers and parapets is enough to make your heart beat faster. Our *first* glimpse of Warwick Castle was one of those "never forget" moments, right up there with the Tower, Windsor and Dover.

Warwick Castle sits atop Ethelfleda's Mound, a high, conical motte named for Alfred the Great's daughter. But the history of the castle really begins in 1068, when William the Conqueror granted his newly built fortress to Henry de Newburgh, the first Norman earl of Warwick. Henry and his sons, Roger of Warwick and the powerful twins, Robert and Waleran Beaumont, were among the most influential players in early English politics. Their strength was underscored by a massive real estate portfolio that stretched across the length and breadth of England. Henry's possession of the strategic Warwick Castle was yet another crucial element in the Beaumont stronghold on the newly conquered nation.

Little remains of the Norman architecture; the castle suffered heavy damage at the hands of Simon de Montfort's forces during the 1264 barons' revolt. De Montfort sacked Warwick and spirited the royalist Earl of Warwick, William Maudit, off to Kenilworth for "safekeeping."

In 1267, the castle and the earldom passed into the hands of the Beauchamp clan, another political powerhouse in the landmark events of England's Middle Ages. The Beauchamps inherited a castle ravaged by time and siege. Finally, in 1331, Earl Thomas Beauchamp, one of Edward III's most distinguished generals, began a massive reconstruction of the castle. The lengthy undertaking was eventually completed by his son Thomas the younger. This Thomas was a virulent opponent of Richard II and one of the most outspoken members of the "Lords Appellant" (*consequently, he spent far more time as a "resident" of the Tower of London than he did in Warwick Castle*). Later Beauchamp earls were equally noteworthy; so well loved was Richard Beauchamp that the town of Warwick paid homage to him with one of the most remarkable tombs in all of Europe (*granted, with funds Richard had set aside for the purpose*).

When Richard Beauchamp's son died in 1449 without an heir, the earldom and the castle passed to Richard's son-in-law, the overmighty noble Richard Neville, Earl of Salisbury. The addition of Warwick Castle to his already bulging real estate portfolio generously increased Neville's wealth and strengthened his might in a way few other peers of the realm could match. Of royal descent, Neville was too far down the hereditary pecking order to hope to ascend to the throne. Instead he settled for the next best thing: using his considerable resources and cunning to play convoluted chess games with his Yorkist cousins. Sir Richard spent most of his

---

☞ Did you know?

Warwick Castle played a pivotal role in the transfer of power between King Stephen and the future Henry II in 1153. The civil war that had raged for 19 years—first between Stephen and Henry I's daughter and rightful heir, Matilda, then between Stephen and Matilda's son Henry Fitzempress—was coming to an end. Disenchanted with Stephen's feckless reign and distrustful of his unsavory son Eustace, the nobility began to view young Henry as an attractive alternative. A groundswell of barons, including the powerful Robert Beaumont, Earl of Leicester, switched their allegiance from Stephen to Henry as the year unfolded. Sometime that spring, the Countess of Warwick, herself a Beaumont, managed to trick the royalist forces billeted in "her" castle, gain control of the stronghold and surrender it to Henry. Her husband, a staunch supporter of Stephen, was fighting elsewhere with the king at the time. Devastated by the news, the Earl of Warwick soon died. Contemporaries attributed the cause of his death to shame over his wife's subterfuge.

adult life attempting to position as monarch whichever relative best served his interests at any given time—a hobby that earned him the nickname "The King Maker" (or, *in Shakespeare's words, "the setter down and plucker up of kings"*). At one point, Neville dared to hold his cousin and sovereign, Edward IV, prisoner at Warwick Castle while he himself attempted to rule as the uncrowned king. Yet, despite the fact that he was a political weathercock, the King Maker was extremely popular in Warwick. He generously improved and endowed such civic enterprises as Beauchamp Chapel, Guy's Cave (legendary home of Warwick's Saxon forefather) and an almshouse for elderly retainers.

After Richard Neville died at the Battle of Barnet in 1471, Warwick Castle was granted to Neville's son-in-law and brother of Edward IV, George, Duke of Clarence (or, *as Shakespeare would describe him,*

Did you know?

The Beauchamp earls of Warwick were among the mightiest nobles of the era—and, more often than not, they used their might to keep the powers of the monarch in check. Early in the 14th century, Guy Beauchamp (nicknamed "The Black Dog of Arden") all but made a career out of making life uncomfortable for Edward II. Sir Guy was one of the leaders of the successful 1312 plot to seize, prosecute (or, *more aptly, persecute*) and execute Edward's alleged paramour Piers Gaveston. Gaveston was hauled away from the Earl of Pembroke's custody in Oxfordshire and held prisoner at Warwick Castle, where he endured a humiliating mock trial destined from the start to find him guilty of treason. Gaveston suffered a traitor's death at the hands of the Earl of Lancaster. Guy Beauchamp did not attend the execution—presumably he was too busy plotting new ways to provoke King Edward.

false, fleeting, perjured Clarence . . ."). Alas, poor Clarence met an early demise when he was drowned—by his brother's orders—in a butt of malmsey while prisoner in the Tower of London. The next tenant of the castle was Richard of Gloucester, yet another son-in-law of Neville and the future King Richard III.

The link between Warwick Castle and the earls of Warwick was severed briefly during the reign of Henry VII—all the rightful heirs were Yorkists, doomed to die or rot in prison. By the time Henry VIII came to power, a distant branch of the Beauchamp family tree — the Dudley clan — had begun to bear fruit. In 1547, John Dudley, a member of the Protectorate for Edward VI, managed to claim both the earldom and the castle that went with it. Dudley would eventually suffer a spectacular fall from glory, losing his life for his role in attempting to place his daughter-in-law Lady Jane Grey on the throne. Remarkably, Elizabeth I restored the earldom, castles and estates to Dudley's son Ambrose — a favor, no doubt, to his brother, Robert Dudley, Earl of Leicester and lord of nearby Kenilworth Castle. (*Elizabeth was ever so fond of Sir Robert . . .*) However, when Ambrose died without issue in 1560, Warwick Castle again reverted to the Crown.

☞ Did you know?

Tragedy loomed large in the house of Clarence. Neville's daughter Isabella, Duchess of Clarence and wife of the ill-fated Duke George, died at Warwick Castle following the birth of her second son, Richard.

The castle and the earldom parted ways again during the reign of King James; Warwick Castle was granted to Sir Fulke Granville (a.k.a. de Greville), Baron Brooke (a descendant of the original Beaumont owners). Members of the family have held the castle ever since.

QUICK TOUR

The castle you see today grew from the interior outward. With the exception of the original Norman defenses, the residential areas of Warwick Castle have always tended to take priority. Even the massive curtain wall with its three defensive towers could be considered more of a showpiece than a military structure — although the entrance to the castle could certainly be very well defended in the event of an attack. While there is a tremendous amount to see at Warwick Castle, your tour will follow a fairly regimented route, well mapped by the castle administrators and largely focused on the castle's interior (*also cleverly crafted to deposit you into as many gift shops as possible*). So you will better understand the individual structures and the role they played in the castle's history, we have provided you with a brief walking tour of Warwick Castle's highlights.

You'll begin your tour at the 14th-century barbican and gatehouse. A set of double portcullises, numerous murder holes and an exhibition on the life of Richard III are the main attractions. To the left of the gatehouse is Caesar's Tower, the most majestic and interesting of the castle's three primary towers. A soaring 148 feet high, the tower was probably built by the first Thomas Beauchamp as a storehouse for spoils taken in the 1356 Battle of Poitiers—including numerous French hostages awaiting payment of their ransom. Descend the steps—if you dare! —to the bleak prison, where inscriptions from the 17th-century Civil War may still be seen. The torture chamber rather gratuitously displays a grim collection of instruments

• •
☞ Did you know?
The design of Caesar's Tower borrows heavily from the fairy-tale style castles of medieval France. (*Somehow, we doubt this made Sir Thomas's French prisoners feel any more at home.*)
• •

of terror (*not our cup of tea, quite frankly*). More to our liking is the extensive collection of arms and armor, rivaled only by the Royal Armories at Leeds Castle and the Tower of London.

Without a doubt, the centerpiece of Warwick is the residential castle. Thomas Beauchamp the elder placed his impressive home on the edge of a striking cliff, overlooking the River Avon. Atop the medieval undercroft are the magnificent 14th-century Great Hall and chapel (c. 1600), plus numerous lesser halls and private residences. The castle's primary living areas were lavishly remodeled in Jacobean times by Baron Brooke; alas, they retain very little of their ancient aura. The medieval era is no stepchild at Warwick Castle, however. A major exhibition in the residential castle lends a dramatic interpretation to a "day in the life" of Sir Richard Neville. Vivid sights, sounds and narra-

tion take you through the tense preparations as the castle min-
ions prepare their lord for the March 25, 1471, Battle of Barnet.
(*We find it ironic that Neville is cast in a military spotlight; his
many strengths did not include battlefield finesse. We also don't
particularly agree with the historical premise of this exhibit. Yes,
Neville did, at one point, fight for the Lancastrian King Henry
VI. However, he did so as a Yorkist turncoat, not because of any
great loyalty to the Red Rose's cause. Neville was first and foremost an opportunist.*)

As you leave the residential castle, proceed clockwise; you'll
pass the provocatively named Ghost Tower. Only recently
opened to the public, this building features another "site and
sound" exhibit focused on the
grim and ghostly story of Sir
Fulke Granville, who was murdered at Warwick in 1628 by a
servant. (*The tale postdates our
era; needless to say, we didn't linger to soak in the details.*)

Next on the circuit, follow
the footpath that leads to the
landscaped Mound, the only
surviving relic from the Norman era. Built by order of Wil-
liam the Conqueror, the high, sweeping vantage was integral to
the castle's defense. Today it provides stunning views of Warwick Castle's grounds. Proceeding clockwise, you'll come to
Bear Tower and Clarence Tower, squat structures that were begun by Richard of Gloucester in 1478 (*we assume he did not
christen the tower after his brother Clarence, for whom he had little use*). The artillery structure was never officially completed,
and the gateway was added much later. It is believed that Bear
Tower served as a kennel for bears used in the pastime of baiting.
You may walk the ramparts between these two towers, if you're
so inclined.

Just before you return to the Barbican, you'll come upon

* *
☞ Did you know?

Throughout your Warwick wander-
ings, you'll frequently happen upon
the "bear and ragged staff" motif. This
is the ancient emblem of the earls of
Warwick, most of whom played an active philanthropic role in the development of the town. Legend claims that
the first "earl" of Warwick, Arthgallus,
was an esteemed member of King Arthur's Knights of the Round Table.
* *

Guy's Tower, built by Thomas Beauchamp the younger and later named for the infamous "Black Dog of Arden." This 12-sided tower encloses a series of residential suites that were used as lodging for the castle's guests. Feeling hearty? You may walk the 127-foot-high ramparts. Like Caesar's Tower, the design here is more French than English.

Although they postdate our era, the grounds of Warwick Castle are worth exploring, weather and time permitting. River walks, a charming island and numerous gardens—including a peacock promenade—provide a peaceful respite from the throngs of school groups and souvenir sellers.

While you're in Warwick . . .

Whether your journey begins or ends at Warwick Castle, be sure to allow enough time to take in the many medieval sites in the town of Warwick. Although a devastating fire in the 1600s destroyed many of the town's ancient residences, several important public buildings have survived. We have listed the highlights here. If you are interested in further investigating Warwick's ancient roots (including the precious collection of homes and churches that *do* predate the fire), a number of inexpensive visitors' guides are readily available from the Warwick Tourist Information Centre. Have fun!

Warwick Tourist Information Centre
The Courthouse, Jury Street

〉〉

PHONE
   01926-492212

TIP!
   The Warwick Society offers guided walks around town on summer Sundays (daily during July and August). The Information Centre can provide you with a schedule and details.

〉〉

Oken's House
Castle Lane and Jury Street

>>

PHONE

01926-495546

OPEN

10:00 a.m.–5:00 p.m. Monday–Saturday, April–September
2:00–5:00 p.m. Sunday, April–September
10:00 a.m.–dusk Saturday, October–March

ADMISSION

Fee charged

>>

This charming Elizabethan residence is now home to the Warwick Doll Museum, perfect for engaging the attention of the youngest members of your party.

Warwickshire County Museum
Market Hall at Market Place

>>

PHONE

01926-410410

OPEN

10:00 a.m.–5:30 p.m. Monday–Saturday, year-round
2:30–5:30 p.m. Sunday, April–October

ADMISSION

Free of charge

>>

If you're visiting Warwick in the summer, this museum is worth a quick stop to check out the small collection of treasures from the region's Middle Ages.

✝ Lord Leycester Hospital
High Street

>>

PHONE

01926-491422

OPEN

10:00 a.m.–5:00 p.m. Tuesday–Sunday, year-round

ADMISSION

£3.20 Adults
£2.20 Children
£2.70 Seniors

CONVENIENCES

Brethren's Kitchens tearoom

TIP!

Behind the main buildings of Lord Leycester Hospital is a walled garden with remnants of Warwick's ancient town walls bearing the telltale Norman arch. Admission is £1.50.

>>

It's hard to say enough about Lord Leycester Hospital—it is, hands down, one of the most interesting and varied medieval attractions we've come across. Abutting the town's medieval west gate, the property offers a varied glimpse at religious, domestic and civic life in the high Middle Ages.

The oldest building on the site is the 14th-century chantry chapel of St. James, which sits atop the medieval gate. The church was built by Thomas Beauchamp, 12th Earl of Warwick. In 1383, the Guild of St. George was granted the benefice of the chapel, and in the late 1300s, more buildings were added to accommodate the Guild of the Blessed Virgin. Several of the buildings on the property date from this era.

When the guilds were disbanded during the Dissolution of the Monasteries, the buildings were saved from destruction; they were given to the Bur-

• •
☞ Did you know?

The chapel at Lord Leycester's is still lit totally by candles. The massive candelabra above the center aisle dates from the Middle Ages.
• •

gess of Warwick and served as the town's guildhall and civic center for several decades. In 1571, the property was purchased by Elizabeth's beloved Robert Dudley, Earl of Leicester, who converted the complex into residential almshouses.

• • • • • • • • • • • • • • • • • • • •

 Did you know?

The rather alarming blue porcupine with the threatening quills that appears in the courtyard outside Lord Leycester Hospital is a symbol of the Sidney family, close kin (and eventual heirs) of the Dudleys. The bear-and-staff emblem is associated with the Beauchamp clan.

• •

Although Lord Leycester Hospital still provides housing for ex-service personnel and their spouses, you are welcome to enjoy the exceptionally well-preserved chapel, kitchens, Great Hall, guildhall and galleried courtyard—together, they offer a diverse and fascinating snapshot of ancient Warwick.

ᴧᴧ

✝ Beauchamp Chapel at St. Mary's Collegiate Church

Old Square and Church Street

>>

PHONE
   01926-403940

OPEN
   10:00 a.m.–5:00 p.m. daily, year-round

ADMISSION
   Donation suggested

CONVENIENCES
   Brass rubbings

TIP!
   Weather permitting, the church tower of St. Mary's is well worth the climb (and the nominal admission fee). Its views of the castle are simply amazing.

>>

The highlight of any trip to Warwick—the castle excepted—has to be the breathtaking Beauchamp Chapel at St. Mary's. The church itself dates from 1123—it was built by Roger Beaumont, the second Norman earl of Warwick—though most of the construction you see today is the result of a postfire remodeling in the late 17th century.

Once you're inside, you're certain to be awestruck by the opulence of the Beauchamp chantry chapel. The focal point is the glorious tomb of Richard Beauchamp, Earl of Warwick —perhaps the greatest of all the Warwick lords. Councilor to both Henry V and Henry VI, Richard was a true hero of his time (although modern judgment sits heavily upon him for the role he played in condemning Joan of Arc to be burned at the stake). His gilded effigy, in full-plate armor, lies atop a magnificent chest adorned with allegorical carvings. Richard "The King Maker" Neville is portrayed as one of the weeping figures on the coffin chest.

◆ ◆

☞ Did you know?

The effigies of Thomas Beauchamp and Katherine Mortimer are depicted holding hands. This seemingly affectionate stance does not signify marital bliss—although theirs may have been a perfectly agreeable marriage. Rather, their hand-holding represents the union of two noble houses.

◆ ◆

The other famous tomb in Beauchamp Chapel is that of Elizabeth I's "Sweet Robin," Robert Dudley, Earl of Leicester. Dudley's effigy lies next to that of his third wife, Lettice Knollys. Dudley's infant son is buried close at hand, as is Sir Robert's brother Ambrose.

In the chancel, look for the tomb of the 14th-century earl Thomas Beauchamp (the elder) and his wife Katherine Mortimer, as well as a small brass plaque marking the burial site of William Parr, brother of Henry VIII's last queen, Katherine. Thomas Beauchamp II and his wife, Margaret Ferrers, are buried in the south transept of the nave.

❖ ❖

RICHARD BEAUCHAMP (1382–1439)

Of all the incredibly interesting and influential earls of Warwick—and, believe us, there were many—none is remembered so fondly by the town of Warwick as Richard Beauchamp. How well regarded is Earl Richard? Just short of glorified. From his stunning gilded tomb (*dare we say "shrine?"*) to the marvelous, if occasionally whitewashed, stories of his heroism and philanthropy,

Richard Beauchamp comes closer to being revered than any noble of his day. (*We find the fact that one biographer has chosen to overlook his role in sentencing Joan of Arc to burn at the stake very telling.*)

Irony aside, there is no arguing that the life of Richard Beauchamp was impressive. Count of Aumale, as well as the 13th Earl of Warwick, Richard was born to greatness. For more than two centuries, the Beauchamps had been at the top of England's political power structure, with clout and wealth virtually unmatched among the nobility. As a warrior, Richard first proved his military prowess against Owen Glendower's Welsh rebellion in 1403, capturing Glendower's banner for King Henry IV. Later that year, at the Battle of Shrewsbury, Richard's bravery (and his men-at-arms) helped assure a victory for the Crown in the struggle against Harry "Hotspur" Percy and his band of disaffected nobles. For these efforts, Earl Richard was made a Knight of the Garter; he continued to be valued on the battlefield until his death, serving as Captain of Calais and as England's commander-in-chief during all French campaigns beginning in 1419.

Surely brains were as crucial as brawn in Richard Beauchamp's success. Returning from a glorious two-year pilgrimage in 1410, Richard was named to Henry IV's newly formed Council; his specific duties were to serve as advisor to Prince Hal, the future King Henry V. His intimate involvement in the inner workings of the royal court would continue until his death, 29 years later. Whether serving as High Steward at the coronation of Henry V, subduing John Oldcastle's Lollard Rising in 1414, or serving as tutor, Council member and protector of young Henry VI, Beauchamp played a diverse role in England's domestic affairs.

His hand in England's foreign policy was even more significant. In 1414, Richard Beauchamp was appointed to head the English delegation to the Central Council of Constance. The council had been convened by Pope John XXIII (a.k.a. the Pisan Antipope) in an attempt to reconcile the schism in the Church and to advise on issues of religious reform. One of the unofficial goals of the council was to mend the differences between England and France, which many believed to be the root cause of Christian dissension.

Unfortunately, the council's mission was largely unsuccessful. Before the year was out, Richard had turned from Church advisor to chief strategist behind a military invasion of France.

Once again, Beauchamp proved to be a powerful warrior—and a brilliant diplomat. His campaign on the Continent resulted in the conquest of Normandy. His skills as a statesman helped him mastermind the hard-earned French treaty of 1419. In 1420, Beauchamp was the chief English emissary in the marriage negotiations between Henry V and the French princess Katherine of Valois—a bridal contract that brought as its dowry the crown of France.

Richard Beauchamp remained one of Henry V's most valued advisors; he was with the king on his deathbed, when he was entrusted with the guardianship of the future Henry VI. Earl Richard remained the principal guardian and tutor of Henry VI until his majority, sharing pride of place with the young king's mother during Henry's coronation ceremonies . . . and handling the delicate issues of royal discipline and punishment during the boy monarch's willful adolescence.

Meanwhile, relations with France had begun to deteriorate. For years, the emotionally disturbed Dauphin Charles had protested the handing over of the French crown by his father, Charles VI. Periodic Dauphin-led rebellions had been effectively quelled, in part through the efforts of Richard Beauchamp. In 1429, events turned dramatically in the Dauphin's favor when a young peasant girl named Joan, fueled by the conviction that she was divinely inspired, led the French armies to victory at Orleans, Beaugency and Patay. Joan of Arc's triumphs paved the way for the Dauphin's coronation as King Charles VII of France.

Needless to say, the English found their defeat in battle and the subsequent loss of "their" French crown alarming. At the request of Henry VI's uncle, the Duke of Bedford, Richard Beauchamp hurried

☞ Did you know?

There is an interesting story connecting Earl Richard Beauchamp and England's patron saint, St. George (*why are we not surprised?*). Anxious to negotiate a treaty in the age-old strife between England and France, the Holy Roman Emperor Sigismund arrived at Dover in 1416, bearing the heart of St. George as a gesture of goodwill toward the English. Apparently, Richard, then Captain of Calais, was the first to officially accept the gift on behalf of his country. The relic was then borne to the royal castle at Windsor, where it was presented to Henry V and enshrined in St. George's Chapel. Awe-inspiring as the gift was, it failed to work miracles where relations with France were concerned. (*And where, we are compelled to ask, had George's heart been in the 1,053 years since his bloody death? It's a mystery.*)

the young English king across the Channel to Rouen, center of the English presence in France; it was here that he awaited *his* coronation as the *real* king of France.

Unfortunately for the French, their victory over the English—and France's possession of the crown—was short-lived. Joan's battlefield strategy took a sudden downturn, hastened, no doubt, by a lack of tangible support from the volatile Charles. After a series of defeats, she was captured by Burgundy, sold to the English and imprisoned at Rouen.

For the following year, Joan of Arc, Richard Beauchamp, Earl of Warwick, and Henry VI, King of England and future King of France, all lived at Rouen

Castle. While Joan withstood a protracted trial on charges of heresy and witch-craft, Earl Richard entertained numerous envoys from both the English government and the Church, all eager to see "The Maid" found guilty and sentenced to death. During this time, Beauchamp lobbied long and hard against Joan and paid numerous visits to her dungeon, berating and humiliating her one moment, then sending his own physician to tend to her the next. (This is not as contradictory as it seems; Earl Richard had a reputation for exacting harsh revenge, and it's likely he wanted to see Joan survive long enough to suffer a witch's death by fire.)

♦ ♦

☞ Did you know?

The ancient lineage of the Beauchamp clan was in a precarious position when Richard's only male cousin died in 1422, leaving the earl last in the Beauchamp line. Father to a parcel of "mere" daughters, Earl Richard eventually embraced his responsibility to beget a boy by remarrying a very wealthy widow, Isabel Despenser. Not fully convinced this ploy alone would assure him the desired "heir and a spare," Richard founded a chantry chapel at Guy's Cliff, outside of Warwick. Here—the legendary home of the Warwick forebear—daily prayers were offered to improve the chances of Sir Richard siring a son. The 1425 birth of Henry, future Duke of Warwick, seemed a godsend. Unfortunately, Henry of Warwick was fated to die young, ending the Beauchamp line. The Warwick title and its vast portfolio of properties passed to Sir Richard's son-in-law Richard "The King Maker" Neville. Neville is depicted as one of the mourners on Earl Richard's tomb (*we bet "The King Maker" cried all the way to the bank*).

♦ ♦

As we all know, the Earl of Warwick had his way. Furious as he was at Joan's unexpected recantation (which would have canceled her fiery demise), he was equally relieved when she abjured of her own free will. Joan was burned at the stake on May 30, 1431; Henry VI was crowned King of France in Paris seven months later. He was accompanied, of course, by his jubilant guardian, Richard Beauchamp.

If Richard Beauchamp's accomplishments were great, his wealth was even greater. At the time of his death, he was the second-wealthiest man in England, trailing only Richard, Duke of York. Heir to properties in 26 counties, he feathered his nest even further by twice marrying important heiresses—his second wife brought him no less than 50 estates as well as the lucrative lordship of Glamorgan. (*Never mind that Richard is known to have settled at least one property dispute by the wholesale slaughter of the town's residents.*) To his credit, Richard was a financially generous earl, and Warwick reaped the benefits of his munificence. Richard Beauchamp rebuilt the medieval walls and gates of the town, richly endowed the collegiate church of St. Mary's, founded the chantry at the Guy's Cliff landmark and gave the funds to build yet another collegiate church at Henley. It is said that when his tomb was opened in the 18th century, local women jostled for the privilege of claiming locks of the earl's hair, which they subsequently wove into highly prized rings. (*We, on the other hand, stand by our skeptical point of view: "If he sounds too good to be true, he probably is."*)

◆◆

Kenilworth Castle
Kenilworth

>>

PHONE
  01926-852078

LOCATED
  Approximately 100 miles from London, off the A452 in Kenilworth

TRAVEL
  Trains depart Marylebone and Paddington stations for both Warwick and Stratford. Taxi service is available from either station. Travel time is approximately 2 hours.

OPEN
  10:00 a.m.–6:00 p.m. daily, April–October
  10:00 a.m.–4:00 p.m. daily, November–March

ADMISSION
  £4.00 Adults
  £2.00 Children
  £3.00 Seniors
  Family ticket available

CONVENIENCES
  Café, gift kiosk, interactive model castle

>>

The once-magnificent seat of so many medieval notables, Kenilworth Castle today stands in ruins. Oh, but what splendid ruins they are! The history of Kenilworth is so compelling, the stones themselves so evocative, that it barely matters that Kenilworth is basically a shell. This is a place to let your imagination run wild, as you call to mind such colorful personalities as King John, Simon de Montfort, Edward I, John of Gaunt, Robert Dudley and the Virgin Queen in action that spans the battlefield to the ballroom. (*If you can't already tell that Kenilworth is one of our very favorite sites, read on . . .*)

The site that would become Kenilworth Castle was originally a royal tract known as Stoneleigh (not to be confused with Stoneleigh Abbey, also in Warwickshire). The property was protected, at first, by a crude Norman fortress of wood and clay. Work on the present Kenilworth began in 1122, when Henry I deeded the property to his Treasurer, Sir Geoffrey de Clinton, but Kenilworth did not remain in de Clinton's hands for long. Henry II appropriated the castle when he prepared to defend himself against his own son, the rebellious "Young King" Henry. The "old" Henry conveniently "forgot" to return the castle to the de Clintons once the threat of rebellion was past.

☞ Did you know?

The first place potatoes were grown in England was at Kenilworth Castle.

Equally paranoid about rebellion (*and with just cause, we might add*), Henry II's youngest son, King John, expanded the castle complex, adding an outer bailey surrounded by a curtain wall and three defensive towers. Despite these precautions, the king (a.k.a. John "Lackland") was forced to surrender Kenilworth, along with three other royal castles, as proof of his intent to honor Magna Carta in 1215. It was returned to the Crown when John's son Henry III ascended to the throne.

For all of his weakness in affairs of state, Henry III had quite an architectural flair; Kenilworth was just one of many royal properties to benefit from his artistic vision. During his reign, the chapel was remodeled on a grand scale, and the king's chambers received a handsome new roof. The queen's chambers were graced with wainscoting and flooded with light from the newly enlarged windows and porch. Exterior improvements were undertaken as well.

Alas, Henry was not the direct beneficiary of these many magnificent touches. Instead, he awarded custody of Kenilworth to his sister Eleanor and her husband Simon de Montfort, whom Henry named Earl of Leicester in 1244. Clearly, this was the highlight of the relationship between the two men. Long infuriated over Henry's whittling away the rights of the nobility, de Montfort—undisputedly the most powerful magnate in England—led a host of dissatisfied barons in open rebellion against the king. Kenilworth Castle served as their command central. In 1264, de Montfort's forces won the pivotal Battle of Lewes, capturing the king and his son Prince Edward as well as the king's brother the Earl of Cornwall and Cornwall's son; all were held, at least for a time, at Kenilworth. Meanwhile, Simon de Montfort, for all intents and purposes, ruled as the "uncrowned king" of England.

This shift in power did not last long, however. Edward eventually escaped (from Hertford, however, not Kenilworth) and quickly mustered his men in retaliation. De Montfort's son (also Simon) advanced to meet the challenge. While en route from London, the young Simon chose to rest his troops at Kenilworth—not within the safe confines of the castle, mind you, but on the exposed lawns surrounding it. The rebels wrongly assumed their enemy was 30 miles away, and no scout was sent nor sentry posted. The woeful ineptitude of de Montfort's intelligence sources, coupled with Prince Edward's brilliant (if morally weak) strategy, resulted in a surprise predawn massacre of the rebel troops by royalist forces. Although young Simon was able to swim to safety (across the man-made lake his papa had cleverly devised as part of Kenilworth's defensive strengthening), the rout gave Edward the momentum he needed to defeat de Montfort's forces at Evesham three days later.

Simon the elder lost his life at Evesham, but his garrison at Kenilworth staunchly refused to surrender. They held the castle for de Montfort's widow, Eleanor, lending credence to Ken-

◆ ◆ ◆ ◆ ◆ ◆ ◆ ◆ ◆ ◆ ◆ ◆ ◆ ◆ ◆ ◆ ◆ ◆ ◆ ◆

🖙 **Did you know?**

In addition to building Kenilworth Castle, Sir Geoffrey de Clinton built a significant priory on the grounds of his property. Every Thursday, the canons of the priory were allowed to take their boats and nets and troll the waters of Kenilworth for fish—evidence that the castle was moated from the very beginning.

◆ ◆ ◆ ◆ ◆ ◆ ◆ ◆ ◆ ◆ ◆ ◆ ◆ ◆ ◆ ◆ ◆ ◆ ◆ ◆

ilworth's reputation as being impregnable. For nearly a year, the Kenilworth troops stood fast against the king's army in what would become one of the most famous sieges of the Middle Ages. Under the leadership of Sir Henry Hastings, the defenders repelled the most fearsome attacks ... and shunned the most generous of terms. Talk about attitude: they proceeded to chop off the hand of a royal messenger and responded to the Church's blanket excommunication of the garrison by, in turn, "excommunicating" both King Henry and the Archbishop of Canterbury. At last, a severe flu epidemic forced the garrison to lay down their arms just before Christmas 1266. Mighty even in defeat, the rebels somehow were able to negotiate an honorable departure.

A royal castle once again, Kenilworth now passed to Henry's son Edmund Crouchback, first earl of Lancaster—and so began the castle's long association with the duchy of that name. The subsequent earls, dukes and kings of the house of Lancaster gave pride of place to Kenilworth. More than a mere stronghold, it became a favorite Lancastrian residence and enjoyed a series of domestic renovations aimed at putting comfort on par with defense.

Grit and violence gave way to more genteel living when Kenilworth passed into the hands of John of Gaunt. This duke of Lancaster, the fourth son of Edward III and powerful uncle of King Richard II, wielded considerable influence throughout the realm, and Kenilworth soon became a symbol of the duke's importance. An extensive sprawl of residential buildings filled the inner bailey during Gaunt's tenancy. Gaunt's stunning Great Hall, with

◆ ◆

Did you know?

Edmund Crouchback's son, Thomas of Lancaster, barely had time to complete his collegiate chapel at Kenilworth Castle before he was executed for his involvement in a treasonous plot against his cousin King Edward II. (You'll see the crime depicted in the ancient wall paintings at the parish church of St. Peter ad Vincula in Oxfordshire.) In an ironic turn of events, Thomas's blind brother, Henry, later held the same king prisoner at Kenilworth—it was here that Edward II was forced to abdicate his throne.

◆ ◆

its plush private apartments and breathtaking views of the shimmering man-made lake, marked Kenilworth's final evolution from fortress to palace. Hints of this splendor can still be seen in the graceful oriel windows preserved in Kenilworth's ruins.

In 1399, Gaunt's son Henry Bolingbroke ascended to the throne as Henry IV. (Albeit, via controversial methods: he forced his cousin Richard to abdicate, then usurped the crown of England, leapfrogging over several cousins whose claims to the monarchy were considerably stronger than his!) As king, Henry re-established Kenilworth as an official royal residence . . . although it was nothing less than "royal" from the time John of Gaunt had finished his remodeling. Gaunt's grandson Henry V continued majestic improvements at the castle, which culminated with a colossal lakeside banquet hall.

For nearly two centuries, the glory of Kenilworth remained unchanged. Virtually no major remodeling was done—indeed, none was needed! The one exception was the now-vanished King's Lodgings complex, built by Henry VIII. Whether for reasons of speed or frugality, the enclave lacked vital structural integrity; it was the first part of the ancient complex to fall to ruin.

Kenilworth's swan song occurred during the Tudor Renaissance, when Robert Dudley, Earl of Leicester, undertook an important expansion and renovation program. In a gesture of undeniable affection, Elizabeth I had given the royal residence to her favorite courtier and friend in 1563. (The castle had been owned by his father, John Dudley, who lost his head—and the castle—as the result of his plans to seat his daughter-in-law Lady Jane Grey upon the throne of Mary Tudor.) Dudley promptly set out to modernize the Norman keep, adding spacious mullioned windows and constructing a Romanesque gatehouse (*"retro" design, Elizabethan style*). No fool when it came to knowing which side of his toast was buttered, Dudley's *pièce de résistance* was the sweeping guest quarters, designed to welcome Glorianna herself—in the style to which she had become accustomed. Known today as Leicester's Buildings, the complex once accommodated the queen and her traveling entourage of courtiers and servants, numbering well over 200. As you wander through this crumbled enclave, imagine the spectacle Dudley prepared to delight and impress his beloved Elizabeth. During her 19-day visit in July 1575, the queen was regaled with pageants, banquets, parades, performances, jousts, concerts, hunts and fireworks, each more lavish than the last. In fact, Dudley spent as much on that summer's merriment—£1,000 per day—as other lords spent on constructing entire manor homes!

The death of Robert and his brother Ambrose Dudley, both without legal heirs, saw the return of Kenilworth into royal hands. Alas, the Stuarts did not share the affection of the Lancastrians, (nor the frivolities of the Tudors) where Kenilworth was concerned . . . and, of course, Cromwell's troops treated the castle with no more regard than they did any royal property. Having withstood centuries of siege and strife, it was the combination of 17th-century disinterest and abuse that set the stage for Kenilworth's decline. It is possible, however, with some help and a bit of imagination, to trace the history of the castle through the rubble that remains.

• •
☞ Did you know?
Elizabeth and Dudley's frolics in the summer of 1575 served as inspiration for Sir Walter Scott's novel, *Kenilworth*, a vivid (if fictional) description of the queen's midsummer pleasures.
• •

QUICK TOUR OF THE PERIMETER

Before you enter the castle confines, take a stroll along what was once the curtain wall. Adjacent to the ticket office, you'll find Mortimer's Tower, which controls access to the Inner Court (where you'll return, momentarily). Look for the arrow slits and portcullis tracks. Once upon a time, someone carved the Mortimer shield into the walls of the tower—history seems to have forgotten which of the many Mortimers connected with Kenilworth did the honors.

Moving counterclockwise, you'll pass the 13th-century

Water Tower, the best preserved of the curtain wall's original three angled towers. Just beyond the Water Tower are Leicester's Stables, a timbered and stonework structure that stretches 160 feet in length. Although they were altered in the 18th century, the stables are the most intact remnants from Kenilworth's past. Inside the stables, you'll find an exhibition on the history of Kenilworth—and a welcome chance to ward off the chill, if you've chosen an inclement day for your visit (*as we* always *manage to do*). The curious foundation in front of the stables is all that's left of Thomas of Lancaster's collegiate chapel.

Continue eastward to Lunn's Tower, one of two towers built by King John; the ground-level guardroom still bears its long arrow loops. Above are two apartments with fireplaces and latrines.

Standing off to itself is the imposing Leicester's Gatehouse; the wing to the right was added after the Cromwellian war. Intent on capitalizing upon Kenilworth's spectacular setting, Dudley moved the main entrance of the castle from the south end of the property to the north. Visitors approaching from London would now have a far more impressive picture of Kenilworth. See if you can spot Robert Dudley's initials—they are carved above the doorway. The interior of the gatehouse is closed to the public, precluding the opportunity to admire the alabaster fireplace and oak mantel—again, carved with Dudley's initials as well as with his motto, "*Droit et Loyal.*"

INTERPRETING THE CASTLE RUINS

You are now ready to venture into Kenilworth's Inner Court. The buildings of the Inner Court are to the left of the main pathway stretching from the ticket office. This was the site of the medieval castle. With its Great Hall, sleep chambers, scullery and stables, the structure measured about 60 meters wide. The area was once accessed by a bridge, but eventually it was torn down and replaced by a causeway leading to Henry VIII's long-vanished buildings.

To your right you'll see a large, oblong building with angled turrets. This is the Norman Keep. Considered in its time to be a masterpiece of defensive architecture, the three-story keep was originally topped with a fighting gallery. Robert Dudley tried to add a touch of élan to the imposing structure by gracing the turret closest to the ticket office with an ornate clock.

Next to the keep are the ruins of the Service Wing and Strong Tower. The foundations of the kitchen's fireplaces and ovens can still be seen; they are lined with tile. Ascend the stairway of the 14th-century Strong Tower for the best aerial

☛ **Did you know?**

Legend has it that the hands of Leicester's Elizabethan clock were permanently set to the hour of feasting. (*We heartily endorse this idea, subscribing as we do to the notion that it's always "happy hour" somewhere in the world!*)

views of the Great Hall and Great Mare (site of Kenilworth's bygone lake).

Although completely open to the elements (*as we are well aware, having visited the castle during a downpour*) and extensively eroded, John of Gaunt's Great Hall still reveals many intriguing hints of life in the Middle Ages. It is accessible from two ground-level stairways, one at either end of the structure. At

☛ **Did you know?**

At the time of construction, Gaunt's Great Hall roof had the widest span of any in the nation.

the far end of the Great Hall, Saintlowe Tower offers sweeping vistas of the entire Kenilworth property. The tower once provided lodging for the castle, as did the adjacent Great

Chamber (a.k.a. the White Hall) and Lesser Chamber (a.k.a. the Presence Chamber). Beyond the Lesser Chamber, you'll glimpse a portion of the original curtain wall, as well as ruins of the 13th-century chapel. Henry VIII's timber-framed King's Buildings, which once separated the chapel from the keep, have now vanished.

Proceed now to Leicester's Buildings, the once-lofty three-story residence designed by Robert Dudley to take the best advantage of Kenilworth's stunning landscape. Clearly, Dudley set out to impress. Unfortunately, he may have been less magnanimous where the quality of construction was concerned, for these buildings (like the King's Buildings) disintegrated well before their medieval counterparts. Still, you can sense the grand scale of the rooms and imagine the decorative touches —the gilded walls, the resplendent tapestries—that made Kenilworth the trendsetter in Elizabethan hospitality.

Complete your tour of Kenilworth by returning to the Outer Court. Just beyond Leicester's Gatehouse are the Tudor Gardens, reconstructed in 1970 following a set of detailed 17th-century landscape plans. Although the waterworks—fountains and small ponds—that were part of the Tudor scheme are not included today, the gardens are still quite handsome and worth a peek.

- -

☞ Did you know?

While in the Tudor Gardens, glance back at the Norman Keep. According to Kenilworth's literature, you'll be able to spot a number of curious balls adorning the walls, relics from the famous 1266 siege. Apparently, this was the ammunition for the medieval catapult (trebuchet)—a mighty weapon, which, nevertheless, failed to oust the even mightier rebel forces holed up within Kenilworth Castle. (*Try as we might, we couldn't identify them. If your eye is more discerning than ours, we'd love to know!*)

- -

Tip!

Time permitting, you may enjoy several different footpaths that wind through the Kenilworth property. Three separate, self-guided walks take you past minor, but interesting ruins, the remnants of the castle's outbuildings. If you're game, you may pick up information at the ticket office. Be certain, however, to wear sturdy walking shoes and be prepared to return from your adventure with your fair share of mud spatters and grass stains (*as we've said before, we're really not big on outdoor experiences*).

While you're at Kenilworth . . .

✝ Stoneleigh Abbey

Kenilworth

>>

PHONE

01926-858585

E-MAIL

enquiries@stoneleighabbey.org

LOCATED

2 miles west of Kenilworth, off the A46/B4115; follow the drive over the Charles Rennie Bridge until you come to Stoneleigh Abbey

OPEN

11:00 a.m.–5:00 p.m. Tuesday, Wednesday, Thursday and Sunday, April–October

Note: Required guided tours are available at 11:00 a.m. and 1:00 and 3:00 p.m. Tours last 90 minutes. Please arrive in advance of tour time.

ADMISSION

£5.00 Adults
£3.00 Seniors
One child admitted free of charge with each paying adult

>>

Founded by Henry II in 1154, the Cistercian abbey of Stoneleigh was once reputed to be the largest "house" in Warwickshire. Beautifully situated close to the River Avon, the abbey was purchased by Henry VIII's brother-in-law, Charles Brandon, Duke of Suffolk, in 1538. Less than 30 years later, it was sold again, this time to wealthy merchant Sir Thomas Leigh, Lord Mayor of London at the time of Elizabeth's accession. When Leigh died in 1571, his widow, Alice, endowed the local almshouse in his memory. Their son set about a major renovation of Stoneleigh's buildings and grounds.

Today, little remains from Stoneleigh's medieval or Tudor heritage. The ancient gatehouse, built by the 16th abbot in 1346, is intact. The stables look convincingly old, but in fact date from 1816 and were later restored in the Gothic style. Much of the recently refurbished abbey focuses on the furnishings, decorative items and history of the 17th century and beyond. However, the abbey's library does contain four Shakespeare folios—worth a peek if you're a die-hard "Bardolator."

Also in the area . . .

Church of St. Mary the Virgin

>>

This handsome Norman church, close by Stoneleigh Abbey, is renowned for its unusual carvings, including an ancient tympanum, symbol of eternal life. In the chancel is the marble effigy of the abbey's benefactor Alice Leigh, reputedly one of the most kind-hearted and generous women of her time.

Baddesley Clinton Hall
Baddesley Clinton
Knowle

>>

PHONE
01564-783294

LOCATED
7½ miles northwest of Warwick, on Rising Lane off Solihull Road near Chadwick End, ¾ mile west of the A4141

OPEN
1:30–5:00 p.m. Wednesday–Sunday, March–October

ADMISSION
£5.80 Adults
£2.80 Children
Family ticket available

Note: A combination ticket is available in conjunction with Packwood House, just 2 miles away. Ask for details at either site.

CONVENIENCES
Café, bookshop

TIP!

As voracious collectors of both fiction and nonfiction related to our favorite era, we were delighted to find that Baddesley Clinton features a secondhand bookshop. Check it out!

>>>

What a treasure! Baddesley Clinton is a rare example of a defensive medieval manor home, beautifully situated and surprisingly well preserved. The site was developed in the 13th century by the de Clinton family, whose name the property inherited. The house that now graces the property was originally built in 1438 by a wealthy attorney and Under Treasurer of England, Sir John Brome. The gatehouse, with its gun holes and provisions for a portcullis, is remaining evidence of Brome's fortification efforts.

Through marriage, the manor eventually passed into the hands of the Ferrers family; they made it their primary residence for the next 500 years. In 1564, Henry Ferrers (*commonly referred to as "The Antiquary," for reasons that elude us*) undertook a major renovation of the interior. The chimneypieces, many of the fireplaces, the rich paneling and the interesting armorial glass date from this 16th-century modernization. In the great parlor hangs a tapestry (c. 17th century) depicting Elizabeth I's 1580 visit to Kenilworth Castle and, in the Blue Bedroom, you'll find a handsome, inlaid "Armada" bed, carved from the timbers of a Spanish galleon.

• •
📖 Did you know?

Providing sanctuary for recusant priests involved more than shoving the clergy in the closet and sliding the bolt in place. A complex choreography of "cover your tracks" tactics had to be implemented speedily whenever the queen's men came galloping down the gravel drive. Even the mattresses had to be flipped and redressed, for fear a soldier might detect the warmth of a recent slumberer among the bedclothes.

• •

Henry Ferrers and his family were staunch Roman Catholics, who nevertheless managed to stay removed from the political and religious turmoil of the latter half of the 1500s. That was not the case for Henry's temporary tenants at Baddesley Clinton, a young widow named Eleanor Brooksby and her sister, Anne, who is believed to have taken the veil secretly. In 1589, the two women rented the manor from the Ferrers while the family was on extended stay in London. The sisters wasted no time turning the property into an illegal sanctuary for Jesuit priests—an enterprise that, fortunately, went undetected during its operation. Numerous clever hiding places, also known as "priest holes," can still be found at Baddesley Clinton . . . including one in a fireplace! (*We were suitably awed by the prospect of fully grown men, along with Eleanor's young children, huddled in uncomfortable silence for hours upon end in these minuscule spaces.*)

Ghost Alert!

The Ferrers family and their tenants may have held their local priests in great esteem. That obviously was not the case for one-time Baddesley Clinton resident, Nicholas Brome. Son of John Brome, Nicholas, who inherited the manor in 1458, had the misfortune of arriving home one afternoon to find his wife in the clutches of a neighboring "man of the cloth." Today there is some question about whether the priest was attempting to *choke* Mrs. Brome or *chuck* her under the chin. Nicholas, however, did not pause to debate semantics. He murdered his wife's assailant on the spot. The bloodstains from this tragedy are still in evidence in front of the living room fireplace. The spectral woman who is occasionally spotted roaming Baddesley Clinton's halls is believed to be Mrs. Brome.

While at Baddesley Clinton . . .

Alongside the carpark, you'll find a meandering, tree-lined path, marked with a discreet directional arrow. This leads you to the petite **Church of St. Michael**. Although the exact age of this church is unknown, the core is believed to date from the 13th century. What is known is that the hot-tempered Nicholas Brome—having received both a papal pardon and a separate pardon from King Henry VII for slaying a priest in his parlor—raised the height of the nave, added the clerestory windows, erected the bell tower and installed three fine bells as his way of balancing his heavenly debit column before the Judgment Day. (*The fact that both pope and king were willing to give Brome dis-*

pensation for his crime leads us to believe the priest in question was doing a wee bit more than "chucking" Mrs. Brome under the chin. Sounds suspiciously like "choking" to us!) Twelve generations of Ferrers family members, from 1535 to 1845, are buried in St. Michael's. As for Nicholas Brome, legend has it he was buried upright beneath the paving of the church porch, so the continual tread of footsteps would disturb his eternal rest. *(Clearly some amateur historian is determined to besmirch this fellow's reputation for all posterity!)*

Also while you're at Baddesley Clinton . . .

Packwood House
Lapworth
Solihull

>>

PHONE
01564-783294

E-MAIL
baddesley@smtp.ntrust.org.uk

LOCATED
2 miles east of Hockley on the A3400, just 2 miles from Baddesley Clinton

OPEN
Noon–4:30 p.m. Wednesday–Sunday, March–October

ADMISSION
£5.20 Adults
£2.60 Children
Family ticket available
Combination ticket with Baddesley Clinton
£8.50 Adults
£4.25 Children
Family ticket available

CONVENIENCES
Gift shop

>>

Packwood House was built in 1550–1595 by John Fetherson on land confiscated from the Benedictine monks during the Dissolution of the Monasteries. Although most of the present house was, by and large, constructed during the 20th century, the owners strived to recreate a close-to-authentic Tudor interior, using recycled ancient materials wherever possible. The medieval-style Great Hall and long gallery are modern, but were converted from an ancient barn and cow byre. The hall's fireplace was rescued from an old Stratford vinery — it dates from Shakespeare's era. Several key pieces of furniture at Packwood House are quite ancient, including the bed where Henry VI's consort, Margaret of Anjou, rested before the Battle of Tewkesbury. This is among the most imaginative architectural meldings we've ever seen and well worth a visit if you combine your trip with nearby Baddesley Clinton.

ANCIENT INNS AND EATERIES

~ Brome House
Warwick
01926-491069
Originally part of the Warwick Castle estates, this once-moated home was built in 1420.

~ Clarendon House Hotel
Kenilworth
This historic inn has been in operation since 1430.

~ Salford Hall Hotel
Wilmcote
01789-267030
Built in the late 1400s, this was once a country retreat for the Evesham Abbey monks.

~ The Tudor House Inn
Warwick
01926-495447
Dating from 1472, this inn makes a nice stop after a busy day of touring Warwick. The guest rooms are comfortable, and meals are served in the home's original Great Hall.

CONTENTS

Stratford-upon-Avon

The Play's the Thing

f there is one thing that competes with our mania for all things medieval and Tudor, it's our passion for plays. We are devoted theater fanatics, and few playwrights rev up our engines the way Shakespeare does. You can imagine, therefore, how we approached the topic of Stratford-upon-Avon: with more than a healthy dose of trepidation. How could we do service to such an important —and popular—destination, without running the risk of falling into overly effusive "Bardolotry"? At last, we resolved to push aside our preconceived notions, dive in and take as objective a look as possible at one of England's best-known and most frequently visited attractions. After all, where there's a Will . . .

Turns out, our fears were unfounded. In many ways, Stratford-upon-Avon is both as humble and as enigmatic as its premier citizen. Yes, there is a sprinkling of ancient buildings—some of which are actually linked to Shakespeare. And yes, there is fabulous, compelling drama—

Did you know?

Although we associate Stratford-upon-Avon with the Elizabethan era, the town itself is quite old. Its name, "street-ford," implies that as early as Roman times, it was a key point for crossing the River Avon. There was a Saxon monastery on the site of the present parish church, and by the end of the 12th century, both population and prosperity had increased enough to justify a major "urban renewal" program. The "new town" of Stratford-upon-Avon was granted its official charter by Richard the Lionheart in 1196.

although during our last visit, more of it was acted out in the controversy surrounding the Royal Shakespeare Company than on the boards of the Royal Shakespeare Theatre (RST). We never encountered the throngs of visitors nor the plethora of Shakespeare *tchochkes* spilling forth from innumerable souvenir stalls that we had imagined . . . then, again, we didn't visit at the height of tourist season. If you go for the theater experience, the town offers pleasant diversions between performances. Otherwise, we found Stratford to be a bit underwhelming. Not *quite* "much ado about nothing." But close.

TIP!

We've been asked, "Can you catch an evening performance at Stratford and return to London that same evening?" The answer is, "Er, yessss . . . if you MUST." To our way of thinking, this would be exceedingly taxing. Evening performances of Shakespeare's works can end as late as 11:00 p.m., leaving you to face a two-hour trip back to the city. However, if you are bound and determined to do this, the Shakespeare Connection bus/ train combination may be your best bet. This service is offered only on performance days and is available only by advance reservation; call 01789-294466 for details.

✝ Stratford-upon-Avon Walking Tour

LOCATED

Take the M40, junction 15, to the A46. Stratford is about 96 miles from London.

TRAVEL

Trains depart Paddington Station for Stratford-upon-Avon (via Warwick) every 2 hours. Travel time is approximately 2 hours.

WEBSITE

There are dozens of websites and pertinent links that can help you plan your trip to Stratford. One we particularly like is *www.shakespeare.uk.org*. It's informative, easy to navigate and updated frequently. Highly recommended!

TIP!

Just north of Clopton Bridge, you'll find ample public parking—use it if you travel by car, for there is virtually no street parking in Stratford. Do not, however, mistake the large "Visitors Centre" on your left as you come into town for a tourist information facility. This is, in fact, a sports complex, as we discovered the hard way. Also, take note of the blue footprints that lead from all the major parking areas—but don't rely upon them. Although these will take you in the right direction for several blocks, they suddenly disappear! Luckily, the phantom footprints fade away in the general vicinity of the "real" Tourist Information Centre, where you'll find numerous maps to help orient you. After that, it's pretty smooth sailing through Stratford.

>>

Despite a somewhat confusing start, we found Stratford very pedestrian-friendly; the streets are well marked and the ancient attractions are very easy to find. We're going to give you a brisk stroll about town as an overview . . . then return for a more in-depth look at the history and present-day appeal of each site.

A convenient starting point is **Bancroft Gardens**, just beyond the two arched bridges that cross the Stratford Canal. The nine-arched bridge, the newer of the two (c. 1823), is limited to pedestrian traffic. **Clopton Bridge**, with its 14 graceful arches, is much older. It was constructed in the 15th century at the behest of Stratford citizen and Lord Mayor of London Sir Hugh Clopton.

After the requisite stop at the **Tourist Information Centre** on Bridgefoot, cross the street to Bancroft Garden's **Gower Memorial**; it's located on the grassy triangle just beyond Clopton Bridge, where Bridgefoot and Bridgeway converge. This is the first of several homages to Shakespeare you'll encounter on your visit. Built in 1888, the memorial features a looming statue of the Bard, surrounded by smaller statues of the Scottish Queen, Falstaff, Prince Hal and Hamlet (representing Tragedy, Comedy, History and Philosophy). If your approach to Stratford is less than academic and your schedule permits some frippery, check out the **Cox's Yard Stratford Tales** exhibit on Bridgefoot at the edge of Bancroft Gardens.

Meander over the footbridge and head—as everyone else does—to Stratford's Number One Shrine: **Shakespeare's Birthplace**. It's readily visible on the east side of Henley Street. The property is entered via the **Shakespeare Centre** on Henley Street; the Centre also features an extensive archive, with a library and study center for those who want a more in-depth examination of Shakespeare and his work.

From the Birthplace, mosey up Meer Street to Rother Street and look for the 15th-century **White Swan Hotel**. With its signature half-timbering and beautiful 16th-century wall paintings, this might be a grand place to spend a night out of London—if you've made your plans *well* in advance. You'll find a smattering of 16th-century buildings in this part of town, but we recommend you proceed along Wood Street and turn right on High Street. At the first intersection, you'll find the lovely **Harvard House**, built in 1594 for Thomas and Alice Rogers, grandparents of the founder of Harvard University. Also keep an eye out for the cluster of three-story Tudor buildings nestled on High Street—these are the finest ancient residences in Stratford today. Contiguous to Harvard House is the **Garrick Inn**, named for famous Shakespearian actor David Garrick. Although the building itself dates from 1595, don't be fooled by its ornate timbering; that's the result of a 20th-century restoration. If you are accompanied by restless teens, you might want to take a moment and veer off onto Sheep Street. Here you'll find the weird and wacky **Falstaff Experience**—definitely a change of pace on your tour of historic houses and churches!

High Street now becomes Chapel Street, where you'll come

◆ ◆

☞ Did you know?

Theater folk are notoriously superstitious about Shakespeare's *Macbeth*, believing the play to be jinxed—and they may be right! Innumerable dire misfortunes have befallen the cast, crew and, in some cases, the *audience* of this dark drama throughout its stage history. To avoid tempting fate, many actors and directors refuse to utter the play's proper name, referring obliquely to "The Scottish Play" or (more irreverently) to "Mackers." (*Lends a whole new meaning to "break a leg," doesn't it?*)

◆ ◆

across the **Town Hall**. Although it postdates our era, its ornamental niche holds a handsome statue of the Bard, presented
to the city by Garrick himself. Opposite Town Hall is the **Old
Bank**. Not to be outdone in its homage to Stratford's premier
homeboy, this Victorian edifice boasts a colorful mosaic portrait of Shakespeare—and some interesting terra cotta panels
depicting scenes from his plays.

If you're looking to spend the night in Stratford, Chapel
Street offers two ancient inns and eateries of note (*remember to
call ahead **well** in advance for room reservations; contact in-
formation follows at the end of this chapter*). The very narrow
Shakespeare Hotel is accented with multiple bay windows and
gables. At the corner of Chapel Street and Scholar's Lane is the
Falcon Hotel (c. 1500). Across the street from the Falcon is
Nash's House and the site of **New Place**, both owned by the
Shakespeare Birthplace Trust. Nash's House was the home of
Shakespeare's granddaughter Elizabeth Hall. Of even greater
interest, its gardens mark the original site of New Place, the
home where Will spent his golden years.

Opposite New Place is another of Clopton's numerous contributions to Stratford, the **Guild Chapel**; it's worth looking
into. Farther along Church Street is the ancient **Almshouse**,
largely unaltered and still serving Stratford's less fortunate citizens; it is closed to the public. At the end of Church Street is the
boundary marker that distinguishes the Saxon village of Strat-
forde and the 12th-century "new town" that was chartered by
Richard I.

Bear left now onto Old Town Street. Here you'll come to
Hall's Croft, where Shakespeare's daughter Susanna and her
husband, Dr. John Hall, made their home before moving to
New Place upon Papa Will's death. Continue at a leisurely
pace—the next site is a bit of a hike—down Old Town Street to
the bottom of Trinity Street, where **Shakespeare's grave** awaits
you. The Bard was buried in the nave of **Holy Trinity Church**,
one of the grandest medieval churches in the Heart of England
and well worth a contemplative visit in its own right.

Return to Old Town Street and watch for the reasonably well-marked pathway that leads to the Avon riverside. If you're looking to take a load off your feet for a moment or two, you can pop into the **Brass Rubbing Centre** for a make-your-own-souvenir respite or hop a ferry to the other side of the river, just for fun. Of course, the main riverside attraction is the massive **Royal Shakespeare Theatre** (*you don't need our directions to find this site . . . you can't miss it*). We hope you heeded our advice in the opening chapter of this book and purchased your theater tickets months in advance. If not, try your luck at the box office to see if any seats have been turned back at the last minute. Even if a play is not in your plans, the RSC's one-time home base offers other diversions, including displayed props, costumes and scripts ("The RSC Collection") and twice-daily backstage tours (hours vary, based on curtain times). The bookstore focuses, as one would expect, on books of theatrical interest.

This concludes your walking tour of downtown Stratford-upon-Avon . . . although no visit is really complete without a visit to **Anne Hathaway's Cottage**. The Bride-of-Bard's homestead *can* be reached by foot (*presumably that's how her famous suitor arrived upon her stoop*), but the journey is about a mile. Since passion isn't propelling you onward (*at least not "that" kind of passion*), you'll probably prefer to hop on one of the open-top shuttle buses that leave from the city center.

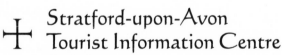

✝ Stratford-upon-Avon Tourist Information Centre
Bridgefoot

>>

PHONE

01789-293127

OPEN

Regular business hours

>>

As you might well suspect, there is seemingly no end to the number of Bard-related pastimes that take place in and around Stratford. This is the place to pick up the latest schedule of "what's on" as well as the requisite walking maps and literature.

~~

✝ The Stratford Tales at Cox's Yard

Bridgefoot

>>

PHONE

01789-404600

OPEN

10:00 a.m.–5:00 p.m. daily, year-round

ADMISSION

£3.95 Adults

£2.50 Children

TIP!

If the idea of walking around Stratford seems daunting to you—or if the weather is simply not cooperating—you can tour Stratford by bus, hopping on and off as the mood strikes. Many of the bus companies depart from in front of Cox's Yard, making it easy for you to do some comparison shopping before you board.

>>

This is the most unusual amalgam of merriment we've seen in a while—sort of an "all things to all people" entertainment complex. Here you'll find an animated time-travel journey through the history of Stratford, an exploration of the Stratford canal waterworks, interactive games, a microbrewery, a traditional English pub, several shops, a tearoom and a wine bar. Have we forgotten anything? Bring your sense of humor and check your Ph.D. at the door—there is nothing in the least "highbrow" about this attraction!

✝ The Shakespeare Centre
Henley Street

>>

PHONE
  01789-204016

E-MAIL
  info@shakespeare.org.uk

OPEN
  Visitors' Centre
    9:00 a.m.–5:00 p.m. Monday–Saturday, April–October
    9:30 a.m.–5:00 p.m. Sunday, April–October
    9:30 a.m.–4:00 p.m. Monday–Saturday, November–March
    10:00 a.m.–4:00 p.m. Sunday, November–March
  Library/Study Room
    10:00 a.m.–5:00 p.m. Monday–Friday, year-round
    9:30 a.m.–12:30 p.m. Saturday, year-round

TIP!
  If you're planning to see "everything" connected with Shakespeare
  during your visit to Stratford, you'll want to check out the "Shakespeare Heritage Trail" ticket, which gains you admission to all five
  of the residences operated by the Shakespeare Birthplace Trust. The
  combination ticket will save you nearly 50 percent over the price of
  individually purchased admissions and includes an insightful guide
  to the properties as well.

ADMISSION
  Shakespeare Heritage Trail Combination Ticket
    £12.00 Adults
    £ 6.00 Children
    £11.00 Seniors
    Family ticket available

>>

Owned and operated by the Shakespeare Birthplace Trust, the
Shakespeare Centre is a must-stop for anyone intent on getting
the absolute *most* from a visit to Stratford. Not only can you purchase a deeply discounted combination ticket to all of the properties owned by the Trust, but you'll also be able to browse
through the wealth of Shakespeare-related acquisitions. The
Trust's archives are extensive, and there is a library and study
room for those who want to dig deeper into Shakespeare's life

and work. On the off chance that none of this interests you in the least (*forsooth!*), you'll want to stop by the Centre anyway —it is, after all, the only way to gain access to Shakespeare's Birthplace.

Shakespeare's Birthplace
Henley Street

>>

PHONE
01789-204016

OPEN
9:00 a.m.–5:00 p.m. Monday–Saturday, March–October
9:30 a.m.–5:00 p.m. Sunday, March–October
9:00 a.m.–4:00 p.m. Monday–Saturday, November–February
10:00 a.m.–4:00 p.m. Sunday, November–February

ADMISSION
£6.50 Adults
£2.50 Children
£5.50 Seniors
Family ticket available

>>

The Shakespeare Birthplace Trust surmises that this is the "most frequently visited literary landmark in England"—and who are we to argue? Careful culling of Stratford's real estate and baptismal records has led scholars to assume this is the house where William Shakespeare was born on April 23, 1564. The family had, in fact, been tenants here for some 12 years before the future playwright's birth, although they didn't officially purchase the property until 1566.

> **Did you know?**
>
> The only surviving letter written to William Shakespeare was a request for a loan, penned by one Richard Quincy in 1598. It is on display in Shakespeare's Birthplace, as is an "almost" contemporary painting of the playwright, dating from 1660–1680, by the artist Gerard Soest.

As you look at the structure from Henley Street, it is apparent that you are looking at two once-separate buildings. The lower left-hand side of the structure and the upper stories of both buildings would have comprised the Shakespeare family's living quarters. To the right was the workshop of John "Father Of" Shakespeare. Upstairs is a small, windowed "birthing room," where Mary Shakespeare (née Arden) gave birth—not only to the Bard, but to his seven brothers and sisters as well! The home is furnished as it would have been during Will's early childhood.

Shakespeare's Birthplace remained in the Shakespeare family until the 19th century . . . although it has not always enjoyed the shrineworthy status it does today. Graffiti scratched into the birthing room windows shows a profound lack of respect—and gratuitous self-promotion—from people who should have "known better," such as Walter Scott, Henry Irving and Ellen Terry. (*Nanny would be appalled, we're certain.*) Indeed, it wasn't until the American entertainment mogul P. T. Barnum made moves to purchase the structure (and ship it across the Atlantic) that the citizens of Stratford, with support from the Crown, formed the Shakespeare Birthplace Trust.

The Trust purchased Shakespeare's Birthplace in 1847. Its subsequent restoration and preservation efforts—which in-

◆ ◆

Did you know?

While not exactly a "Renaissance man," John Shakespeare was, nonetheless, multifaceted. Although commonly referred to as a "tanner," the elder Shakespeare was more specifically a "glover," or maker of gloves. He was also a wool merchant, moneylender, real estate investor, beer-taster, lawmaker . . . and law breaker! John was not a Stratford native; he was born in nearby Snitterfield and moved to Stratford after marrying Mary Arden in 1552. His handwear handiwork provided him with the financial means to purchase investment properties throughout Stratford, send his sons to the local grammar school and earn the honor of serving as Town Bailiff—a job whose duties included the "tough-work-but-*somebody*-has-to-do-it" privilege of tasting and approving the quality of all the locally produced beer. Alas, the measurable rise in status did not translate into a rise in "class." Town records report that John Shakespeare allowed such a heinous muck heap to grow in front of his Henley Street house that he was fined 12 pence and ordered to remove the offensive waste posthaste.

◆ ◆

cluded tearing down adjacent buildings to reduce the threat of fire—were truly visionary for their time. Vast portions of the original construction have been maintained, and, over the years, the home has been carefully decorated with furniture representative of a middle-class Elizabethan household.

As you approach the residence from the Shakespeare Centre, you'll pass through a lovely garden, where many of the flowers, herbs and trees mentioned in Shakespeare's plays make for a particularly charming setting.

While you're in the area . . .

Don't miss **The Shakespeare Bookshop**, opposite the Shakespeare Centre at 39 Henley Street. What a treasure trove for anyone mad about theater! Scripts, critiques, photographs of your favorite actors, videos, CDs and an extensive Tudor history section are just some of the shop's pleasures. There's even a thoughtfully culled collection of children's books, any of which would make a great gift for a budding thespian. Phone: 01789-292176.

✝ Harvard House
High Street

≫≫

PHONE
   01789-204507

OPEN
   11:30 a.m.–4:30 p.m. Friday, Saturday and Sunday, May–July and
   September–October
   11:30 a.m.–4:30 p.m. Thursday–Monday, July and August
   Closed Tuesdays and Wednesdays, year-round
   Closed November–April

ADMISSION
   £1.50 Adults
   50p Children
   Free of charge with the Shakespeare Heritage Trail combination ticket
≫≫

One of the best-preserved Tudor houses in Stratford has nothing whatsoever to do with Shakespeare. Scholars may find themselves making this pilgrimage for a different reason: Harvard House was the birthplace of Katherine Rogers, whose son John Harvard (1607–1638) founded—or at least funded—America's best known and highly esteemed college of the same name.

On September 22, 1594, a devastating fire swept through Stratford, destroying many of the timber-framed houses on High, Chapel and Henley streets. Thomas Rogers—who had made his fortune as the town's leading butcher, maltster and grazier—set about rebuilding his residence in a style that reflected his fine taste and net worth. It was completed in 1596. Rogers managed to preserve the beautiful 14th-century stained glass windows, which are handsomely offset by intricate 16th-century carved timbers.

◆ ◆

☞ Did you know?

Yes, the dates we quote for the life of John Harvard are correct! Harvard emigrated to the New World in the summer of 1637, with the intent of working on a body of law for the colony of Massachusetts. By September 1638, he was dead. A mere 31 years old, young John clearly had no premonition that his life would be cut short—he left no legal will. However, on his deathbed, he verbally expressed his desire to leave his extensive library and half his estate for the establishment of a "new college" in the aptly named village of Cambridge, Massachusetts.

◆ ◆

Now owned by Harvard University, Harvard House displays a fine collection of period furnishings and is home to a renowned collection of pewter. (*For those of you who wave the Crimson and Gold pennant, there is also an interesting exhibit on the life of John Harvard.*)

While you're in the vicinity . . .

✝ The Falstaff Experience

Shrieves House Barn, Sheep Street

>>>

PHONE

01789-298070

WEBSITE

www.falstaffexperience.co.uk

OPEN

10:30 a.m.–5:30 p.m. Monday–Saturday, year-round
11:00 a.m.– 5:00 p.m. Sunday, year-round

ADMISSION

£3.50 Adults
£1.50 Children

TIP!

Some of the displays in the Falstaff Experience may be too intense
for young children. We rate this attraction PG.

>>>

No doubt about it—the Falstaff Experience is definitely an acquired taste. The name is somewhat misleading; the Disneyesque displays in this, er, "museum" have little to do with
Shakespeare's jolly "Fat Jack." What you'll get is a peek at the pe-
culiarities of history, starting in 1196, with an eye toward the
spooky and strange. Adolescents (*or those with an adolescent
sense of humor*) will love this. Everyone else: you're on your
own!

✝ New Place Ruins and Nash's House
Chapel Street

>>

PHONE

01789-204016

OPEN

9:30 a.m.–5:00 p.m. Monday–Saturday, March–October
10:00 a.m.–5:00 p.m. Sunday, March–October
10:00 a.m.–4:00 p.m. Monday–Saturday, November–February
10:30 a.m.–4:00 p.m. Sunday, November–February

ADMISSION

£3.00 Adults
£1.50 Children

>>

Some of us dream of retiring to someplace warm and exotic. Others agree with Dorothy Gale: "There's no place like home." Clearly, Shakespeare was of the latter sentiment. After a long and exciting career in *le beau monde* London, the Bard headed back to his hometown of Stratford, where he spent his final six years . . . well, we're not exactly sure *how* he spent them. Reading penny dreadfuls? Raising a pint or two at the local boozer? Catching the occasional football match, perchance?

What we *do* know is that Shakespeare must have been planning ahead for his golden years. He purchased New Place for £60 in 1597, 13 years before he finally left London. New Place had been built by the magnanimous Sir Hugh Clopton and, typical of Clopton, the house was (by Stratford standards, at least) grand. It was the second-largest home in town and the only one made of brick. With its beautifully landscaped courtyard, gracious gardens, fruit or-

- -

👉 Did you know?

So much of the lore and legend surrounding Shakespeare is just that: so much lore and legend. One of our favorite stories, however, assures us that Will spent his final hours entertaining Ben Johnson and Michael Drayton. Whether it was bad food or a bad heart that killed the Bard on his 52nd birthday in 1616, no one knows for certain. (*Frankly, we'd like to think he died laughing!*)

- -

chard and stables, New Place was hardly the "starving artist's garret" typically associated with actors and artists of the time. Certainly no dramatist before the Bard (*and relatively few since*) ever enjoyed such high style!

Shakespeare left New Place to his daughter Susanna Hall. (*Susanna fared* considerably *better than Anne Hathaway; the Bride of the Bard merely inherited her husband's "second-best" bed . . . theirs was not a particularly cozy marriage.*) Susanna and her husband, noted physician John Hall, spent the rest of their lives at New Place. John's infirmary—where he treated such notable patients as poet Michael Drayton and the Bishop of Worcester—can still be seen at New Place today.

Susanna and John Hall had but one daughter, Elizabeth. The proverbial "girl next door," Elizabeth married her New Place neighbor, John Nash, who eventually inherited his father-in-law's lucrative medical practice. Upon Elizabeth's death, New Place returned, once again, to the Clopton family. Sir John Clopton made extensive renovations to New Place and was the first owner to open the home for public viewing.

● ●

🖙 Did you know?

John Clopton may have been sympathetic to the interests of the touring public, but the next New Place owner was not so congenial. In fact, the Reverend Francis Gastrell was decidedly eccentric and downright antisocial. Annoyed to the point of distraction by the number of tourists who passed through his yard, Gastrell whipped out his axe and felled a massive mulberry tree said to have been planted by Shakespeare himself. This reduced the locals to hooliganism; they retaliated by smashing all of the New Place windows. But wait . . . there's more! In one of the most extreme cases of tax evasion we've *ever* heard of, Gastrell sought to avoid an increase in his real estate assessment by razing New Place to the ground. Stratford citizens literally ran Gastrell out of town (*we're amazed he wasn't hanged, drawn and quartered . . . or at least tarred and feathered*). From that day forth, anyone with the surname of Gastrell was forbidden to live in Stratford.

● ●

Today, a painstakingly accurate Elizabethan knot garden covers the foundation of New Place. The garden is accessed through Nash's House, where John and Elizabeth once lived. Although the half-timbered facade is a replica, the interior re-

▪ ▪

☞ Did you know?

A series of colossal garden statues, each evoking the spirit of one of Shakespeare's plays, is being erected in the Shakespeare Memorial Garden. Upon our last visit, three of the great sculptures were in place. Plans are to add one per year.

▪ ▪

veals much of its 16th- and 17th-century past. There is a very nice collection of Shakespeare-era furniture, as well as a local history museum that traces Stratford's growth from Roman river ford to a thriving theater town. A second garden (in addition to the New Place knot garden) can be entered via Chapel Lane. This is the Shakespeare Memorial Garden, maintained by the Birthplace Trust. Note the massive mulberry tree smack in the center of the yard—legend has it that it was grown from a cutting rescued from Gaskell's midnight ravages.

∿

✝ Guild Chapel and King Edward VI School
Chapel Lane at Church Street

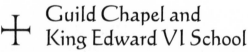

PHONE
None

OPEN
King Edward still functions as a private school and is not open for touring when school is in session. Limited public viewing hours are scheduled on Saturday and Sunday afternoons in July and August. Please check with the Tourist Information Centre as close as possible to your intended visit for specific times and entry fees.
The Guild Chapel is open at random hours daily, year-round.

With the exception of Holy Trinity Church and the Almshouse, these are the only true medieval buildings in Stratford. With any luck, you'll be able to schedule your visit during one of the few days when both King Edward School and the Guild Chapel (a.k.a. Gild Chapel) are open. Although very different in nature, both buildings offer rare-for-Stratford insights into the town's pre-Shakespeare days.

The school and the chapel both trace their beginnings to Stratford's medieval guildhall. The Guild of the Holy Cross was founded in 1269 by Robert de Stratford. Unlike the trade guilds, which focused primarily on the procedures and practices of money-making enterprises, Stratford's guild was a spiritual fraternity, concerned with the souls and the social well-being of the townsfolk and offering succor for the poor priests of the diocese. As part of their mission of service, the Guild of the Holy Cross ran a hospital and almshouse; the latter still serves the needs of the town's less fortunate citizens. In addition, the guild provided Stratford with its first structured education programs, employing a schoolmaster in 1295 to teach Latin to its members and their sons.

By the early 1400s, the Guild of the Holy Cross had outgrown its ancient buildings and a major expansion program was begun. A grand feast hall (ideal for staging spectacular Holy Day festivals) was constructed in 1416—that building serves as the primary building for King Edward School. The town's first formal schoolroom, now known as the Pedagogue's House (*would we lie?*) was added in 1427; it is the oldest half-timbered school room in England, but unfortunately, it's closed to the public. Stratford's guild-run school was further elevated in 1482 when one of its successful—and grateful—alums, Thomas Jolyffe, gave a sizeable endowment, enabling the school to hire a full-time master suited to teach grammar to all interested local students (*by which we mean "boys"; we all know what a medieval girl's chances of receiving in-school education were*). Among the illustrious masters secured under this endowment were Richard Fox, chief minister for Henry VII (and Bishop of Winchester, to boot), and William Smyth, founder of Brasenose College, Oxford. About this time, the munificent Sir Hugh Clopton funded construction of the Guild Chapel, an edifice so impressive that to this day it is mistaken for the primary church of Stratford (that honor belongs to Holy Trinity Church). Clearly, the Guild of the Holy Cross was on the ascent!

Unfortunately, the glories of that ascent would be relatively short-lived. With its financial security and impressive real estate portfolio, the Guild of the Holy Trinity was a natural target for Henry VIII during his dissolution of religious institutions. The Guild was suppressed in 1547 and its assets seized. The school was allowed to continue as an independent entity and was re-endowed in 1553 by King Edward VI as the Stratford Grammar Free School. This is the school young William Shakespeare would have attended. Judging from the breadth and depth of his vocabulary (estimated at 21,000 words; the King James Bible, by comparison, uses a mere 17,000 different words) and his vast understanding of geography, history and philosophy, the quality of education in 16th-century Stratford wasn't half bad!

The school Shakespeare "probably" attended is still attended by Stratford's aspiring young scholars. That means that it is exceedingly hard for visitors to get a glimpse inside King Edward School. If your visit brings you to Stratford on a summer weekend afternoon, call and see if there is a guided tour available; you might get lucky.

◆◆

WAS SHAKESPEARE "SHAKESPEARE"?

Mark Twain. Sigmund Freud. Charlie Chaplin. What did these gentlemen all have in common? Each was a devout "anti-Stratfordian." Translated, that means these otherwise rational fellows allowed themselves to get caught up in what is known in Shakespeare circles as the "authorship question."

Never before in the history of literature and letters has the identity of an author created such a furor (*after all, did anyone really care who the "Anonymous" author behind* Primary Colors *was?*). Do educated adults spend time and money trying to determine if the chap who penned the *Odyssey* was really Homer or Homer's next-door neighbor? Of course not. Yet, for reasons that escape us, passions roil and tempers flare over the authorship of the 154 sonnets and 38 (or more) plays credited to William Shakespeare of Stratford-upon-Avon. The idea that a man of common birth and ordinary education could compose the greatest canon of work in the English language tests the credulity of many to the absolute breaking point.

Well, *somebody* wrote this stuff! If not Shakespeare, who? Through the ages, any number of contenders have been put forth by their various erudite advocates. To date, the most convincing case has been made by proponents of Edward de Vere, Earl of Oxford (*to learn more about the compelling Oxfordian argument, visit* www.shakespeare-oxford.com). Other names bandied about include Francis Bacon, Christopher Marlowe (*who would have required a miraculous level of posthumous prolificacy*) and the teamwork theory, also known as "Shakespeare-by-Committee."

We find this debate to be tedious in the extreme. We *know* that if Shakespeare had a ghost writer, it was most certainly Elizabeth I. No doubt about it! Plays, poems, politics—all in a day's work for the brilliant, witty and imaginative Glorianna. Perhaps in the next world, Bess and the Bard continue to collaborate . . . heaven only knows.

❖❖

Most days, Clopton's handsome Gild Chapel is open at random during daylight hours. The most significant features of the church are the medieval wall paintings of the Last Judgment and the Dance of Death, and the murder of St. Thomas à Becket. (*Led by our Internet surfing to believe that these paintings were "spectacular," we were rather disappointed. We found many churches in the Heart of England with better-preserved and more vividly rendered wall paintings.*) As you stroll around, admire the stained glass windows. They pay tribute to the individuals most closely associated with the Guild of the Holy Cross and its buildings: Robert de Stratford, Thomas Jolyffe, Hugh Clopton, King Edward VI and John Shakespeare.

❖❖

SIR HUGH CLOPTON,
THE BENEVOLENT BACHELOR (D. 1496)

Although he was born at Clopton House in the Warwickshire countryside, Hugh Clopton always considered himself to be a Stratford native—lucky for Stratford he did! Even after establishing himself as a successful London mercer, Clopton kept a home in Stratford-upon-Avon and became one of the town's most important benefactors. Sir Hugh's most visible contribution is the impressive 14-arch bridge (c. 1490) that has borne the bulk of Stratford's traffic . . . as well as Clopton's name . . . for over 500 years. Clopton was also a generous patron of the Guild of the Holy Cross; his munificence enabled the Guild to erect its handsome Gild Chapel in 1495. Clopton's generosity also funded the building and maintenance of many of Stratford's roads and a late 15th-century expansion of Holy Trinity Church. As the town archives explain, "having never wife nor children [Clopton] convertid a great peace of his substance in good works in Stratford."

For his own pleasure, Clopton built the gracious estate of New Place; at the time, it was the town's second-largest residence and the first Stratford home to be built of brick. New Place eventually would become Shakespeare's "retirement home." Yet, despite Clopton's devotion to Stratford and his generosity to Holy Trinity Church, Sir Hugh was not buried in the town. He was laid to rest in London, where he served as Lord Mayor in 1491–1492. His nieces, nephews and other family members are buried in Clopton Chapel at Holy Trinity, just a few yards away from Shakespeare's grave.

◇ ◇

While you're in the vicinity . . .

Stroll over to Rother Street and admire **Mason's Court**. This rare 15th-century Wealdon house was built by John Hodgkins on land owned by the Guild of the Holy Cross. The recessed center portion of the home was the original Great Hall; the side wings are from a later expansion.

⌁

✝ Hall's Croft
Old Town Street

≫≫

PHONE

01789-204016

OPEN

9:30 a.m.– 5:00 p.m. Monday–Saturday, April–October
10:00 a.m.–5:00 p.m. Sunday, April–October
10:00 a.m.–4:00 p.m. Monday–Saturday, November–March
10:30 a.m.–4:00 p.m. Sunday, November–March

ADMISSION
  £3.00 Adults
  £1.50 Children
CONVENIENCES
  Tearoom
>>

The last of the "Shakespeare Houses" on your tour of down-town Stratford, Hall's Croft was built in the 16th century as one of a bevy of small Tudor buildings in the area now known as "Old Town." The structure was purchased in the early 1600s by Dr. John Hall, who set about expanding and remodeling the property to serve as both residence and medical facility. In 1607, Dr. Hall married Susanna Shakespeare, the playwright's daughter. The couple lived at Hall's Croft until moving into the more gracious accommodations at New Place in 1616.

Hall's Croft is furnished as one might imagine it would have been when Dr. and Mrs. Hall were in residence. Those with an abiding interest in medicine will appreciate the exhibition on Jacobean medical practices, some of which are nothing short of hair-raising. There is also an in-depth exploration of the life of Dr. Hall, one of the best-regarded physicians of his time. Outside, the lush walled garden focuses on plants with medicinal properties, most of which would have been well known to Dr. Hall and his colleagues.

Holy Trinity Church
Trinity Street

>>
PHONE
  01789-266316

OPEN
  8:30 a.m.–6:00 p.m. Monday–Saturday, April–October
  9:00 a.m.–4:00 p.m. Monday–Saturday, November–March
  12:30–5:00 p.m. Sunday, year-round

Note: There is no touring during Sunday worship, and touring during weekday worship is limited. There is also no touring at times when the church is closed for official functions. Please call ahead on the day of your visit for any last-minute closings.

WORSHIP

Sunday: 8:00 a.m. Holy Communion
    10:30 a.m. Parish Communion (sung)
    6:00 p.m. Evensong
Weekday Holy Communion: 10:00 a.m. Tuesday

ADMISSION

Church: Donation suggested
Shakespeare's grave: £1.00 Adults
    50p Children

>>

Looking at your walking map of Stratford, you may have been wondering why the parish church is removed from the center of town—and why we insisted you get there "on foot." Once you approach Holy Trinity, however, any reservations you have had will almost certainly be cast aside. With its postcard-perfect riverside ambience, this is one of the prettiest settings for an in-town church we've seen—spiritually removed from the commercial hustle and bustle of Stratford, ideal for a contemplative moment in a busy day of touring. Sure, chattering tourists are paying homage at Shakespeare's grave. That's to be expected. Just step outside and enjoy the serenity . . . it makes your pilgrimage to Stratford easier to manage.

There has been a church on this site since 845 when Beorhtwulf (Bertulf), King of Mercia, authorized construction of a small wooden chapel. It is believed that this Saxon church was replaced by a Norman stone church, but no trace of either remains. However, the present limestone structure is no "newcomer." The oldest parts of the cruciform building date from 1210.

By comparison, the front entrance to Holy Trinity is relatively new—it was built in 1500. The heavy wooden main door is accented by a massive metal knocker. This is a "sanctuary knocker"—fugitives who were lucky enough to grab the knocker's ring before the authorities reached them could claim a safe haven from the long arm of justice for 37 days before being handed over for trial.

The oldest portion of the church is where the nave's main aisles intersect. The four massive pillars that soar skyward support the tower and ringing chamber, home to Holy Trinity's signature chimes. Holy Trinity Church was greatly expanded in 1280 and again in 1330, through endowments made by the town's Guild of the Holy Cross. The Guild's munificence paid for the graceful tower and enabled the original nave to be re-built to accommodate the wide side aisles you see today. As you admire the space, take extra note of the ancient corbels and carved misericords—they're some of the best you'll come across.

Before you hustle off to pay your respects to Shakespeare, be certain to admire the Clopton Chapel. Although the benevolent Sir Hugh Clopton is buried in London, the chapel is an enduring tribute to this most

• •

🐾 Did you know?

Holy Trinity Church is approached via an avenue of 24 fragrant lime trees. The trees represent the 12 Apostles and the 12 Tribes of Israel.

• •

generous of Stratford citizens. Originally Holy Trinity's Lady Chapel (dedicated to the Blessed Virgin Mary), this is but a small portion of the improvements Clopton funded in this parish church. Sir Hugh was a childless bachelor; the Cloptons you see here are descended from his nieces and nephews.

Ghost Alert!

One of the creepiest stories we've encountered in our travels centers around the Clopton Chapel. Years ago (just how many years ago, no one could verify for us), a deadly sweating illness swept through Warwickshire. The Cloptons of Clopton Hall were not spared. Among the first of the family members to suffer from the attack was the adolescent Charlotte. After hours of agonizing pain, young Charlotte fell into a coma, was shriven, pronounced dead and buried in the family vault at Holy Trinity Church. Within days, her kin gathered to mourn yet another family member and, upon entering Clopton Chapel, were met with the most gruesome of sights. Propped against the wall was the shroud-clad body of Mistress Charlotte. She was quite dead ... but apparently she had NOT been "quite" dead when she was buried! Reviving from her coma, the girl had managed to pry her way out of her sarcophagus. Whether she died from the complications of her illness, starvation or the sheer horror of her plight, no one knows for certain.

There have been no further posthumous sightings of Charlotte Clopton—and that doesn't surprise us in the least. After that ordeal, why would she *want* to come back?

~~

Now the moment you've been waiting for: Shakespeare's final resting place. (*Just how much "rest" poor Will gets with so many people milling about is open to debate.*) As a share-owner since 1605 in the church's tithe privileges, William Shakespeare earned the right to be buried in Holy Trinity's sanctuary. His gravestone is quite simple—none of the elaborate frills and carvings so popular in his time. It's the epitaph that makes the marker remarkable—was it penned by the Bard himself, or by a loved one attempting to mimic the poet's inimitable style?

> *Good frend for Jesus sake forbeare*
> *To digg the dust encloased heare;*
> *Bleste be ye man y spares thes stones,*
> *And curst be he yt moves my bones.*

Close by the grave of Shakespeare are several of his family members, including his wife Anne Hathaway, his daughter Susanna and her husband, Dr. John Hall, and their son-in-law John Nash.

✝ Brass Rubbing Centre
The Royal Shakespeare Theatre Summer House
Avon Banks Gardens

>>

PHONE

01789-297671

OPEN

10:00 a.m.–6:00 p.m. daily, April–October

11:00 a.m.–4:00 p.m. Saturday and Sunday, November–March

ADMISSION

Free of charge

The cost per rubbing ranges from 95p to £15, depending on the size
of your selected brass.

>>

If the children on your tour have had their fill of old homes and
gravestones, this stop is certain to appease them. The center
offers a great variety of ancient (and ancient-style) memorial
brasses—including the requisite Shakespeare-related selections, which can be used to create your own take-home souvenir. It takes about 45 minutes to complete a rubbing—more if you're a perfectionist or if you've chosen one of the biggest brasses.

• •

☞ Did you know?

One hundred years after the death of Shakespeare, his plays continued to provide popular entertainment for English audiences. His hometown of Stratford, however, all but ignored the playwright. It took the renowned actor—and keen entrepreneur—David Garrick to remedy the situation. On tour in Stratford in 1717, Garrick expected superlative publicity for playing Shakespeare in Shakespeare's territory. Dismayed at the lack of hoopla paid to the poetic homeboy, Garrick set about raising funds for the first-ever Shakespeare festival, to be held on the banks of the River Avon. It took him a while, but Garrick's vision of turning Stratford into a Shakespeare Mecca was finally realized with a grand jubilee in 1769. Since then, Stratford-upon-Avon has been one of the world's most popular cultural destinations, and the rich experience of enjoying multiple works of Shakespeare in a festival atmosphere has been successfully imitated internationally.

• •

✝ Royal Shakespeare Theatre
Waterside

>>

PHONE

01789-296655 (general information)

01789-403403 (box office)

WEBSITE

www.rsc.org.uk

OPEN

Theatre Complex

10:00 a.m. daily, year-round

Closing and tour times vary, depending on curtain times; call for details on the day of your visit.

Box Office

9:00 a.m.–8:00 p.m. Monday–Saturday, year-round

Box office closes at 6:00 p.m. on non-performance days

Note: As we went to press, the Royal Shakespeare Company (RSC) was embroiled in a controversial dispute regarding its mission and its future. Certain powers within the organization were championing disbanding the resident acting company in favor of an international touring company that would focus on "big name" stars. The ultimate outcome of this debate will affect the number of plays presented on the Stratford stage as well as the nature of the plays and the length of the season. Such controversy makes great theater gossip — unfortunately, it also challenges our ability to give you specific advice if a "night at the theater" is high on your list of priorities!

ADMISSION

Theatre Tour

£4.00 Adults

£3.00 Seniors

Family ticket available

CONVENIENCES

Two restaurants and the be-all-and-end-all Shakespeare gift shop/ bookstore

>>

Home to the Royal Shakespeare Company, this complex is worth a drop-by, even if you're not going to take our advice (*gasp!*) and center your visit to Stratford around attending the

theater. Three separate stages highlight the plays of Shakespeare and his contemporaries as well as works by other classical
playwrights and modern dramatists influenced by the Bard.
The fascinating behind-the-scenes tours of the theater complex
surpassed even our jaded "been-there-done-that" expectations.
The gift shop is the ultimate in Bardolotry—you can spend
hours browsing through the books and marveling at the endless
ways marketers can spin Shakespeare.

 # Anne Hathaway's Cottage
Cottage Lane
Shottery

>>>

PHONE
   01789-212800

LOCATED
   Anne Hathaway's Cottage is about 1 mile from downtown Stratford-
   upon-Avon.

TRAVEL
   A very pretty and well-marked footpath (perhaps the very path the
   amorous Will Shakespeare traversed) will take you from Evesham
   Place in Stratford, or you can hop the shuttle bus from Bridge Street.

OPEN
   9:00 a.m.–5:00 p.m. Monday–Saturday, April–October
   9:30 a.m.–5:00 p.m. Sunday, April–October
   9:30 a.m.–4:00 p.m. Monday–Saturday, November–March
   10:00 a.m.–4:00 p.m. Sunday, November–March

ADMISSION
   £3.50 Adults
   £1.50 Children
   Family ticket available
>>>

Of the five residences operated by the Shakespeare Birthplace
Trust, this is by far the most charming. The childhood home of
Shakespeare's wife, Anne Hathaway, it is the quintessential En-

glish country domicile, from its thatched roof, to its wattle-and-daub walls, to the profusion of wildflowers that blanket the picturesque yard.

As we soon recognized, the term "cottage" is a bit of false modesty. Anne's father was a yeoman (or gentleman) farmer and his was a sizeable Elizabethan* farmhouse, generously proportioned with 12 comfortable rooms and over 90 acres of land. The Trust does a convincing job of portraying the lifestyle a prosperous squire and his family would have enjoyed in the late 16th century. Their task is made all the easier by the many original furnishings that remained in the Hathaway home through the centuries — even some of the original kitchen utensils are on display.

◆ ◆

☞ Did you know?

The amorous William Shakespeare was 18 years old when he found himself obliged to marry his lady love, Anne Hathaway. The Bride of the Bard was eight years older. She was also more than a "little bit pregnant." So hasty were their nuptials that Anne's father had to pay a staggering £40 fee for the rush job on the marriage license. Further penalties were charged to waive the traditional announcing of the banns of matrimony. The fact that the playwright left Stratford for London relatively early in his marriage, visiting his wife and three children only infrequently, has led to speculation that young Will may have been unwillingly nudged to the altar . . . if not with the muzzle of a shotgun per se, then with an equally inarguable threat. (*On the other hand, we find his behavior a mere foreshadowing of today's typical Hollywood marriage!*)

◆ ◆

---

*The core construction of the house dates from the 15th century; some portions are believed to be even older.

✝ Mary Arden's House and The Shakespeare Countryside Museum

Wilmcote

>>

PHONE
01789-293455

LOCATED
3½ miles from Stratford-upon-Avon on the A34

OPEN
9:00 a.m.–5:00 p.m. Monday–Saturday, April–October
9:30 a.m.–5:00 p.m. Sunday, April–October
9:30 a.m.–4:00 p.m. Monday–Saturday, November–March
10:00 a.m.–4:00 p.m. Sunday, November–March

ADMISSION
£4.00 Adult
£2.00 Children
Family ticket available

>>

It wasn't until the late 18th century that Shakespearean scholars identified this lovely thatched-roof farmhouse as the childhood home of Shakespeare's mother, Mary Arden. Even then, the remarkable Tudor timbering you see today remained hidden beneath a thick layer of stucco until the home was purchased by the Birthplace Trust in the 20th century. The heavy cladding served as a sealant, making Mary Arden's House one of the best-preserved Tudor residences in the Heart of England . . . even though the furnishings are largely Edwardian.

👉 **Did you know?**

When the aspiring glover John Shakespeare married Mary Arden, he elevated his social status considerably. Mary was the youngest of eight daughters born to Robert Arden, a well-established—and well-heeled—Warwickshire gentleman farmer, who traced his lineage to Saxon nobility. The Forest of Arden, with its fairy-tale beauty, bears the family name and inspired the settings for many of William Shakespeare's plays. Indeed, Mary's genteel upbringing and ancestral pride may well have contributed to the playwright's uncommon insight into matters and mannerisms typically alien to a merchant's son.

With its thatched roof, irregular walls, primitive handmade tiles and miniature dormer windows, this is a most whimsical home, surrounded by acres of rich green pasture. A working farm since its inception, the property features a multitude of Tudor-era (and later) outbuildings, which serve as a hands-on museum of English rural life. In addition to rare farm tools, some of which date from the 15th century, amateur historians might be lucky enough to catch a falconry exhibition (there's an extensive bird-of-prey aviary) or a gypsy caravan re-enactment.

St. Peter's Wootton Wawen
Wootton Wawen

>>

PHONE
01564-792659

LOCATED
Take the M40, junction 15, to the A46 south. At the second round-about, pick up the A3400 toward Henley-in-Arden and proceed 4 miles to the church on the right.

OPEN
Daylight hours daily, year-round
Limited touring during worship or when the church is closed for official occasions

ADMISSION
Donation suggested

>>

St. Peter's is the oldest parish church in Warwickshire—so old, in fact, that it's more commonly known as "The Saxon Sanctuary" than "St. Peter's Wootton Wawen." (*Here's another for the Britspeak handbook—Wawen is pronounced "Warin," except when it's pronounced "Wagen." We are now convinced they do this just to trip us up!*) To make things even more challenging, St. Peter's claims to be three separate churches. But that's another story, best told by the dioramas in the church's exhaustive historical exhibition.

The Saxon Sanctuary traces its roots to 900 CE. The tower and a crossing in the heart of the main church are the primary traces of this ancient beginning. Parts of the nave are Norman, the chancel is Early Gothic and the southwest chapel was built in the 14th century. The southeast Lady Chapel, built to resemble a barn, is also medieval. Here you can wander at leisure through the informative Millennium Exhibition, which explores the 1,000-year history of the church and the hamlet it serves.

In truth, the whole of St. Peter's Wootton Wawen is a museum of sorts, an amalgam of curious architectural whimsies, monuments and memorials that span centuries, and no small number of legends and folklore. Luckily, an on-site guidebook and numerous helpful signs steer you through these complexities. One of our favorite "ah ha!" moments was when we discovered stone carvings of King Edward III and Queen Philippa on either side of the great *"Te Deum"* window. Their granddaughter, Anne, married two consecutive earls of Stafford, both of whom were lords of Wootton as well. Just a sample of the myriad pleasures that await you in this fascinating church.

● ●

🔖 Did you know?

Wootton Wawen takes its name from the Saxon lord Wagen, on whose manor St. Peter's church was constructed. The possibility that the poor fellow suffered a speech impediment (or enjoyed talking with his mouth full), leading to constant mispronunciation of his surname, is a matter of mere speculation.

● ●

Ghost Alert!

Generations of St. Peter's parishioners have claimed they've encountered a wraithlike "gray lady" wandering through the church. Popular opinion deems she's the secret wife of a past Prince of Wales. Unfortunately, no one seems to agree which prince kept such a sullied consort or what her exact connection to Wootton Wawen might be.

☦ Charlecote Park

Wellesbourne/Warwick

>>

PHONE

01789-470277

E-MAIL

charlecote@smtp.ntrust.org.uk

LOCATED

5 miles east of Stratford-upon-Avon or 6 miles south of Warwick on the north side of the B4086

TRAVEL

Take the train from Marylebone or Paddington Station to Warwick or Stratford-upon-Avon stations; taxi to Charlecote Park

OPEN

Noon–5:00 p.m. Friday–Tuesday, March–November
Closed Wednesday and Thursday

ADMISSION

£5.80 Adults
£2.90 Children
Family ticket available

CONVENIENCES

Restaurant, brewhouse, gift shop

>>

Charlecote has an ancient lineage—the property was owned by the Lucy family from 1247 to 1946, when it was given to the National Trust. The present home was begun by Sir Thomas Lucy in 1551, starting with the demolition of the semisqualid medieval residence—a structure so rank that Lucy's tutor, John Foxe, complained he needed to have his "nose cut off" just to tolerate the smell. Construction was completed in 1558, a date reflected in the heraldic glass of the manor's Great Hall. Sir

• •

☞ Did you know?

Local legend tells that William Shakespeare was caught poaching game on the Charlecote grounds in 1583—the character of Justice Shallow in *Merry Wives of Windsor* is said to be based on Sir Thomas Lucy.

• •

Thomas was knighted here in 1565 by Robert Dudley, Earl of Leicester, who was acting in the stead of Queen Elizabeth. Glorianna herself visited Charlecote in 1572.

Alas, Charlecote Park was extensively remodeled in 1823. (*We will always marvel at the Victorians' sentimental attempts to "Tudorize" what was already authentically Tudor.*) The two-story Elizabethan gatehouse is authentic, but the Great Hall's barrel-vaulted ceiling is faux-timbered—you'll have chances to see the real thing in many other manor homes. However, there *is* a contemporary painting of Elizabeth I on view, a rarity that makes up for all the surrounding Victoriana . . . at least in Sarah's eyes.

~

 ## Coughton Court
Alcester

>>>

PHONE
01789-762435

WEBSITE
www.coughtoncourt.co.uk

LOCATED
2 miles north of Alcester on the A435, 8 miles northwest of Stratford-upon-Avon

OPEN
11:30 a.m.–5:00 p.m. Saturday and Sunday, March and October
11:30 a.m.–5:00 p.m. Wednesday–Sunday, April–September
Also open Bank Holiday Mondays and Tuesdays in August
Closed November–February

ADMISSION
£9.45 Adults
£4.75 Children
Family ticket available

CONVENIENCES
Family-run restaurant, gift shop, plant sales

>>>

Although Coughton Court is owned by the National Trust, it has been the home of the Throckmortons since 1409 — the family still lives in the house and manages the property.

This is one of the grandest Tudor manor homes you'll come across (*a grandeur reflected in the price of admission, we might add*). The imposing gatehouse was built in 1530; the balance of the home was completed 10–20 years later and remains, by and large, unaltered. Inside, amateur historians are treated to an interesting journey through the Throckmorton family history, underscored with numerous portraits, porcelain, tapestries and furnishings from the Tudor era.

Staunch Catholics, the Throckmortons maintained their allegiance to Rome throughout the religious turmoil of the Tudor period. Sir Nicholas Throckmorton, Elizabeth's one-time ambassador to France, was imprisoned by his queen because of his close friendship with Mary, Queen of Scots. Sir Nicholas's nephew was executed in 1583 for his role in the "Throckmorton Plot" to assassinate Elizabeth and restore a Catholic monarch to the English throne. Despite ongoing persecution, imprisonment and fines, the family continued to harbor renegade priests at Coughton Court, where secret, illegal Masses were celebrated for generations. The estate also has important connections to the Gunpowder Plot; although that incident postdates "our" era, we were fascinated by the well-told story.

It is most unusual that the manor has two churches on its property, both of which are still used today. St. Peter's church was built in 1450; the confusingly named church of St. Peter, St. Paul and St. Elizabeth is Victorian. The grounds of Coughton Court are particularly lovely, if strolling is "your thing." A lake and several very special gardens (including an Elizabethan knot garden) enhance the beautiful riverside setting. If you must pick and choose among manor homes, this is one you won't want to miss. It's worth the price of admission.

While you're in the area . . .
✝ Henley-in-Arden

>>>

One of the things we enjoyed most about researching this book was happening upon numerous ancient villages, each charming and worth a visit in its own right. As you drive around the Heart of England, you'll make discoveries of your own that will delight you just as much. One village we heartily recommend is the beautifully preserved medieval "street village" of Henley-in-Arden. Officially made a borough in 1296, the town grew up around the line of Feldon Street, which was the original route out of the Forest of Arden. During the Norman era, Henley thrived as a trading post for nearby Beaudesert Castle, built in 1140 by Thurstan de Montfort, a staunch supporter of Empress Matilda. All that remains of that stronghold is the motte, or mound, just outside the village. However, two ancient churches—**St. Nicholas** and **St. John the Baptist**— a restored 15th-century **Guildhall**, a medieval market cross, and numerous timbered residences along High Street provide a particularly authentic medieval atmosphere. Stop for tea at the 16th-century **White Swan**, opposite the Guildhall. Most enjoyable!

ANCIENT INNS AND EATERIES
Inside Stratford

~ The Vintner
  4–5 Sheep Street
  01789-297259

Built in 1600, the Vintner was once the shop of Stratford's leading wine merchant. (*We like to imagine Shakespeare picking up a bottle of Beaujolais on his way home to New Place.*) This is where we had lunch during our visit. The welcome was warm, the food—and wine—delicious.

~ Lambs
   12 Sheep Street
   01789-292554
Once a Tudor-era coaching inn, this is now a restaurant serving fine cuisine.

~ The Shakespeare Hotel
   Chapel Street
   0870-400-8182
This elegant hotel features beautifully preserved Tudor architecture, luxurious surroundings and a gourmet restaurant.

~ The Swan
   Rother Street
   01789-297022
Built in 1450, this hotel combines ancient atmosphere with modern conveniences.

~ Alveston Manor
   Clopton Bridge
The oldest hotel in Stratford. Shakespeare staged a production of A *Midsummer Night's Dream* on the lawn of the inn.

~ The Garrick Inn
   25 High Street
Stratford's oldest pub—ancient ambience with your ale!

Outside of Stratford ...

~ The Arrow Mill

Arrow Street
Alcester
01789-762419

Listed in the *Domesday Book*, this ancient mill serves lunch and dinner.

~ Billesley Manor

Alcester
01789-400888

This Elizabethan manor home is just 3 miles from Stratford, although not all of the accommodations are in the ancient portion of the home.

LEICESTERSHIRE

DERBYSHIRE

NOTTINGHAMSHIRE

Belvoir
Castle

LINCOLNSHIRE

Ashby de la Zouch
Castle

Donnington-le-Heath

Rutland

Oakham

Kirby
Muxloe
Castle

Leicester

Oakham Castle Hall

Bosworth
Battlefield

Lyddington
Bede House

WARWICKSHIRE

Key

Cathedral

Abbey or Priory

Castle

Notable building or structure

This map provided for orientation purposes only.
You will need to acquire a detailed roadmap of
The Heart of England if you plan to drive.

NORTHAMPTONSHIRE

0 Miles   10
0 Kilometers   16

Leicestershire

CONTENTS

TRIP 1

Leicestershire

My Kingdom for a Horse

 t's pretty fair to say that most amateur historians have a peculiar passion for one particular period of history. Some are Conquest Crazed, obsessed with William the Bastard's invasion and the creeping Normanization of England. Others are Totally Tudor, gripped by the stories of Henry VIII, his ill-fated wives and his ambitious children. But few are as fanatical as those whose imaginations have been fired and fertilized by the Wars of the Roses. The towering personalities, on-again/off-again loyalties, crimes, usurpations, mysteries and controversies loom large and linger long in this proverbial Family Feud. For those of you who find these waning years of the medieval era supremely compelling, this is the trip for you—from the town of Leicester with its Richard III connections, to the castles of Yorkist supporters, to the Battle of Bosworth, where the Wars of the Roses came to a bloody end. Even if your interests are not *so* specific, there is enough variety to keep you—and any children you have in tow—thoroughly engaged. We loved this journey; we think you will, too.

✝ Leicestershire Tourist Information Centre

7–9 Every Street
Town Hall Square

>>

PHONE
01162-650555

LOCATED
On the M1, junctions 19–24

TRAVEL
Four trains an hour depart St. Pancras Station for Leicester. Travel time from London is about 1½ hours.

OPEN
Regular business hours

TIP!
Most—but not all—of the historic buildings in downtown Leicester are centrally located in an area collectively referred to as "Castle Park." The town does an excellent job of "marketing" the Castle Park attractions with Heritage Trail signs, site guides, brochures and maps, even an audio tour and a children's treasure trail. You can walk the entire Castle Park trail in about three hours, depending on how long you choose to linger at any given site. Please note that the remains of the castle, per se, are in Castle Gardens, somewhat removed from the other "Castle Park" buildings. This is not as confusing as it sounds; everything is pretty well marked. Docents at each attraction can readily direct you to the next site on your list, and we found the residents eager to help us when we momentarily lost our bearings.

>>

A bustling university city, Leicester traces its heritage to the Roman era. Amid the many eclectic modern buildings, the intrepid amateur historian can still nose out remnants of Roman, Saxon and Norman architecture. We were sorely disappointed that the *most* important historic site, Leicester Castle, is largely closed to the public. Still, if you're touring Leicestershire's many other castles, ancient homes and battlefields, you might want to take the time to walk around the city of Leicester. The Tourist Information Centre can provide you with maps that will help orient you before you take to the streets.

SARAH AND CAROLE'S RICHARD III TREASURE HUNT

He was titled "Duke of Gloucester," but the city of Leicester, after York, may well be the number one contender for sites associated with Richard III. The last of the Plantagenet kings, Richard stayed at Leicester Castle while on progress in 1483 and spent his final earthly night in Leicester, before meeting death on the battlefield at Bosworth. Legend to the contrary, Richard was the only king to be buried in Leicester—his defiled body was brought to the church of the Grey Friars, and after the mandated public viewing (or in Richard's case, ridicule, for he was hung naked from a tree), he was laid to "rest" in the walls of the monastery church. Unfortunately, it was a fairly short rest. The monastery was ransacked and ruined during the Dissolution and Richard's ill-treated remains are believed to have been unceremoniously dumped into the River Soar. Grey Friars (sic) was located approximately across the street from the present-day **St. Martin's Cathedral**, near the intersection of Greyfriar's and Peacock Lane. A handsome memorial tablet to Richard can be found in St. Martin's.

* *

☞ Did you know?

Richard Plantagenet was the last of England's medieval monarchs . . . and certainly one of its most maligned. His sullied reputation is due in no small part to William Shakespeare (*dare we say* "*Shake*-smear". . .) whose vilified *Richard III* became the benchmark against which Machiavellian rulers have since been measured. Don't get us wrong, we love Shakespeare, but there's no doubt he took great liberties in his telling of history. Speaking of which, one of Shakespeare's plays alleges that there was a king *other than* Richard buried in Leicester. Buy yourself a pint if you can guess who. (*Answer: King Lear*)

* *

Another lost treasure in the pursuit of "Ricardifacts" is the Blue Boar Inn, where the last medieval monarch spent his final night (and not, as Shakespeare would have us believe, tossing and turning in nightmarish anxiety on some cot in a pup tent). Could Richard have chosen this hostelry because of its name? At the time, it was known as the White Boar Inn—the white boar being one of Richard's chosen emblems. If so, the sentiment held little sway with the innkeeper. Upon hearing of the Yorkists' defeat at the Battle of Bosworth, the boorish landlord hastily changed his sign to read "Blue."

Despite these lost landmarks, several tangible tributes to Richard are worth seeking out as you tour Leicester. Chances are, you'll enter the city by way of King Richard's Road, which crosses the River Soar via the highly decorative **Bow Bridge**. Rebuilt in 1863, this is the bridge King Richard proudly crossed en route to Bosworth . . . and the bridge over which his defiled corpse returned. A

> ◆
>
> ☞ Did you know?
>
> Richard was so confident of victory over Henry Tudor that he brought his own bed to Leicester. He left it at the White Boar Inn, where he expected to return in due course for an evening of well-deserved comfort.
>
> ◆

sorrowful legend tells us that one of the king's spurs struck against the bridge wall as he left Leicester. Watching the military parade, a local crone prophesied that where Richard's foot had struck, so would his head strike before the day was done. Indeed, by nightfall, Richard was dead. Bare and battered, flung across a horse, the crownless Richard struck his crown on Bow Bridge. On the town side of the bridge, look for a plaque declaring the spot where Richard III's remains were discarded during the Reformation. On the far end of the bridge are two separate plaques; the north side bears the arms of Richard III, the south side bears the arms of his foe, Henry Tudor.

Perhaps you won't mind being shut out of Leicester Castle *quite* so much when you happen upon the stunning **Richard III Monument**, just inside Castle Gardens. It was built in 1980 and portrays a mighty monarch, crown held aloft (*presumably* *this was before Henry Tudor stole it from a briar bush, where it had become entangled during the heat of battle).*

Finally, as you near the church of St. Mary de Castro, pay close attention to the wall of **Castle House**. You'll spot a tablet that marks the uncommon occasion when two kings of England graced Leicester within two days: King Richard III, on August 21, 1485 . . . and his usurper, Henry VII, on August 22.

••••••••••••••••••••••
☞ Did you know?
King Richard III's motto was *"Loyaulte Me Lie"* (Loyalty Binds Me).
••••••••••••••••••••••••

We hope you enjoyed this fleeting glimpse of Richard III's final days . . . just a little something to whet your appetite before proceeding to Bosworth Battlefield!

✺

✝ Leicester Castle and the Castle Gardens Buildings

Castle Gardens

⟫⟫

PHONE

The Guildhall handles inquiries about the Castle: 01162-532569.

LOCATED

Castle Gardens is located between the River Soar and Castle Street, across from De Montfort University. You may avoid crossing the busy highway by using the Southgate Pedestrian Underpass. Signs from the center of Leicester can be confusing, so don't hesitate to ask directions. Unfortunately, the Great Hall is obstructed by the Court House. However, fragments of the castle, including the motte, are scattered throughout Castle Gardens.

OPEN

The Great Hall is open only on rare occasions. Call the Guildhall, or try your luck and inquire at the Court House.

ADMISSION

Free of charge (*if you're lucky enough to get in!*)

Note: It is hard for us not to rant and rave over the fact that the primary remnants of this extraordinary castle are virtually inaccessible.

Leicester Castle played a pivotal role in the history of England, and the very idea that medieval enthusiasts are essentially barred from admiring the inside of the surviving Great Hall is incomprehensible to us. However, those are the facts—we only hope that by determination, cunning or charm one day we can talk our way in. If you succeed where we have not, we hope you'll let us know! (We have heard that plans are afoot to open a castle-related museum in the Great Hall, but no specific timetable has been determined.)

>>

Although Leicester has Roman and Danish roots and was fortified several times during those eras, its first real castle was built just after the Norman Conquest. It was constructed at the command of William the Bastard by Hugh de Grentmeisnil, Sheriff of Leicester. By the reign of Henry I, all of Grentmeisnil's estates, including the castle, had passed into the hands of Robert Beaumont, Earl of Leicester, who set about improving their defensive structure. Unfortunately, his "upgrades" were short-lived; Beaumont's son, Robert Blanchemains, rose with Prince Henry in the 1173 rebellion against Henry II. The king retaliated by sacking both the town and the castle, which was, for all intents and purposes, demolished. Only the Great Hall, believed to have been constructed in 1150, remained relatively unscathed.

Of course, the city of Leicester was far too strategic to go unprotected for long. In 1239, Henry III's powerful brother-in-law Simon de Montfort was invested with the earldom of Leicestershire. Under his patronage, Leicester Castle was reconstructed; here, in the castle's ancient Great Hall, de Montfort —who had successfully led a barons' revolt to curtail the might of the monarchy—held the first English Parliament in 1264. De Montfort's victory had its limits, however. Within a year, the royalists forces, under the leadership of Prince Edward, rallied. De Montfort was killed at

• •
☞ Did you know?
The first proto-Parliament was not the only parliament to meet at Leicester Castle. In 1425, Henry VI convened the great deliberative body in the castle's Great Hall.
• •

the Battle of Evesham; his earldom and Leicester Castle were awarded to King Henry's son Edmund "Crouchback," Earl of Lancaster.

So began a long relationship between Leicester Castle and the house of Lancaster. De Montfort's stronghold was remodeled to become one of the primary Lancastrian residences. The castle was further enlarged in the 1330s by Henry, Earl of Lancaster and Leicester, who added the large Newarke ("new work") outer court. The Newarke functioned as an enclosed religious complex, which compared in its day to the lower ward of Windsor Castle. Within its confines were the church of St. Mary of the Annunciation (now demolished), old Trinity Hospital and several medieval houses used as rectories for priests.

When the Duchy of Lancaster fused with the Crown in 1399, Leicester Castle gradually fell from political prominence, although it continued to domicile the great Lancastrians. It was particularly favored by Edward III's powerful son John of Gaunt, who died at Leicester on February 3, 1399. A vaulted medieval cellar, known as John of Gaunt's Cellar, is located at the south end of the Great Hall. It is just one of several remnants of Leicester Castle we are sorry not to be able to see.

Leicester Castle took a beating during the Cromwellian Wars. Fragments of the castle's defensive structure are scattered around the area known as Castle Gardens, but they are very hard to distinguish from the remaining bits and pieces of the Leicester Roman Wall. However, two important buildings from the medieval complex are very well preserved (*and the fact that they're not conveniently accessible . . . well, don't get us started again!*).

> ☞ **Did you know?**
>
> After the Reformation, Newarke's role as a quiet religious enclave was suddenly transformed. Virtually overnight, the castle's outer court changed from spiritual haven to tax haven, as Leicester's wealthiest residents flocked to the spacious green ward in hopes of avoiding the hefty in-town real estate taxes. Ironically, the gate into Newarke was converted into a prison—whether for Robin Hood-ish thieves or tax-evading fat cats is a matter of conjecture!

Hidden behind the 17th-century facade of the Court House is the stunning medieval **Great Hall** (c. 1150). This is believed to be the oldest surviving aisled and bay-divided castle hall in Europe, though our sources claim the interior has been largely partitioned into individual offices and courtrooms.

Another tantalizing, mostly off-limits relic from our era is the ancient church of **St. Mary de Castro**. Originally the castle's lavish chapel, it was founded as a collegiate church by the first Robert Beaumont in 1107. Although the church has been heavily Victorianized, portions of the Norman architecture (including remarkable Norman sedilia carvings) have remained intact. Sadly, unless you care to attend church services, the church is only open for touring on summer Saturday afternoons. You'll find a schedule of religious services posted at the door. Phone 01162-628727 for further information.

☞ **Did you know?**

Henry VI was knighted at St. Mary de Castro. It is also believed that Geoffrey Chaucer was married in this church.

As you meander through Castle Gardens, climb the **castle motte**. An information panel, which relates a few highlights of the castle and Newarke's history, will help orient you. From this vantage, you'll be able to identify old **Trinity Hospital**, to your left as you face the river. Trinity was founded in 1331 by Henry, Earl of Lancaster and Leicester as an almshouse. Most—but by no means all—of the medieval hospital was torn down during rebuilding programs in 1776, 1898 and 1901. The new Trinity hospital was erected in 1995, and the remaining ancient buildings were taken over as offices for De Montfort University. Looking at Trinity, you can still spot the arcades of the ancient castle's second chapel and infirmary. The ancient chapel within Trinity can be viewed by prior appointment. Again, contact the Guildhall for information.

The only remaining defensive portions of Leicester Castle are three of its gates. The **Turret Gate**, c. 1423, was the castle's southern gate. Along Castle Street, you'll find **Castle Gate**, adjacent to the medieval timber-framed buildings of **Castle House**.

Also of 1400s vintage, this gateway would have served as lodging for the porters who guarded the main approach to the castle. Finally, across Oxford Street, is **Magazine Gateway**. Built in 1400, this was the original entry into the Newarke. The Magazine Gateway is occasionally open for touring. Check with the Newarke House Museum for a schedule of opening times.

Good luck on this most frustrating of "Lost Treasure" tours!

✚ While in Castle Gardens . . .
Newarke House Museum
The Newarke, Castle Gardens

>>
PHONE
01162-473222

OPEN
10:00 a.m.–5:30 p.m. Monday–Saturday, year-round
2:00–5:30 p.m. Sunday, year-round
>>

The fascinating history of Leicester is revealed through numerous artifacts and displays spread through two 16th-century residences, Wygston's Chantry House (c. 1513) and Skeffington House (c. 1560). Although you'll be treated to scads of information that postdates our period, there's enough focus on medieval and Tudor times to hold your interest. Check here to see if the Magazine Gate is open during your visit.

• • • • • • • • • • • • • • • • • • • •
🐟 Did you know?

Wygston's Chantry House was built by William Wygston, Leicester's wealthiest citizen. The house provided lodging for the two priests who had been retained to sing masses for Wysgton's soul's salvation. The priests pealed the appeal (sang the request) at the Newarke church of St. Mary of the Annunciation. The church was closed in 1548, the year Parliament decreed that ritualized prayers for the dead were superstitious and illegal. (*One can safely assume that Heaven had received Wygston's musical message loud and clear well before then!*)
• •

❖❖

ROBERT BEAUMONT, SECOND EARL OF LEICESTER (1104–1168)

To understand the power of Robert Beaumont and his twin brother, Waleran, one must first take a look at Beaumont's father, Robert, Count of Meulan. A descendant of Charlemagne and the son of a mighty Norman magnate, this Robert was already Lord of Meulan and Beaumont when he proved his prowess at the Battle of Hastings. A series of fortuitous inheritances and honors, including first Earl of Leicester, helped secure his material strength and assured that all three of the first Norman kings of England would hold Meulan in the highest esteem. By the end of his career, he had served as the chief lay advisor to both William Rufus and Henry I, paving the way for his children's subsequent rise to prominence. (Another of the twins' brothers was Roger of Warwick, who also was no small potatoes in the 12th-century English power structure.)

The Beaumont twins were a force to be reckoned with, a political one-two punch who used their connections, money and even their "twinship" to form one of the most formidable power structures of the early Middle Ages. Raised in the court of Henry I, who took an almost fatherly interest in the boys, they had an exceptionally privileged childhood, with a superior education that stretched beyond scholarly pursuits to the nuances of political subterfuge.

Of the two brothers, Robert was the more conservative — careful and circumspect where Waleran was impulsive and passionate. Robert's cautious nature ultimately proved to be the more successful. While his brother suffered a series of devastating setbacks, Robert slowly and methodically continued to build influence — and the wealth that comes with it — throughout his long career. By the time he was in his 50s, Robert Beaumont was easily the most powerful baron in England and one of the nation's most esteemed lawyers, diplomats and administrators to boot.

☞ Did you know?

Several of the women in Robert Beaumont's life seemed to have enjoyed a rather liberal, if not libertine, sex life. Beaumont's mother, Isabel of Vermandois, eloped with William de Warenne *twice* — once before she married Robert of Meulan and once after. Robert's sister Elizabeth was one of Henry I's many mistresses, bearing at least one of the king's out-of-wedlock children (he had 21). Of course, his sister's special relationship with the king may have been yet another safeguard to Robert's already ironclad position at court.

When Robert of Meulan died, his English lands and the earldom of Leicester went to the younger twin, Robert, while the family lands in Normandy and France passed to the minutes-older Waleran. Although Robert Beaumont would eventually acquire a sizeable Norman fiefdom when he married Amice of Breteuil, the brothers' division of English/Norman assets served them well during the 19-year civil war between King Stephen and Empress Matilda. With one brother protecting the domestic front and the other defending lands abroad, the Beaumont boys were assured that one of them would always be on the "winning" side. Robert's success in helping Stephen defeat Matilda's supporter Robert of Salisbury earned him the earldom of Hereford and secured the confidence of the king. However, Robert was not blind to the fragilities of Stephen's monarchy. While remaining loyal to Stephen during most of the civil war, Beaumont skillfully negotiated treaties with England's pro-Matilda magnates to ensure that destruction of his vast English lands—which stretched from Wales to East Anglia—would be kept to a minimum.

By 1153, it was clear that, although Stephen had managed to hold onto his throne, the war would ultimately be won by his enemies. By the time Matilda's son Henry Fitzempress was crowned Henry II, Robert's loyalties had wisely changed course—in fact, Beaumont is credited with helping to mastermind the treaty that enabled Henry to secure the throne. Robert's unparalleled knowledge of the inner workings of England's power structure helped elevate him in fairly short order to the role of justiciar, a position in which he co-served with Richard de Lucy. As justiciar, Beaumont was deeply involved in the Crown's fight with Thomas à Becket, yet he managed to be exempted from the widespread excommunications inflicted by Rome in support of the Archbishop of Canterbury. He also represented the king in England when ongoing struggles in Normandy and Aquitaine called Henry II abroad. He died in 1168, having served the king for 14 years in such an exemplary manner that several historians cite Robert Beaumont as the benchmark against which future medieval administrators must be measured.

◆ ◆ ◆ ◆ ◆ ◆ ◆ ◆ ◆ ◆ ◆ ◆ ◆ ◆ ◆ ◆ ◆ ◆
☞ Did you know?

Sadly, Robert Beaumont's political savvy was not part of his son's massive inheritance. Robert Blanchemains was temporarily stripped of the earldom of Leicester (and a host of other lands and honors) for the role he played as one of the primary supporters of the 1173 uprising against Henry II. He languished in the king's prison for four years before deciding it was in his best interests to offer a humble apology and plea for mercy. Henry was surprisingly lenient—but no earl ever served in that king's closest circle again.
◆ ◆ ◆ ◆ ◆ ◆ ◆ ◆ ◆ ◆ ◆ ◆ ◆ ◆ ◆ ◆ ◆ ◆

Ghost Alert!

The cells beneath Leicester Castle's Great Hall are famously haunted. The sound of long-abandoned cell doors banging, as well as unearthly weeping and wailing, continue to disrupt the court proceedings from time to time. Officials also complain they hear the unexplained peal of chimes. (*We, of course, assume these are amateur historians from ages past who share our frustration over being denied access to the castle.*)

➤➤

 # Jewry Roman Wall and Museum
St. Nicholas Circle

➤➤➤

PHONE
01162-473021

LOCATED
On St. Nicholas Circle in the center of Leicester

OPEN
10:00 a.m.–5:30 p.m. Monday–Saturday, April–September
2:00–5:30 p.m. Sunday, April–September
10:00 a.m.–4:00 p.m. Monday–Saturday, October–March
2:00–4:00 p.m. Sunday, October–March

ADMISSION
Donation requested

➤➤➤

Nearly 2,000 years old, the Jewry Wall at Leicester once formed the foundation of the city's public Roman baths. Today it takes pride of place as the largest surviving Roman civic building in Britain. The wall originally separated the exercise room (located on the site of the current St. Nicholas Church) from the bathing area.

◆◆◆◆◆◆◆◆◆◆◆◆◆◆◆◆◆◆◆◆◆◆◆
👉 **Did you know?**
In Roman times, Leicester was known as *Ratae Corieltauvorum*.
◆◆◆◆◆◆◆◆◆◆◆◆◆◆◆◆◆◆◆◆◆◆◆

Although no one knows for certain how the wall received its name, it is widely believed to have been named after Leicester's sizeable Jewish community, which was banished from the town by official charter in 1250. There is also conjecture that the name stretches back even further, a reminder of Jerusalem's Wailing Wall, which is all that survived when Rome devastated the great Jewish temple.

Extensive excavation in the 1930s revealed not only the

baths, which date from about 150 CE, but also the forum, which sits below St. Nicholas Circle. Information and artifacts revealed by archeologists are on display in the Jewry Wall Museum, including beautiful mosaic tiles, wall paintings from a 1958 excavation of the Blue Boar Inn, and a Saxon woman's skeleton. Two millennia of Leicester's history are brought to life in a multimedia exhibition. There are several hands-on projects to entertain children while parents admire the ancient treasures.

✝ St. Nicholas Church
St. Nicholas Circle and Vaughn Way

PHONE
01662-858943

LOCATED
Adjacent to the Jewry Wall and Museum

OPEN
2:00–4:00 p.m. Saturday, year-round
12:30–3:00 p.m. Tuesday, year-round
The key to the church is available from the staff of the Jewry Wall and Museum.

This is the oldest building in the city of Leicester. Believed to have been the site of a pagan temple, St. Nicholas Church was built by Saxon Christians using tiles reclaimed from the adjacent Roman baths. Although it was remodeled in the Norman, Plantagenet and Victorian eras (*look for the telltale Norman arches!*), much of its fabric remains intact, including the rare windows in the north wall.

☞ **Did you know?**

English law required that the body of a deceased monarch be publicly displayed before burial—a custom that made it hard for pretenders to emerge "after the fact," claiming to be the late, great ruler. After the Battle of Bosworth, Richard III's body was terribly defiled. The public was not spared the pitiful sight of his abused corpse, however. Legend has it that before being removed to Grey Friar's, the last of the Plantagenet kings was exhibited in the church of St. Nicholas.

✝ Leicester Guildhall
Guildhall Lane

>>

PHONE
01162-532569

WEBSITE
www.leicestermuseums.ac.uk

LOCATED
Adjacent to High Street and St. Nicholas Place in central Leicester

OPEN
10:00 a.m.–5:30 p.m. Monday–Saturday, year-round
2:00–5:30 p.m. Sunday, year-round

Note: Hours may change according to Guildhall functions; please call in advance for current schedule.

ADMISSION
Free of charge

CONVENIENCES
Gift shop, guided tours upon request

>>

Leicester Guildhall was originally constructed in 1390 as the official meeting place for the Corpus Christi Guild, an exclusive but influential group of merchants and gentry. By 1500, the Great Hall had been expanded significantly and the two wings at either end added. About this time, the Corporation of Leicester began to share the premises with the guild; when the guild was dissolved in 1548, the property passed to the city for the paltry sum of less than £26.

The Guildhall is considered to be one of the best of its kind in England. Although many of

• •
☞ Did you know?

Leicester was the first county in England to engage in the nasty pastime of bear-baiting. Although 21st-century sensibilities cringe at the idea, the sport was wildly popular during Elizabethan times. The poor bear would be lashed to a post and five mastiff dogs would be unleashed upon it. Bets would be placed on both the bear's and the dogs' success. Leicester's Bear Garden was adjacent to the Guildhall, and guests at mayoral banquets would frequently pause between courses to watch the gory sport. Apparently, it did little to curb their appetites.

• •

the rooms and attractions postdate our period, it is well worth stopping by to admire its ancient timber-framed halls and to read about the building's vital role in the city's rise to fortune. There are portraits of Leicester's mayors dating back to the Tudor era, and the painted ceiling panels sport the arms of the influential Hastings family, whose strongholds peppered the Leicestershire countryside. We particularly enjoyed the display of Tudor costumes, which span ages and occupations from 1485 to 1603.

Ghost Alert!

The Guildhall has earned the reputation for being Leicester's most haunted building. No fewer than five different specters are believed to "inhabit" the site, including two cunning female pickpockets. Hang onto your wallets!

✝ Leicester Cathedral (a.k.a. St. Martin's Cathedral)
Guildhall Lane

>>

PHONE
  01662-625294

LOCATED
  Across from the Guildhall

OPEN
  Daylight hours daily, year-round
  Limited touring during services

ADMISSION
  Donation suggested

>>

Your first reaction as you come across St. Martin's will no doubt be "Victorian." You're right and you're wrong. Although the church was heavily restored during the 1800s—and again when it was consecrated as a cathedral in 1927—there are slivers and slices of the ancient parish church that make a visit worth your while. Besides, the cathedral houses a handsome memorial to Richard III—reason enough in our book to stop and pay homage.

The nave of St. Martin's was built 800 years ago. Look up; although heavily "touched up," the ceiling features some of the most splendidly colored carved angels you're likely to see in all your church visits. To the right of the nave is the south aisle, originally built in the 14th century. It was here that members of the Corpus Christi Guild used to come and worship before beginning their business meetings.

Without a doubt, the most interesting part of the cathedral is the chancel. Here is where you'll find the striking marble floor panel honoring King Richard III. But take a close look at the chancel seats—each is named after an important figure in Leicester's history, and the names read like the *Amateur Historian's Guide to Medieval Luminaries* (*a book we have yet to write, but it's not a bad idea . . .*).

Of the two smaller chapels, St. Katherine's is older. Built in the late 1400s, it was dedicated to the patron saint of pregnant women and has held a special place in the hearts of the women of Leicester for well over 500 years.

While you're in Leicester . . .

Although far-flung from Leicester's other ancient sites, there is one more medieval church in Leicester. It's **St. Margaret's Church**, which sits on the northeast outskirts of the borough boundaries, well away from the hustle and bustle of Leicester's busiest streets. Originally constructed in 1086, the current building features a 13th-century nave and 15th-century chancel. Unfortunately, St. Margaret's is generally closed for touring. A schedule of church services can be obtained from the Tourist Information Centre.

While you're in the area . . .

✝ Kirby Muxloe Castle
Kirby Muxloe

>>

PHONE
  01604-735400

LOCATED
  4 miles west of Leicester off the B5380

OPEN
  Noon–5:00 p.m. Saturday and Sunday, April–October

ADMISSION
  £2.00 Adults
  £1.00 Children
  £1.50 Seniors

>>

When William, Lord Hastings, was granted the estates of Ashby-de-la-Zouch, he cleverly incorporated an existing manor home into a "state-of-the-art" residential castle. With Kirby Muxloe, Hastings had the opportunity to use his architectural talents from the ground up. Defying the trends of the day, he chose an oblong, rather than square, structure and selected brick over the more popular stone for the exterior. Serious attention was paid to defense at Kirby—a water-filled moat accessed by drawbridge, two gatehouses and multiple gun ports were integral to the plan.

• •
☞ Did you know?
In the category of "Jobs We're Glad We Don't Have": Lord Hastings retained the services of a watchman who was paid to remain awake at night, simply to be certain water in the moat did not exceed an acceptable level. (*Snore . . .*)
• •

Hastings received the license to crenulate Kirby Muxloe in 1474, but he did not begin construction until 1480. Unfortunately, his execution in 1483 put a halt to his ambitious building scheme. Today the castle seems a particularly evocative ruin— picturesque, yes, but somber when viewed as a symbol of the fickle winds of medieval politics.

✝ Bosworth Battlefield and Visitor Centre

Sutton Cheney
Market Bosworth

>>

PHONE

01455-290429

LOCATED

Off the A5, A444, A447 and B585; travel time from London is approximately 2 hours.

OPEN

Visitor Centre
    11:00 a.m.–5:00 p.m. Monday–Saturday, April–October
    11:00 a.m.–6:00 p.m. Sunday and Bank Holiday Mondays, April–October
Battlefield
    Daylight hours daily, year-round

ADMISSION

Visitor Centre
    £3.00 Adults
    £1.90 Children and Seniors
    Family ticket available

Note: Prices are slightly higher on event days.

Battlefield
    Free of charge

CONVENIENCES

Ranger-guided tours of the battlefield are held on the first Sunday of every month, from Easter through October; tours leave at 2:00 p.m. from the Visitor Centre. There is a restaurant on the premises as well as a bookstore.

TIP!

The Battle of Bosworth is re-enacted on the battlefield every summer. The event is staged on the weekend closest to the battle date (August 22); please call ahead for details.

>>

Of all the many reasons to visit Leicestershire, the lure that grabbed us and would not let go was "Bosworth Battlefield." As enthusiastic as we are about England's medieval and Tudor history in general, certain people, places and events really stir our imaginations, and the culminating 1485 confrontation between Richard III and Henry Tudor is one of our personal hot buttons. The battle, which decided the Wars of the Roses, marked the end of England's medieval era and rang in the Tudor age, was one of the most dramatic moments in ancient history. Imagine our delight when we discovered that Bosworth Battlefield and Visitor Centre not only lived up to our lofty expectations, but managed to exceed them at every turn!

It is enormously hard to embody the excitement and passion of such a pivotal historic moment when most of what you're working with is essentially a *field*. With imagination, thoroughness and exquisite taste, the Visitor Centre sets the stage for your battlefield tour, explaining the politics, culture, daily life and military strategy that led up to the final confrontation between the House of Lancaster and the House of York. The exhibition center at Bosworth ranks, along with the Tower of London and Dover, as the best we've seen: creative, engaging and *clear*. We only wish we had visited on a day when the battle is re-enacted with armored men and mounts . . . knowing what this team can do with inanimate portrayals, we just bet their flesh-and-blood events are spectacular!

Bottom line: if you've been disappointed by other battlefield experiences (as we were at the Battle of Hastings exhibition), fear not—Bosworth won't let you down. Whether or not you're a military aficionado, a passionate Ricardian or simply an amateur historian gripped by the drama of ancient times, we recommend this visit unreservedly.

❖❖

THE WHITE ROSE, PRUNED

The Wars of the Roses had dragged on for more than 30 years by the time the Battle of Bosworth was fought. As a matter of political debate, the struggle between the houses of York and Lancaster for the English throne began in 1399, the moment Henry Bolingbroke (heir to the Lancastrian title), usurped the crown from his cousin Richard II . . . bypassing such possible rival claimants as the descendants of their uncle the Duke of York, who were technically next in line for the throne. When out-and-out fighting over succession issues actually began in 1455, England's nobility was sharply divided, highly impassioned and willing to stake much on the outcome of the quarrel.

By the Battle of Bosworth, passions had clearly waned; the debate over "York or Lancaster" was simply less compelling. Many of the key nobles were war-weary and tired of the family feud that had ravaged their lands and squeezed their coffers. Richard III's tainted public image further strained support for him. Although Richard was a Yorkist king, many Yorkist supporters felt he had come by the title unfairly, snatching it from his nephew Edward, Prince of Wales (whom Uncle Dick then imprisoned in the Tower of London and even-tually murdered . . . or so Richard's detractors were quick to claim). In short, the Yorkists themselves were a house divided. Richard was faced with apathy on the one hand and hostility on the other when appealing to his peers to raise an army that would help him defeat a fresh onslaught by Lancastrian forces, led this time by Henry Tudor, Earl of Richmond.

The Welsh-born Henry, great-great-great-grandson of Edward III, had been living in self-imposed exile in Brittany during the longest stretch of Yorkist rule, between 1471 and 1484. Now, with the Yorkist cause so fragmented, Henry saw the chance he had been waiting for. On August 7, 1485, he landed in Wales and, along with 2,500 men, proceeded into England via Shropshire, recruiting the Earl of Oxford's troops and a nominal number of additional reinforcements along the way. Henry was in great need of support from his stepfather, Thomas, Lord Stanley, who, together with his brother, William Stanley, could deliver a crucial 6,000 soldiers. But Thomas and William were self-serving strategists and they declined to declare for either side so early in a questionable match.

Difficult as it may have been for Richard III to rally fervent support, he was still king and, as such, commanded 10,000 men-at-arms. A highly capable sol-dier with an enormous investment in winning the conflict, Richard seemed to have every advantage in the looming confrontation. Yet his position was by no means secure; he, too, was des-perate for the fair-weather Stanleys' make-or-break patronage. Although he held Thomas Stanley's young

☞ Did you know?

Richard III was only 32 years old when he died on Bosworth Battlefield.

son, Lord Strange, as surety, when it came to the duplicitous Stanley brothers, nothing could be counted as certain.

The morning of August 22 saw Richard and his troops positioned on top of Ambien Hill, just outside Market Bosworth. Wearing a bejeweled coronet, with his troops gloriously arrayed, the king must have presented a fearsome sight to Henry Tudor, who had never before seen battle. Richard was, in theory, sup-ported by the dukes of Norfolk and Northumberland; little did he know that before the day was over Norfolk would be slaughtered by the Earl of Oxford's vanguard and that—in one of medieval history's most appalling instances of betrayal—Northumberland would turn and flee the battle, leaving his king fatally exposed. True to form, the Stanleys had positioned their troops between the two armies, still declining to commit to either side.

Richard may have seemed supremely confident, but he was not. His taut nerves gave way when he saw the Earl of Richmond's banner approaching the Stanley camp. Richard charged, attempting to cut off Henry before he reached his stepfather. Thanks to the lily-livered Northumberland, an insufficient number of horsemen followed their king into battle. Seeing the king's vulnerability, the Stanley forces threw their might behind the Tudor cause. Richard was unhorsed and slaughtered by Stanley men, his body defiled and his crown retrieved from the bloody battleground and placed upon Henry Tudor's head.

◊ ◊

Your visit to Bosworth will consist of two very different activities. We suggest that you start at the Visitor Centre, where a short film and extensive exhibition hall will give you the background and insights necessary to help you appreciate your next activity: a self-guided tour of the battlefield itself. Thanks to the cooperation of local farmers and landowners, a series of footpaths traverse Bosworth field. Plaques along the way describe key maneuvers by the Yorkist and Lancastrian forces. Depending on the route you choose to follow, you may pass by King Dick's Well (c. 1813), which for many years was the only tribute to the Battle of Bosworth. The spot where Richard III fell is marked with a small memorial in King Richard's Field; his banner, depicting a white boar, flies over the site.

Back in the Visitor Centre,

• •
Did you know?

The Battle of Bosworth marks the last time the Crown of England changed hands on a field of battle. It was also the last time the country's king personally led mounted knights in a charge.

• •
Did you know?

Excavations near Sutton Cheney in 1748 revealed a cache of weapons, believed to have been cast aside when the yellow-bellied Northumberland and his troops abandoned the Battle of Bosworth. Had Northumberland stood fast for his king, the outcome of the battle most certainly would have been different.

• •

you might want to take a closer look at the excellent battlefield models, replica armor, shields, flags and other medieval military memorabilia. We found that a "before and after" look at the displays helped deepen our appreciation for what we had experienced on foot.

✝ While you're in the area . . .
St. James Sutton Cheney Church

No one knows for certain where Richard III and his soldiers gathered for their last Holy Communion, but it stands to reason that this church—a mere mile from Bosworth Battlefield—could well have been the spot. The Richard III Society has given the nod to St. James, installing a commemorative plaque on the church's wall and holding its annual service of worship here on the Sunday closest to August 22. Take time to appreciate the kneelers; the cushions were all hand-worked by the Richard III Society and are resplendent with white boars, white roses and the "Sun in Splendor," emblems associated with Richard.

✝ Ashby-de-la-Zouch Castle
South Street
Ashby-de-la-Zouch

PHONE
01530-413343

WEBSITE
www.english-heritage.org.uk

LOCATED
12 miles south of Derby on the A511, in the town of Ashby-de-la-Zouch

OPEN
  10:00 a.m.–6:00 p.m. daily, April–October
  10:00 a.m.–6:00 p.m. Wednesday–Sunday, November–March

ADMISSION
  £3.00 Adults
  £1.50 Children
  £2.50 Seniors

Note: Your admission ticket also allows you to visit the nearby Ashby Museum.

>>

Long before it was a castle, Ashby-de-la-Zouch was the seat of the prominent Zouche family. Their rather posh (by medieval standards) 12th-century manor home became the centerpiece for the balance of Ashby Castle, when the property was granted to William, Lord Hastings, in 1464. (The Zouche family line had become extinct in 1399).

What, you may ask, happened to Ashby-de-la-Zouch between 1399 and the time it was acquired by Lord Hastings? The property changed hands in rapid succession, eventually passing to James Butler, Earl of Ormonde. Butler, an avid Lancastrian, was captured at the Battle of Towton in 1461 and beheaded. As a traitor, his lands were forfeit to the Crown and were held by the Yorkist king Edward IV, until gifted by the monarch to Hastings.

Lord Hastings was a loyal Yorkist defender during the Wars of the Roses, and Edward IV rewarded him well for his support. Together with the office of Lord Chamberlain, the gifts of Ashby Castle, nearby Kirby Muxloe Castle and several smaller estates provided Hastings with a tidy income, indeed. He, in turn, turned both Ashby and Kirby into significant defensive structures. Working around the existing early Norman buildings, Hastings modernized and expanded Ashby-de-la-Zouch, adding a spectacular Perpendicular chapel, an extensive curtain wall and an imposing square "residential" tower, aptly named the Hastings Tower. The four-story tower provided Hastings with the necessary blend of security and luxury, with a separate well, storeroom, kitchen, Great Hall and solar. A separate seven-story annex provided additional accommodations.

Although much of the castle is in ruins, you can still climb the 90-foot-high Hastings Tower and enjoy some breathtaking views of the Leicestershire countryside. In addition, Ashby-de-la-Zouch features a totally spooky underground tunnel that links the tower with the cellar of the original manor house—a journey you'll either love or hate, depending on your tolerance for confined, lightless spaces.

◆◆◆

GREAT SCOTT!

If the name "Ashby-de-la-Zouch" has set bells ringing for you literature lovers out there, it is because Sir Walter Scott, the father of historical fiction, used the castle as a primary backdrop for the first half of his saga, *Ivanhoe*. As you will recall, *Ivanhoe* is the story of a disinherited knight who won fame and fortune with a little help from friends like Richard the Lionheart and Robin Hood.

In the opening pages of the book, most of the main characters are introduced as they are preparing for a grand tournament that is to be held at the castle. And it is during the tournament at Ashby-de-la-Zouch that Scott chooses for Prince John to receive a major shock. This is when he learns the news from his partner in treachery Philip of France that, despite their best efforts to keep him chained, King Richard has been freed from captivity in Germany. Philip's oblique warning, "Take heed to yourself, for the Devil is unchained," was all too clear to the traitorous prince. He cut short the tournament and prepared to usurp his brother's throne by force of arms. Unbeknownst to John, his mighty brother was already in England, masquerading at the tournament as the Black Knight.

◆◆◆

WILLIAM, LORD HASTINGS (1431–1483)

The Wars of the Roses were peppered with fascinating, if controversial, figures—persons whose actions were so pivotal that it is hard to remain neutral, much less objective, about the roles they played in the great drama of English history. William, Lord Hastings, is no exception. Hastings met a tragic (some would argue *dubious*) end when he was confronted by Richard of Gloucester, Protector of England, arrested for treason, and hauled off for a very hasty execution at the Tower of London. Just what had Hastings done to warrant such a demise? Detractors of Richard claim that the former Lord Chamberlain was summarily dispatched because he stood between Richard and the throne Gloucester coveted. Defenders of Richard, you can be certain, are not convinced.

As early as 1458, Hastings was a staunch supporter of the Yorkist cause; he was also a particularly close friend of Edward IV, retreating into exile with Edward and Richard in 1459 and 1470 and taking up arms in pivotal battles during the prolonged hostilities against the Lancastrians. Edward repaid Hastings's loyalties with a host of royal perks, elevating him to the peerage in 1461, naming him Lord Chamberlain and Captain of Calais, providing him with extensive Leicestershire land holdings, and granting him permission to be buried near Edward in the Royal Chapel at Windsor.

Despite his unquestionable loyalty to King Edward, Hastings was no friend of the king's consort, Elizabeth Woodville. Not only did the queen suspect that Hastings was leading Edward astray with saucy wenches and intoxicating drink (*given Edward's reputation for licentious behavior, this was probably not a Herculean effort for Hastings*), she also recognized that Hastings presented her own relatives with stiff competition for the king's favor. Hastings had won out over the queen's brother Anthony, Earl Rivers, for the captaincy of Calais and, as Lord Chamberlain, Hastings controlled access to the king . . . which made it especially hard for Elizabeth's self-serving brothers and sons by her first marriage to rise as rapidly as they (and she) desired. When Edward died in 1483, Hastings half-heartedly allied himself with the late king's brother Richard against the Woodville faction—but (or so the anti-Richard argument goes) Hastings's overarching affection and concern lay with the new king, 13-year-old Edward.

If the queen's dislike for Hastings was strong, her disdain for her brother-in-law Richard was vehement. Relations between them had been strained for years, each tolerating the other merely to appease Edward IV. Upon Edward's death, Richard—appointed by the late king as Protector of England—wasted no time in taking the Prince of Wales and his younger brother under his "protection." Elizabeth viewed the move as hostile and sought sanctuary with her younger children in Westminster Abbey. A tense standoff between the two camps escalated in the weeks approaching the young Edward's anticipated coronation. During that time, Richard began to form his own circle of advisors, the Protectorate that would help him govern England during the new king's minority.

Some veterans of Edward IV's inner circle—Hastings, Lord Stanley and Edward's former mistress Jane Shore (now Hastings's paramour) among them—were not pleased with this turn of events. Whether they were truly skeptical of Richard's motives or merely jealous over their loss of power, this group, headed by Hastings, made covert gestures of alliance toward the Woodvilles. Together, the disaffected hoped to wrest power from the Protectorate and set up their own interim government to steer England in young Edward's stead.

If they thought such a coup could be pulled off with ease, the Woodville/Hastings alliance severely underestimated Richard. Counterintelligence sources informed Gloucester of the plot and, true to form, Richard acted quickly and decisively. In a scene immortalized in Shakespeare's *Richard III*, the Protector called a council meeting at the Tower of London's White Tower, opened the proceedings by announcing his knowledge of the conspiracy and promptly accused Hastings, Stanley and their co-conspirators of treason. Hastings was sentenced to death without trial and was hauled from the chamber to Tower Green, with barely enough time to be shriven en route by a priest.

Despite the fact that he suffered a traitor's death, Hastings was indeed buried at St. George's Chapel, Windsor, close by his friend Edward IV, just as the late king had dictated. Richard was also lenient in his treatment of Hastings's family; they did not forfeit their holdings in Leicestershire, as was typically required of a traitor's heirs. Indeed, Hastings's widow continued to oversee construction of Kirby Muxloe for a brief period of time, before eventually losing interest—or heart—in the castle's construction.

◇ ◇

While in Ashby-de-la-Zouch . . .

✝ St. Helen's Church

Lower Church Street
Ashby-de-la-Zouch

≫≫

PHONE
01530-412180

LOCATED
Next door to the castle

OPEN
Daylight hours daily, year-round

≫≫

• • • • • • • • • • • • • • • • • • •
☞ Did you know?
When William, Lord Hastings, erected the massive 90-foot tower at Ashby-de-la-Zouch castle, he thoughtfully raised the ancient tower of St. Helen's Church (c. 1200). The impressive sundial that graces the church tower is believed to have been a gift from Lord Hastings.
• • • • • • • • • • • • • • • • • • • •

St. Helen's is a fascinating find, particularly if you have an abiding interest in Edward IV or the Wars of the Roses. We were intrigued by the carved heads of Edward and his boon companion William, Lord Hastings. There is also an impressive array of heraldic glass; see if you can pick out the arms of various Plantagenet kings and their courtiers. Another "eureka" moment came when we realized that the chief mourner depicted below the elaborate effigy of Lord Huntingdon must be none other than Henry VI.

 # Ashby-de-la-Zouch Museum
North Street
Ashby-de-la-Zouch

>>

PHONE
01530-560090

OPEN
11:00 a.m.–1:00 p.m. and 2:00–4:00 p.m. Monday–Friday, April–October
10:00 a.m.–4:00 p.m. Saturday, April–October
2:00–4:00 p.m. Sunday, April–October

ADMISSION
Entry to the museum is included in your ticket to Ashby-de-la-Zouch Castle

>>

You might want to take the time to check out this museum for additional insights on the castle's history, including a model of the castle under siege. There is also a "time travel" exhibit based on Sir Walter Scott's 19th-century novel of a disinherited medieval knight, *Ivanhoe*.

While you're in the area . . .

 # Donnington-le-Heath Manor Home
Donnington-le-Heath

>>

PHONE
01530-831259

LOCATED
½ mile southwest of Coalville, 4½ miles west of the M1, junction 22

OPEN
> 11:00 a.m.–5:00 p.m. daily, April–September
> 11:00 a.m.–3:00 p.m. daily, October–March

ADMISSION
> Donation requested

CONVENIENCES
> Café and bookshop

>>

One of the prettiest medieval manor homes we've seen, Donnington-le-Heath dates from 1290. Although it was altered in both the 16th and 17th centuries, the home's ancient integrity remains largely unhampered — even the roof frames are original. If you're looking for a place to take children, you could hardly do better. The period gardens feature a maze, and there are extensive rotating exhibits on medieval life as well as frequent hands-on activities, all of which make Donnington particularly child-friendly.

〜

Essendine Castle Ruins
Essendine

>>

PHONE
> None

LOCATED
> 4 miles north of Stamford on the Leicestershire/Rutland border

OPEN
> Daylight hours daily, year-round

ADMISSION
> Free of charge (donation suggested for the church)

>>

Although nothing remains of Essendine Castle, per se, the large square enclosure, surrounded by a deep ditch, shelters the parish church of St. Mary. Believed to have once been the castle's chapel, St. Mary dates back to the Norman era, as evidenced by its arched entry portal. The portal is of particular note, with its fine panel portraying Christ and a host of heavenly angels.

Little is known about Essendine's origins. There is some speculation that the castle may have been built by Gilbert de Grant, immediately following the Norman Conquest; others assert that the castle was constructed a century later by the powerful de Busseys.

Bradgate Country Park and Visitor Centre

Bradgate Park
Newtown Linford

>>>

PHONE
01162-236713

LOCATED
6 miles northwest of Leicester; enter the park gates at Newtown Linford and walk ¼ mile to the ruins

OPEN
Ruins
Daylight hours daily, year-round
Visitor Centre
Noon–5:00 p.m. Tuesday–Sunday, April–October
1:00–4:00 p.m. Saturday and Sunday, November and March
Closed December–February

ADMISSION
Ruins
Free of charge (you must pay for parking)
Visitor Centre
£1.20 Adults
60p Children and concessions
Family ticket available

>>>

If you're a Tudor fanatic, the reason to make this trek is to poke around the ruins of the Grey family manor, childhood home to

Lady Jane Grey. (*There's also a medieval deer park, if, by chance, you haven't had your fill of those.*) Stop by the Visitor Centre for greater insight into Lady Jane, her power-hungry kinfolk and her tragically brief reign as England's "Nine Days Queen."

∿

┼ Rutland

>>

Although Rutland is not technically part of Leicestershire, we noticed in our research that the two counties are typically grouped together . . . at least for travel purposes. Since there are really just four sites in Rutland that we want to call to your attention, we decided to follow suit. **Belvoir Castle, Oakham Castle, St. Mary Lady of the Vale** and **Lyddington Bede House** are very close to one another and make for an easy side trip during your exploration of Leicestershire.

Tip!

As you approach Rutland from Leicestershire, make time to stop in the market town of **Melton Mowbray**. This is one of England's oldest market towns, dating back 900 years. It is also home to some gastronomic treats the hungry historian won't want to miss. Look for the authentic Melton pork pies, for which the town is famous, then sample some locally made Stilton, Red Leicester cheese and Melton Hunt Cake—heavily laced with Old Jamaica Rum!

Belvoir Castle
Grantham

>>>

PHONE

01476-870262

LOCATED

Off the A1, A607 and the A52, 7 miles west of Grantham; travel time is about 30 minutes from Leicester.

OPEN

11:00 a.m.–5:00 p.m. Saturday and Sunday, April
11:00 a.m.–5:00 p.m. daily, May–September
11:00 a.m.–4:00 p.m. Sunday, October
Closed November–March

ADMISSION

£6.00 Adults
£3.50 Children

>>>

As you approach Belvoir Castle, it's hard to comprehend just what you're seeing. Castle? Country home? Movie set? Belvoir is an amalgam of architectural styles, which may be why it's earned the reputation for being the most re-built castle in England. And that's just the start of a series of oddities that make Belvoir Castle interesting.

The first castle at Belvoir was constructed by Robert de Todeni, who had the distinction of being William the Conqueror's standard bearer during the Battle of Hastings. Judging from a contemporary seal, the castle consisted of a large, rectangular stone keep and a masonry curtain wall. Perhaps out of gratitude for having survived his role as Primary Conspicuous Target at Hastings, de Todeni built a substantial priory next to the castle, where he was laid to rest in 1088. Peculiarly, his grave was ex-

Did you know?

Although the name Belvoir translates from Norman French into "beautiful view," it's pronounced "beever" (*trust us on this one—we wouldn't set you up for making such a potentially embarrassing faux pas*). Truly, the view across the Belvoir Vale is beautiful and one of the primary reasons why you might want to seek out this castle.

cavated in the 18th century, and de Todeni was moved to the castle proper, where he remains to this day—albeit in his coffin.

De Todeni's descendants were the powerful de Albini clan. William de Albini married Adeliza, widow of Henry I. As stepfather to Empress Matilda, he had the honor of being the first to welcome her to Arundel Castle when she invaded England, the first aggression in a 19-year-long battle for the English throne. By 1247, the de Albini clan was extinct, and Belvoir Castle passed through marriage to Robert de Roos.

Belvoir remained in control of the de Roos clan for just over 200 years. In 1461, the castle managed to survive a serious attack from Yorkist forces. By 1464, Thomas, Lord Roos, had been executed by Edward IV for his Lancastrian activities, and the castle was awarded to the king's man, William, Lord Hastings.

This was not the end of the onslaught Belvoir Castle would suffer in the Wars of the Roses. Loyal supporters of Lord Roos besieged the castle with stone and lead salvaged from a nearby ruin. Greatly undermined, the castle fell into serious decline upon the death of Lord Hastings. It was restored to the de Roos family by Henry VII and, with the marriage of Eleanor de Roos, passed into the ownership of Sir Robert Manners.

In 1523, Belvoir Castle finally enjoyed rebirth. Now owned by Thomas Manners, first Earl of Rutland, most of the castle's medieval fortifications were sacrificed in favor of a sumptuous Tudor manor home, one befitting a peer of the realm. The earls—and later the dukes—of Rutland have owned Belvoir Castle since.

That still was not the end of Belvoir's trials, tribulations and reconstructions. Attacked twice in the Cromwellian wars, Belvoir again fell to ruin. By 1668, another "castle" graced its site, although much of this incarnation was eventually torn down. In the early 1800s, construction on yet another building was begun; a devastating fire in 1816 created still another setback. Finally, during the reign of Victoria, work was finished on the castellated home that you see today.

True, when you visit Belvoir Castle today there is nearly nothing left of its tumultuous medieval or Tudor past, aside from a wonderful portrait of Henry VIII. Still, with a history this steeped in ancient politics, Belvoir would be hard to overlook.

⋀

While you're in the area . . .

✝ St. Mary Lady of the Vale
Bottsford

>>

PHONE
None

LOCATED
From Belvoir Castle, head northwest along the A52 and follow signs to Bottsford.

OPEN
Hours vary

ADMISSION
Donation suggested

>>

The parish church of Belvoir Castle, St. Mary is significant for its mausoleum housing the remains of the earls and dukes of Rutland. There are some well-worn ancient carvings of the Seven Deadly Sins in the nave, but the interior is largely post-Reformation. It was then that the tombs of the de Roos and Manners families were moved to the chancel; here the early Rutland nobility lies in extraordinarily tight but evocative confines (members of the family who died after 1828 were buried in the newer mausoleum at Belvoir Castle).

The first through the fifth earls served and died during "our" period of history; all are buried here. The remaining 18 graves postdate the Elizabethan era. As you pay your respects to these Rutland nobles, you will see two handsome Elizabethan wall memorials for the third and fourth earls facing one another

across the north-south aisle. Rendered in 1591, they were commissioned for a hefty £100 each. Farther along is the stunning
monument to the second earl and his wife, its carved effigies depicted beneath a communion table, surrounded by grief-stricken mourners.

* * * * * * * * * * * * * * * * * * * *

☞ Did you know?

No doubt your attention will be drawn to the spectacular tomb of the sixth earl of Rutland. Even though this monument is Jacobean, its fascinating inscription bears a story worth telling. It seems the earl's two baby sons — shown at his feet and grimly embracing skulls — were murdered "by wicked practice and sorcerye." A mother and two daughters, all in service at Belvoir Castle, were arrested on charges of witchcraft and murder. During the trial, the mother choked on a piece of bread — proof positive in the eyes of the officials that she was, indeed, a witch. She was burned at the stake. Her daughters confessed their crimes and were hanged in 1618 at Lincoln gaol.

* *

〜

✝ Lyddington Bede House
Blue Coat Lane
Lyddington

>>>

PHONE
01572-822438

LOCATED
6 miles north of Corby in the village of Lyddington, 1 mile east of the A6003

OPEN
10:00 a.m.–5:00 p.m. daily, April–October

ADMISSION
£2.75 Adults
£1.40 Children
£2.10 Seniors

>>>

Also known as The House of Prayer, Lyddington Bede was founded in the 1300s as a palace for the Bishops of Lincoln. In

1600, it was converted into an almshouse, a service it provided for three centuries. The rooms you tour date primarily from the 16th century. The ancient fireplace and ceilings in the upstairs rooms are particularly noteworthy.

Oakham Castle
Market Place
Oakham

>>>

PHONE

01572-758440

LOCATED

East of the town center, near the parish church

OPEN

10:00 a.m.–1:00 p.m. and 1:30–4:00 p.m. Monday–Saturday, year-round

1:00–5:00 p.m. Sunday, year-round

ADMISSION

Free of charge

>>>

Oakham was once the Great Hall of a fortified Norman manor home (c. 1180), although you'd never guess it from its unusual exterior. We saw things at Oakham we've never seen before—some beautiful ancient sculptures of musicians and a curious collection of ceremonial horseshoes. We're not sure why, but it seems the 200 horseshoes were "paid" to Oakham's Lord of the Manor as a form of symbolic tax, whenever the monarch passed this way. They date from the reign of Edward IV.

BEDFORDSHIRE, BUCKINGHAMSHIRE, HERTFORDSHIRE, NORTHAMPTONSHIRE

LEICESTERSHIRE

Rockingham Castle

Kirby Hall

Corby

Deene Park

Prebendal Manor House

Rushton Triangular Lodge

Geddington

Lyveden New Bield

Fotheringhay

Barnwell Castle

NORTHAMPTONSHIRE

Boughton House

CAMBRIDGESHIRE

Holdenby House

BEDFORDSHIRE

Northampton

Castle Ashby

Bushmead Priory

Canons Ashby

Sulgrave Manor

Bedford

De Grey Mausoleum

Elstow Abbey

HERTFORDSHIRE

Buckingham

Woburn Abbey

Knebworth

Bishop's Stortford

OXFORDSHIRE

BUCKINGHAMSHIRE

Hertford

Aylesbury

St. Albans (Verulamium) Roman Town and Theatre

Hatfield

Berkhamsted Castle

LONDON

Key

♨ Cathedral
♙ Abbey or Priory
♜ Castle
⌂ Notable building or structure

This map provided for orientation purposes only.
You will need to acquire a detailed roadmap of
The Heart of England if you plan to drive.

5

Buckinghamshire, Northamptonshire, Bedfordshire & Hertfordshire

CONTENTS

Buckinghamshire

The Varied, Verdant Vale

 e have to admit it—there always comes a point in our travels when we're ready to trade "mega-history" for a bit of bucolic beauty. A visit to Buckinghamshire —also known as the Vale of Aylesbury—fits the bill perfectly. The countryside is green and rolling, dotted with thatched-roof cottages and old stone walls that are postcard-perfect. *Of course*, there's a variety of manor homes and churches to top off your thirst for all things ancient (*speaking of topping off your thirst, there's also one **very** ancient pub you won't want to miss*). But this is a trip best suited for meandering, stopping to poke around the ruins of an ancient hill fort, wander through a museum, sample the local delicacies in the market square. When you're ready for a take-it-easy day, take in the Vale of Aylesbury. We bet you'll find it restorative.

✝ Aylesbury

›››

PHONE

01296-330559 (Tourist Information Centre)

E-MAIL

info@aylesbury-tourist.org.uk

LOCATED

62 miles from London on the A41

TRAVEL

Trains depart London's Marylebone Station for Aylesbury regularly; travel time is approximately 1 hour.

TIP!

Aylesbury is a difficult town to navigate by car. There are many one-way streets and portions of the town have been blocked to automobile traffic. We recommend that you park at the car park on Friarage Road, near the train station, and follow the well-marked pedestrian walkway to Friar's Square Shopping Centre, where you'll find the Tourist Information Centre.

›››

Since the reign of King Henry VIII, Aylesbury has had the distinction of serving as the "county town" or seat for Buckinghamshire. The history of the town, however, stretches back to the Anglo-Saxon era; the first reference to "Aegel's Burgh" was in 571. In the 7th century, the citizens of Mercia converted to Christianity and erected one of their minsters on or near the site of the present St. Mary's Church. In the 13th century, Aylesbury established its reputation as a market town, famous for the highly prized

> **☞ Did you know?**
>
> For many decades, the towns of Buckingham and Aylesbury competed heavily for the privilege of serving as county town for Buckinghamshire. Could the fact that Henry VIII awarded the honor to Aylesbury have *anything* to do with the fact that Anne Boleyn's father was Lord Mayor of Aylesbury? Surely not!

Aylesbury duck. You can still visit this bustling market on Wednesdays, Fridays and Saturdays. A most unusual museum, an early Tudor coaching inn and the requisite medieval church are other lures to Buckinghamshire's charming capital.

Buckinghamshire County Museum
Church Street
Aylesbury

>>

PHONE

01296-331441

LOCATED

In the old quarter of Aylesbury, next to St. Mary's Church;
follow the signs from Market Square

OPEN

10:00 a.m.–5:00 p.m. Monday–Saturday, year-round
2:00–5:00 p.m. Sunday, year-round
The Roald Dahl Gallery is open 3:00–5:00 p.m. on school days

ADMISSION

Free of charge

CONVENIENCES

Café and gift shop

TIP!

To see the old portion of this building, meander behind the building
to Pebble Lane. You'll also find a small cluster of Tudor residences
between the museum and St. Mary's Church.

>>

We found the most interesting thing about this museum to be
the fact that it's housed in a portion of Aylesbury's 15th-century
grammar schoolhouse. However, if you have children in your
party who are growing a bit bored (*gasp!*) with all things ancient, this museum will give them a welcome break. Cleverly
integrating artifacts, science and technology, the Roald Dahl
Children's Gallery is a phantasmagoria of discoveries. Who
knows? A ride in the Glass Elevator or a stroll through the Giant
Peach just might change your historical perspective as well!

✝ The King's Head Inn

King's Head Passage
Market Square
Aylesbury

>>>

PHONE
01296-318501

LOCATED
On the northwest corner of Market Square, via a narrow passage
Don't hesitate to ask directions!

OPEN
During regular pub hours daily, year-round

ADMISSION
(House Tour)
£2.00 Adults
Children free of charge

Note: Although the King's Head still operates a pub where you may slake your thirst, you won't want to miss the opportunity to tour the house. Reservations MUST be made in advance and no more than four persons may tour at a time.

>>>

During its medieval heyday, Aylesbury's busy market square was once chock-a-block with now-vanished coaching houses and inns. Luckily, the King's Head has remained virtually intact, giving visitors a very authentic glimpse of ancient English hospitality.

Originally built in the 14th century as the local Greyfriars's monastery guesthouse, the King's Head was converted into a coaching inn during the 15th century. Note the extra-wide archway and spacious, cobbled stable yard; both were built to accommodate carriages, horses and grooms.

• •
☞ **Did you know?**

The Greyfriars's monastery at Aylesbury was founded by James Boteler, Earl of Ormonde. Boteler was a loyal Lancastrian who was captured at the bloody Battle of Tewksbury. The Yorkist king Edward IV wasted no time in beheading Boteler for treason.
• •

The small pub was reconstructed from the Great Hall of a local medieval manor home. Other parts of the building that you will see on your tour date from the 1450 renovation; expanses of wall expose the telltale wattle-and-daub construction. However, the set piece at the King's Inn is the incredible ancient window paying homage to the last Lancastrian royals. A host of heavenly angels is shown bearing shields upon which are emblazoned the arms of Henry VI, his queen, Margaret of Anjou, and their son, Prince Edward, who was killed at the Battle of Tewkesbury.

• •

🖙 Did you know?

We know, we know, it's a "George Washington slept here" sort of claim, but legend insists that King Henry VIII wooed Anne Boleyn at the King's Head Inn.

• •

Sure, you can enjoy the King's Head over a pint at the bar, and far be it from us to deter you from that! But we do urge you to plan ahead; a tour of the rest of the inn is one of Buckinghamshire's *not-to-be-missed* attractions.

✝ St. Mary's Church
Market Square
Aylesbury

≫≫

PHONE
    None; call Tourist Information Centre

LOCATED
    Off Market Square at the corner of Church Street and Parson's, near the Buckingham County Museum

OPEN
    St. Mary's is open at random hours throughout the week and for worship on Sunday. Try your luck at the door, or call the Tourist Information Centre.

ADMISSION
    Donation suggested

≫≫

Christianity came to the kingdom of Mercia early in the 7th century. One of the region's earliest missionary churches was founded by the Mercian king Wulfhere in Aylesbury, sometime between 657 and 674. Based on the discovery of Saxon graves to the south and southeast of the parish church, it is likely that St. Mary's sits on (or very near) the original ancient minster.

Major portions of St. Mary's date from the 13th century, although the soaring spire and clock tower are of the 17th century. If you are lucky enough to get inside the building, you will find a number of medieval and Tudor tombs and memorials, although all are heavily eroded. Among the more interesting is the partly gilded effigy of a knight, elaborately detailed, though well worn. This is believed to be the likeness of James Boteler, Earl of Ormonde, who founded the local Greyfriars's monastery in 1387. Another compelling monument is that of Lady Lee, whose father, William Lord Paget, served as Lord of the Privy Seal for Queen Mary Tudor. As you walk around, admire the exceptionally well-preserved angel corbels and the splendid "Aylesbury Font" that dates from 1180.

☞ Did you know?

Not only was Lady Lee the daughter of a Tudor courtier, her husband, Sir Henry Lee, was personal Champion to Queen Elizabeth I. For all this prestige, the poor woman's tomb evokes sorrow rather than stature. Two of her children died in infancy; they are depicted in their swaddling clothes along with Lady Lee and her elder daughter, Mary. The tomb's inscription mourns the death of the babies and requests that a red flower perpetually adorn Lady Lee's grave. That request is honored to this day.

✝ Nether Winchendon House
Aylesbury

>>>

PHONE
01844-290199

LOCATED
Halfway between Aylesbury and Thame, 2 miles north of the A418

OPEN
By prior appointment only, 2:30–5:30 p.m.
Please inquire in writing to:
Mr. Robert Spencer Bernard
Nether Winchendon House
Aylesbury, Buckinghamshire HP18 ODY

ADMISSION
£4.00 Adults
£2.00 Children
£2.00 Seniors

>>>

If you haven't visited your share of medieval and Tudor manor homes, write ahead and secure a tour of Nether Winchendon House. The 16th-century frieze and linenfold paneling seem to sum up the artifacts from our period of history. In short, probably not worth the effort unless you suffer from Manor Madness, in which case, be our guest (or the guest of Mr. Bernard)!

∿

✝ Chenies Manor
Chenies

>>>

PHONE
01494-762888

LOCATED
4 miles east of Amersham off the A404

OPEN
2:00–5:00 p.m. Wednesday, Thursday and Bank Holiday Mondays, April–October

Note: The only way to tour the house at Chenies Manor is escorted by a guide. You will be asked to stroll the gardens or enjoy a cup of tea until your tour group has assembled. Tours of the house last approximately 90 minutes.

ADMISSION
£5.00 Adults
£3.00 Children

CONVENIENCES
Tea garden, shop

»»

All but forgotten to history, the ancient manor of Iselhampsted was once a royal palace, enjoyed by Edwards I and II before ultimately being awarded to Thomas Cheyne, shield-bearer to King Edward III. Ancient records refer to Iselhampsted-Cheyne, a relatively small medieval manor home built by Sir Thomas, but all traces of this estate have long since vanished.

The handsome Tudor manor home of Chenies Manor was built by Sir John Cheyne in 1460. The manor's unusual fortified tower bears testimony to the sensitive role Cheyne played as a key advisor to Edward IV at the height of the Wars of the Roses. The estate passed through the will of Lady Agnes Cheyne to the Sapcotes in 1494 and by marriage to the Russells, future earls of Bedford. The first earl, Sir John Russell, ex-panded the house in the 1560s, and if his signature chimneys remind you of Hampton Court, that's no coincidence. The same group of master builders lent their talents to both residences.

☞ **Did you know?**

Elizabeth so enjoyed her visits to Chenies Manor that she chose to hold court there in 1592. Her fondness for the estate must have been sorely taxed in 1602, when its owner the Earl of Bedford joined the notorious Essex rebellion, aimed at dethroning the queen.

The interior of Chenies Manor offers a charming and in-structive glimpse of the evolution of design and furnishings during the Tudor era and beyond. Each room has a different theme. Naturally, we are partial to Queen Elizabeth's Room, with its oak floors, carved furnishings and glorious tapestries.

Glorianna herself was a frequent guest at Chenies Manor, extending her visit in 1570 for a full month.

There are several unexpected treats at the manor, including a 13th-century undercroft, secret chambers and hiding places and an underground tunnel that leads to the woods (*the better for randy residents to meet their illicit paramours, perhaps?*). The gardens, too, are worth a look about. You'll find a sunken Tudor garden, a spectacular all-white garden, a physic garden full of apothecary herbs and two mazes.

Ghost Alert!

"*Cur-thump, cur-thump, cur-thump.*" What is that dreadful sound that numerous visitors to Chenies Manor claim to hear? Many believe it is the cuckolded Henry VIII, ulcerated and overweight, limping toward the Chenies bedchamber, where his fifth wife, saucy Catherine Howard, was enjoying an adulterous romp with Thomas Culpeper.

While you're in Chenies . . .

The Bedford Chapel
St. Michael's Church
Chenies

>>>

PHONE
01494-762223 or 762888

LOCATED
Immediately next door to Chenies Manor

OPEN
St. Michael's Church is open on a very limited basis; phone ahead for the schedule.
The Bedford Chapel is not open to the public, but is partially visible from inside the church.

ADMISSION
Donation suggested
>>>

We cannot tell you how disappointed we were that the important Bedford Chapel is not open to the public. True, if you're lucky enough to find St. Michael's Church open, you can peer through the windows and grating that divide the church from the chapel . . . but, believe us, it's just not the same as seeing this spectacular monument firsthand.

The Bedford Chapel, built in 1556, has been described as one of the richest collection of funeral memorials in England. It is here that the earliest earls of Bedford, the Russells, and many of their successive heirs are laid to rest. With its hammerbeam roof, resplendent with the colorful Bedford banners, and its evocative array of carved alabaster and marble effigies, the chapel begs to be explored. Luckily, a plaque just outside the chapel window helps you distinguish who's who in this noble mausoleum.

The oldest tomb in the chapel is that of the Russells' ancestor and earliest occupant of Chenies Manor, Sir John Cheyne. The loyal Yorkist knight is portrayed in chain mail, side by side with his wife. Their unfinished tomb gives the eerie impression that the Cheynes are rising like specters from the grave. At the far east end of the chapel, you'll spy the tomb of Sir John Russell (1486–1555), first earl of Bedford, and his wife, the heiress Anne Sapcotes. Sir John led a distinguished political career that spanned the reigns of Henry VII, Henry VIII, Edward VI and Mary Tudor. Sir John's daughter Anne (d. 1604), wife of the Earl of Warwick, lies on the north side of the altar. The memorials surrounding her, by and large, postdate our era, but they are striking, nonetheless. Just south of the altar, you can barely make out the tomb of the fourth earl (1593–1641), his wife and their infant. At the foot of the altar itself lies Francis Russell, second Bedford earl (1527–1585).

As for the church of St. Michael's . . . well, it's not its fault the Bedford Chapel is off limits. The architecture is almost completely 19th century, although there was a much earlier church on the site. A Norman baptismal font dates from this ancient incarnation. As long as you're here, you may want to take a look at the brasses and inscriptions that line the walls; many are from the late 1400s–early 1500s. Of particular interest is the tribute to Agnes (d. 1494), widow of Sir John Cheyne. Apparently, Agnes's remarriage kept her separated from her first husband's Bedford Chapel tomb.

∼

While you're in the area . . .

Amersham Museum

49 High Street
Amersham

≫≫

PHONE
01494-793700 or 725754

LOCATED
Off the A413 in Amersham

OPEN
2:00–4:30 p.m. Saturday, Sunday and Bank Holiday Mondays, April–October
2:00–4:30 p.m. Wednesday, Saturday, Sunday and Bank Holiday Mondays, June–September
The museum is closed November–March

ADMISSION
£1.00 Adults
Children admitted free of charge

TIP!
Amersham is a delightful town with many ancient buildings, most of which are privately held. The museum offers walking tours of the old sector, peppered with historical insights—and tall tales, galore! Call the museum in advance for an updated schedule.

≫≫

This fascinating museum offers a wealth of engaging vignettes about Amersham's ancient past. Much of the museum is housed in a 15th-century half-timbered house and visitors will find its architectural highlights helpfully called to their attention. A collection of locally crafted medieval floor tiles, a detailed history of the 14th-century Shardeloes manor home and a display on the art of Amersham lace are of interest. We were particularly moved by the story of Amersham's Lollard martyrs. Followers of John Wycliff, these local "heretics" were burned at the stake in the 16th century. Their story is depicted in a handsome panel of illuminated glass.

* *

☞ Did you know?

In 1200, King John granted Amersham a charter permitting the residents to hold an annual market and fair, a tradition that continues to this day.

* *

◇ ◇

THE HILLFORTS OF BUCKINGHAMSHIRE AND SOME ALL-BUT-LOST MOTTE-AND-BAILEYS ...

We've never found them particularly interesting, but many people are greatly drawn to England's very ancient (*we're talking BCE in some cases!*) hillforts. If you're one of those military strategists who can't stand the thought of leaving a fortress unvisited, you're in luck! Buckinghamshire is peppered with an unusual number of these early defensive structures. Let us steer you in the right direction.

~ Boddington Hillfort
Wendover
You'll find a single rampart standing, constructed of chalk, flint and earth.

~ Bulstrode Fort
Gerrards Cross
This particularly large fort offers double ramparts for your touring pleasure.

~ Cholesbury Fort
Cholesbury
Oddly enough, this ancient fort surrounds the local church.

~ Ivinghoe Beacon
Ashridge
Dating from at least 700 BCE, this is surely one of England's oldest fortifications. All that remains are traces of round and rectangular huts—but the views are special!

~ Pulpit Hill
Princes Risborough
Can't tell you much about this one.

~ West Wycombe Hillfort
West Wycombe
Very unusual: the parish church was built within the ramparts of this small, round fort.

In addition to the hillforts, there are a handful of "blink-and-you'll-miss-'em" motte-and-bailey structures where you can muck about to your heart's content. One or two, we admit, have pretty interesting history. We haven't visited them all, but we didn't want to be accused of *overlooking* them . . .

~ Bolbec Castle
Whitchurch
Naughty, naughty! The builder of this castle, one Hugh de Bolbec, constructed his motte-and-bailey structure illegally in 1147 — and garnered a nasty smack on the wrist from the Pope in return. The castle was allowed to stand, however, and during the reign of Henry II passed into the hands of the de Vere family, better known as the earls of Oxford. The castle was eventually rebuilt in stone, but was not strong enough to withstand the punishing Parliamentary forces during the 16th-century Civil War. None of the masonry remains.

~ Castlethorpe (a.k.a. Hanslope Castle)
Castlethorpe
Hard by the River Tove are the earthwork remains of an early Norman castle. This is another unusual instance of the castle walls once enclosing the parish church. During the reign of King John, the castle was owned by one of the Magna Carta barons Robert Maudit. John, as he was wont to do, destroyed the castle in retaliation for Maudit's rebellion. Castlethorpe did not remain ruinous for long; William de Beauchamp rebuilt it in 1292. By and large, what you'll see at Castlethorpe are the earthworks from the later structure.

~ Lavendon
Lavendon
No bailey, alas, but three mottes for you to climb.

~ Wycombe Castle
Castle Hill, High Wycombe
The 18th-century folly that caps this Norman motte makes it rather distinctive.

◇◇

✝ Boarstall Tower
Boarstall

≫≫

PHONE
01884-237488 or 239339

LOCATED
Off the B4011, 2 miles west of Brill, between Bicester and Thame

OPEN
2:00–6:00 p.m. Wednesdays and Bank Holiday Mondays, April–October
Saturday showings available by prior appointment with the tenant

Note: The only way to visit Boarstall Tower is on a tour led by the tenant.

ADMISSION
£2.10 Adults
£1.05 Children
≫≫

Sad to think that these are the only *significant* castle remains in Buckinghamshire, but that's the long and the short of it. Boarstall Tower is exactly that: a tower built in 1312 to serve as the gatehouse for John de Haudlo's fortified manor home. Although there were substantial alterations in both the 16th and 17th centuries, you can still appreciate the medieval belfry, crenelation and crossloops used by archers defending the property. Inside the tower, a number of rooms maintain their 14th-century flavor.

⊥ Buckingham

>>

PHONE

01280-823028 (Tourist Information Centre)

LOCATED

Off the M1 and M40, on the A432 in the heart of the Aylesbury Vale.
The Tourist Information Centre is in the Old Gaol Museum.

TRAVEL

Trains depart Euston Station for Milton Keynes Central. From
there, you can catch an express bus to Buckingham. Travel time is
approximately 1½ hours.

>>

Although Buckingham is possibly much older, its first official
reference dates from 914. That year, the *Anglo-Saxon Chronicles* tell us, Edward the Elder stationed his troops on what is now
Castle Hill, in preparation for an attack on the invading Danish
army. By the time of the Norman Conquest, Buckingham
was a royal borough, boasting
a mint, two mills, a wealthy
church and no fewer than 53
burgesses making certain that
the civic wheels were churning
smoothly. Castle Hill would continue its tradition of defense.
In 1071, a Norman castle was erected on the site by the Conqueror's crony Walter Giffard, the first earl of Buckingham. Although the estate wasn't significant enough for the well-heeled
Giffard to actually take up residence, it provided perfectly adequate lodging for one of its earliest "guests": the Crown's prisoner Hereward the Wake.

> ◆◆◆◆◆◆◆◆◆◆◆◆◆◆◆◆◆◆◆◆◆◆◆◆
>
> 🖙 Did you know?
>
> Translated from the Anglo-Saxon, the
> name Buckingham means "meadow
> of Bucca's people." (*Three points for
> anyone who can tell us who the heck
> Bucca was!*)
>
> ◆◆◆◆◆◆◆◆◆◆◆◆◆◆◆◆◆◆◆◆◆◆◆◆

Eventually, the manor of Buckingham passed through marriage into the hands of the de Braose family. Like the Giffards,
the de Braoses were absentee landlords. They made several attempts to position Buckingham as a viable market town, but
lack of convenient transport and navigable waters resulted in
lackluster success. Records show that by 1305, the castle was in

shambles and the shire assizes (courts) had moved to more viable Buckinghamshire locations, such as Newport Pagnell and Aylesbury. Buckingham had lost whatever hope it may have held for being the county's primary town. Both the famine of 1316 and the Black Death of 1349 hit Buckingham particularly hard. By the turn of the 14th century, fewer people lived in the vicinity than had during the Roman era.

In the 15th century, the tide began to turn for Buckingham. A host of ambitious, civic-minded landowners replaced the absentee gentry, gradually rebuilding the town on income generated from crafting local clay into Buckingham brick. Buckingham Castle's prominence resurfaced when it passed to Humphrey Stafford, first duke of Buckingham in the early 1400s. Unfortunately, the Staffords' tenancy was relatively short-lived. In 1521, the third duke, Edward Stafford, was convicted of treason and the estate reverted to the Crown. However, royal disfavor did not frown upon Buckingham for long. The pro-Catholic town made the brilliant move of being one of the first English towns to proclaim Mary Tudor "Queen of England." She, in turn, conferred a royal charter upon Buckingham, confirming its rights and making its incorporation official.

Perhaps Mary's charter was just the boost Buckingham needed to fulfill its highest potential. During the reign of Elizabeth, tanning, bell casting and lace making joined the local brick works as major industries, increasing the town's prosperity—and population—significantly. (*We're talking the "Tudor-Era Award for Urban Economic Development" here!*) Prosperity and expansion continued until 1725, when a devastating fire destroyed a major portion of the town. More than a third of Buckingham's residents were left homeless, and all but a smattering of the town's medieval and Tudor buildings were reduced to ash. In 1777, the ruins of the castle were carted away and its motte leveled to make way for a new parish church. All that remains of ancient Buckingham is the Buckingham Chantry Chapel.

HEREWARD THE WAKE (D. 1071)

If history had to choose a great-great-grandfather for Robin Hood, Hereward the Wake would be a likely candidate. Noble by birth, outlaw by choice, Hereward was ousted from his Lincolnshire estates by order of Edward the Confessor who concurred with the verdict reached by Hereward's own father — "This boy's up to no good!" (*or ancient words to that effect*). Just what the renegade blue blood did to create such a nasty reputation in his youth is lost to time. However, the record does show that when his lands were divvied up among the Norman carpetbaggers after the Conquest, Hereward sought revenge. Raising a band of disaffected rebels and anti-Norman patriots, Hereward launched a series of hit-and-run attacks on the new French gentry, eventually joining forces with the Danish invasion of Ely in 1070. Eluding his captors after this escapade, he led his gang on a raid of Peterborough Abbey when the abbot refused to restore a portion of Hereward's confiscated estate. Captured and held briefly at Buckingham Castle, Hereward once again managed to escape. He eventually made an uneasy peace with the Conqueror, but was murdered shortly thereafter by a Norman squatter reluctant to relinquish any of Hereward's lands (*a heck of way to settle a property dispute!*).

"Cruel in act, severe in play" is the *Peterborough Chronicle*'s bottom line on Hereward. His countrymen saw him a bit differently. Appealing to deep-seated anti-French sentiment, Hereward soon became a posthumous celebrity. Legends were told about him, ballads paid tribute to him, children were named for him. By the 12th century, his "resistance" had been romanticized, his banditry turned to patriotism and Hereward's original sin, all but forgotten.

Buckingham Chantry Chapel
Market Hill
Buckingham

PHONE

01494-528051

OPEN

Daily year-round, by written appointment only:
  Buckingham Heritage Trust
  c/o Old Gaol Museum
  Market Hill, Buckingham MK18 1JX
Phone: 01280-823020

ADMISSION
Free of charge

TIP!

Every Saturday, the Buckingham Chantry Chapel is home to the
Buckingham Women's Institute Market. This is a great way to see
the chapel and stock up on some locally produced goodies as well!
The hours are 8:00 a.m.–1:00 p.m. — prior booking not needed.

>>>

Avid supporters of both Katherine of Aragon and her daughter,
Mary Tudor, the citizens of Buckingham were thoroughly dis-
gusted with the Reformation and the changes it wrought.

• •

☞ **Did you know?**

Katherine of Aragon was held in great
regard by the citizens of Buckingham
and vice versa. The queen was the
guest of her friends the Fowlers in
1513. It was during her visit that Katherine introduced the ladies of the
town to the Spanish art of tatting,
which would eventually become a
Buckingham cottage industry. To this
day, Buckingham lace is considered
among England's finest.

• •

Perhaps they should have
considered themselves lucky.
Rather than reducing the Buckingham Chantry Chapel to
rubble (the fate of so many
religious establishments in
the 16th century), Edward VI
ordered that the building be
converted into the Royal Latin
School, a role it played until
1907.

Today, the chapel is the only
medieval building still standing in Buckingham. Dating from
the 12th century, it sports the usual array of telltale Norman details and a smattering of medieval touches, somehow more
compelling because of their rarity in this town.

◆ ◆

ST. RUMBOLD, RELIGIOUS PRODIGY

What will this child turn out to be?
—Luke 1:66

Whatever baby Rumbold's parents were expecting, we bet they hadn't bargained for an infant saint—and a precocious, preaching infant saint at
that. Legend tells us that Rumbold was born in the mid-7th century into the
royal family of the kingdom of Mercia. His mother was Christian, his father pa-

gan . . . but little Rumbold made it clear from the start that he had inherited his mamma's faith, declaring, "I am Christian," when he was just three hours old.

Rumbold died three days later, having in that remarkably brief time quoted Scripture, asked for (and received) the sacraments and preached his first sermon. (*In a play group with baby Jesus, Rumbold would have shone as the prototypical alpha-kid!*) Born in Banbury, buried in King's Sutton, Rumbold's relics were later transferred to Buckingham, a town that continues to honor his memory through churches, street names and the continual retelling of his incredible feats.

❖❖

〰

While you're in Buckingham . . .

Old Gaol Museum
Market Hill
Buckingham

>>

PHONE
01280-823020

OPEN
10:00 a.m.–4:00 p.m. Monday–Saturday, year-round

ADMISSION
£1.50 Adults
£1.00 Children
£1.00 Seniors

CONVENIENCES
Gift shop, bookstore

TIP!
The museum doubles as Buckingham's Tourist Information Centre.

>>

Although the building itself is not ancient, the Old Gaol Museum should be included on your list for the many interesting artifacts it displays from "our" era. Thematic rooms span medieval and Tudor times (and beyond). Of particular note is a lovely carved crucifix that once belonged to Katherine of Aragon.

ANCIENT INNS AND EATERIES

~ The Royal Oak Inn
Wingrave Road
Aston Abbots
01296-681262

This 500-year-old thatched-roof pub features open fireplaces and a beamed ceiling.

~ The Lowndes Arms
4 High Street
Whaddon, near Milton Keynes
01908-510706

A 16th-century restaurant with beamed bars and an outdoor terrace.

~ Hickwell House
Botyl Road
Botolph Claydon
01296-712217

Thatched late-Tudor residence, now a B&B with handsome gardens.

~ Dinton Cottage
Dinton, near Aylesbury
01296-748270

Quaint thatched-roof cottage offering B&B.

~ The Oak
119 Green End Street
Aston Clinton, near Aylesbury
01296-630466

Romantic thatched-roof restaurant serving gourmet food.

~ The King's Head

Market Square
Aylesbury
01296-718812

Although you can get a meal or a drink at the King's Head, the *real* reason to visit is to tour the ancient building. (*See our entry earlier in this chapter for details.*)

CONTENTS

TRIP 2

Northamptonshire

Convicts and Convictions

he religious strife that rocked England during the Tudor era left an indelible mark on the country's domestic landscape as well as on the grounds of leveled churches and ruined monasteries. Families, both royal and common, were ripped asunder and private residences became refuges of asylum—or virtual prisons—depending upon the religious convictions of their owners. In a few remarkable cases, architecture itself took on a theological spin, with the builder's theology symbolized in the very bricks and mortar of his home. As you tour Northamptonshire's many attractions, you'll be reminded repeatedly of the seismic effects of the Reformation and its aftershocks. (Of course, conflicts between the Church and Crown were not unique to the Tudors; Henry II and Thomas à Becket set the stage for their famous fallout in the halls of Northampton Castle!) From the ruins of Fotheringhay, where the captive Catholic Mary, Queen of Scots lost her life to her Protestant "protectors," to the highly symbolic Rushton Triangular Lodge—homage to the

• •

☞ Did you know?

Talk about "lost treasures"! Although 47 castles once dotted the Northamptonshire landscape, little lives on of these once mighty fortresses, with the exception of Rockingham. Small portions of medieval buildings have been subsumed by palatial 17th- and 18th-century manors—interesting to visit, but having little or no trace of their ancient heritage, except in name.

• •

Holy Trinity—the convictions of Northamptonshire's ancient residents continue to resound. The scenery is inspiring . . . the stories woven into it are no less so.

✺

✝ Astwell Castle Ruins
Astwell—Privately Owned

>>

Although Astwell Castle is privately owned and not open for public touring, it has an interesting history worth sharing. At the time of the Norman Conquest, Astwell was owned by Saxon brothers Leofric and Alfric. The specifics of how they came to lose their estates are no longer known; however, by the time the *Domesday Book* was compiled, Astwell was in the firm grasp of two *Norman* brothers, recorded simply as "Geoffrey and Robert" (*we couldn't help but wonder if the Saxon brothers were wily enough to change their names in an attempt to placate the Conqueror's new regime*).

In 1471, Astwell's owner, one William Broke, sold the property to Sir Thomas Lovett, Lord High Sheriff under Edward IV. It is worth noting that Sir Thomas had among his descendants two latter-day Sir Thomas Lovetts, both of whom also held the position of Lord High Sheriff, the first under Henry VII and the second under Elizabeth I. The last Sir Thomas died in 1586—but not before "depopulating" the village of Astwell in order to create a deer park worthy of the royal hunt. Upon his death, Astwell Castle passed through marriage to the Shirley family.

In 1606, the Astwell estate was totally rebuilt; most of the medieval castle was pulled down to make way for a sprawling manor home. All that remains of Astwell Castle is the fortified gate tower, built by Edward IV's pro-Yorkist courtier during the Wars of the Roses.

✝ Canons Ashby
Canons Ashby
Daventry

>>

PHONE
01327-860044

E-MAIL
ecaxxx@smtp.ntrust.org.uk

LOCATED
Approximately 13 miles southwest of Northampton, off the B4525.
As an alternative, take the M40, junction 11, or the M1, junction 16,
then follow the signs from the A5.

OPEN
House
1:00–5:00 p.m. Saturday–Wednesday and Bank Holiday Mondays,
April–November
Church
Noon–5:00 p.m. Saturday–Wednesday and Bank Holiday
Mondays, April–October
Noon–4:30 p.m. Saturday–Wednesday and Bank Holiday
Mondays, November–March
Closed Thursday and Friday

ADMISSION
£5.00 Adults
£2.50 Children
Family ticket available

CONVENIENCES
Tearoom; gift shop

>>

We just *love* "twofers" and Canons Ashby is no exception! In
one short but fascinating visit, you can tour a handsome Elizabethan manor home *and* a medieval priory church, both nestled in a beautiful 70-acre park.

Canons Ashby was the home of the Dryden family for nearly
500 years, before the National Trust took ownership several
years ago. Built by John Dryden in 1550, the manor was expanded in the 1590s. Although there are later alterations,

• • • • • • • • • • • • • • • • • • •

 Did you know?

Canons Ashby has associations with two great English poets. John Dryden, Poet Laureate in the 1650s, frequently visited his cousins at the manor. More relevant to our era, Edmund Spenser (1552–1599), author of *The Faerie Queen*, was an Oxford classmate and close friend of Sir Erasmus Dryden. Spencer visited Canons Ashby on several occasions—which makes every bit of sense: his mistress, Rosalind, was a Dryden relation.

• • • • • • • • • • • • • • • • • • • •

much of the original detailing remains to be seen, including the cobbled interior courtyard, leaded windows and some truly impressive Elizabethan wall paintings.

Stroll through the lovely Canons Ashby gardens and you'll reach the glorious medieval church, all that remains of the 13th-century Augustinian priory from which the property takes its name. One of the few privately owned churches in England, Canons Ashby has been lovingly maintained through the years.

✝ Castle Ashby

Castle Ashby
Northampton

>>

PHONE
  01604-696696

LOCATED
  Off the A428 between Northampton and Bedford

OPEN
  Castle Ashby is only open for private events, such as weddings. Rental rates are available upon request; please telephone the number above.

>>

It's no secret that Elizabeth I was partial to luxury. She traveled frequently and in high style, expecting to be entertained lavishly and accommodated graciously by the hosts and hostesses lucky enough to welcome her into their homes. The opulent remodeling of Castle Ashby was begun in 1574 by Henry, Lord Compton, whose overarching goal was to create an environment worthy of hosting his queen. Work was completed in 1600; Elizabeth and her entourage promptly descended upon the Compton household. Gazing upon the manor home today, one can only assume she was suitably impressed!

The history of Castle Ashby predates the reign of Elizabeth by 500 years. The first castle was built in the 11th century on land given by William the Conqueror to his niece Judith in honor of her wedding to Waltheof, Earl of Northampton and Huntingdon. Rather than live at Castle Ashby, the newlyweds chose to lease the castle to Hugh of Ashby. Descendants of Sir Hugh held the castle until 1300, ultimately selling it to Langton, Bishop of Coventry, whose license to crenulate — or "embattle" — the castle was granted by Edward I.

In 1512, Sir William Compton purchased Castle Ashby and promptly dismantled it. Reconstruction did not begin until his son Henry felt the burning desire to impress Good Queen Bess. The castle is still owned by Sir William's descendants. With its 26 spectacular bedrooms and beautifully tended gardens, Castle Ashby is a favorite venue for special events such as weddings and board retreats. Unfortunately, the only way you'll see the castle is to be a guest at — or the host of — one of these grand occasions.

ᴧᴧ

┼ Northampton

>>

PHONE
  01604-622677 (Tourist Information Centre)

LOCATED
  Take the M1 to junction 15, 15a or 16

TRAVEL
  Trains depart London's Euston Station on a regular basis; travel time is about 1 hour.

>>

Very little of Northampton's ancient past remains for you to explore today. Still, it seems a shame to have an entire chapter, entitled *Northamptonshire*, and ignore the county seat entirely.

So here's what you'll want to nose out. One of the three remaining original **Eleanor Crosses** is in the city of Northampton on the A508. Also of interest is the **Church of the Holy Sepulchre**. Located in the center of town, this is one of four round churches remaining in England. It was built by crusaders in 1100 as a replica of the shrine of the Holy Sepulchre in Jerusalem. Unfortunately, the open hours are erratic. Phone 01604-754782 for a current schedule.

Tip!

We'll let you in on a little secret: we're both absolutely ga-ga about shoes. Painstaking as our research *always* is, we pride ourselves on poking around ruins and rubble without ever . . . well, *hardly* ever . . . resorting to "sensible" footwear. Imagine our giddy delight when we discovered that the **Northampton Central Museum & Art Gallery** is primarily a "Shoe Zoo"! Yessiree, an entire museum devoted almost entirely to trotter accoutrements. Two new galleries, *Followers of Fashion Shoe* (*that would be us!*) and *Life and Sole*, feature a dizzying array of pumps, slides, mules, boots. Hey—any museum whose logo is a hot pink sequined stiletto with a peek-a-boo toe is worth a peek. It's enough to make us forget about ancient history . . . for a moment or two. (*On a redeeming note, the museum is located on "Guildhall Road," former site of the medieval civic seat. So much for frippery!*)

〰

A lost treasure . . .
✝ Northampton Castle

≫≫≫

Like the vast majority of Northamptonshire's castles, the fortress that bears the county's name has long since vanished. In its heyday, however, Northampton Castle was one of the Crown's preeminent strongholds, and as such, it suffered no lack of historical drama.

Long before it sported a castle, Northampton played an important role in the politics of England, serving as an administrative center for the Danes. The town was reclaimed for the English throne by King Edward the Elder, son of Alfred the Great, in 913. On the heels of the Norman Conquest, William the Bastard wasted no time in seizing control of the region, erecting a comparatively crude motte-and-bailey structure that was rebuilt in much grander style by Simon de Senlis in 1100.

Perhaps Senlis came to feel that he had been just a bit too grand for his own good; the castle's commanding size and exceptionally thick curtain walls made it all too attractive (*or threatening*) to the Crown. The castle was seized by Henry I and became not only a pivotal command post but a favored royal residence of every subsequent king, through Richard II. Northampton Castle was the scene of the emotionally fraught trial of Thomas à Becket in 1164 and, at various times during the Plantagenet era, served as the seat of Parliament. In fact, during King John's reign, Northampton served as a virtual backup English capital, second only to London.

The presence of the monarch did not keep Northampton — nor its castle — from attracting popular dissent. If anything, the town seems to have been a rallying point for the contrary and the disgruntled. In April 1215, during the tense negotiations surrounding Magna Carta, armed baronial forces descended upon Northampton to continue their "discussions" with the implacable John. John never showed up at the Northampton bargaining table; he had fortified the castle well and was confident that his presence would not be needed to keep the unruly barons in hand. In fact, the barons failed to take the town, but their anger over John's Northampton effrontery was the final straw; by May, the rebels had broken their allegiance to the king and civil war ensued.

◆◆◆◆◆◆◆◆◆◆◆◆◆◆◆◆◆◆◆◆◆◆◆
☞ Did you know?
Don't go getting all excited when you hear that Northampton has a cathedral. Lovely as it is, Northampton Cathedral was built in the 19th century. Sorry.
◆◆◆◆◆◆◆◆◆◆◆◆◆◆◆◆◆◆◆◆◆◆◆

Another baronial uprising roiled at Northampton during the reign of John's son, Henry III. The leader of the opposition was Simon de Montfort, who as earl of Leicester enjoyed strong support in this area of the east midlands. De Montfort rallied local troops in 1264 and, on April 6, these troops, led by de Montfort's son, confronted the royalist forces at Northampton. Again, the Crown had done a fine job of fortifying the castle. The rebel barons were defeated by Henry's troops—but only temporarily. Just six weeks later, de Montfort went on to lead the disaffected nobles in a stunning victory at the Battle of Lewes.

Hard hit by the plague and a downturn in the local economy, Northampton began to recede in prominence by the late 14th century. Its decline in stature did not spare the town from experiencing further political bloodshed, however. Just beyond the castle walls, one of the most important confrontations in the Wars of the Roses, the Battle of Northampton, ended in an unqualified Yorkist victory on July 10, 1460. Two of the leading Lancastrian supporters, the duke of Buckingham and the earl of Shrewsbury, were killed in the battle. King Henry VI was captured in the fray by the future Edward IV and was briefly imprisoned in the Crown's own castle of Northampton, before being moved to the Bishop of London's palace in the capital city.

The ensuing years were ones of abject neglect for Northampton Castle. Although it remained a property of the Crown,

---

☛ Did you know?

Passions ran deep during the Wars of the Roses and they weren't always stirred by the "York versus Lancaster" debate. One of Henry VI's erstwhile supporters, Sir William Lucy, lived close enough to the Northampton battlefield to hear the melee. To his merit, Lucy hastened to the aid of his king. What awaited him was more than he could have foreseen. For some time, his wife had been carrying on an adulterous affair with Sir John Stafford, kin of the duke of Buckingham and himself an ardent supporter of the king. The fact that both men were ostensibly fighting on behalf of the Lancastrians did not prevent Stafford from seizing the opportunity to kill his lover's husband. (*We can't help but wonder how Mrs. Lucy reacted to that news . . .*)

the castle's useful purpose seems to have been spent; it was destroyed by Oliver Cromwell during the 17th-century Civil War. Only the postern gate, now on private property, remains of this once-mighty Norman fortress.

◇ ◇

TURNABOUT IS UNFAIR PLAY:
BECKET AND HENRY AT ODDS

Perhaps the most infamous event to center upon Northampton Castle was the tension-filled trial of the Archbishop of Canterbury in 1164. To fully understand the stunning implications of the trial, one needs to look at the complex history of the relationship between prosecutor and defendant: Henry II vs. Thomas à Becket.

Thomas à Becket was born in London's Cheapside in 1118. Although his family was far from impoverished, Thomas seems to have spent an inordinate amount of time, energy and money trying to overcome the stigma of "common" birth. His father was a wealthy merchant and onetime Sheriff of London. His mother, Matilda, was a devout Catholic, who no doubt instilled in Thomas the religious convictions that would influence the later years of his career. Even when you consider his somewhat privileged upbringing, Thomas was exceptionally well educated, first at Merton College in Oxford and then in the leading schools of Paris. He returned to England in 1140 and, at the age of 22, hooked up with his first professional mentor, Theobald, Archbishop of Canterbury. Under Theobald's guidance, Becket studied both canon and civil law before being promoted to Archdeacon of Canterbury. His strong administrative skills and overarching interest in politics prompted Theobald to recommend Becket, in 1154, to the newly crowned King of England, young Henry of Anjou.

♦ ♦

☞ Did you know?

To Henry, Thomas à Becket may have seemed the ideal choice to be Archbishop of Canterbury. Yes, there was the small problem that Thomas was merely a clerk in the minor orders: he was hurriedly ordained a priest on June 2, consecrated as a bishop on June 3 and enthroned as archbishop just after lunch the same day. Once Henry II wanted something done, waiting was never an option!

♦ ♦

Henry II and Thomas à Becket struck up a remarkable friendship, based on trust, mutual respect and a common *joie de vivre*. Both were primary personalities: strong, decisive and passionate, with a shared zest for living "fine and fast." It must have appeared to be a match made, if not in heaven, at least in the most blessed of earthly realms. Henry himself considered Thomas, now Lord Chancellor of England, to be "closer than a brother" . . . perhaps in that context what ensued between the two could be deemed "Major Sibling Rivalry."

In 1162, Henry appointed Thomas to succeed his mentor Theobald as Archbishop of Canterbury. Henry's fondest hope was that Thomas would assist in extending the Crown's authority over the Church, specifically on issues of taxation and disposal of Church property and the right to try errant clerics in secular court. Surprisingly, Becket—largely seen as Henry's "yes-man" until now—had a sudden change of heart. Taking his duties (or his newfound powers) as archbishop more seriously than anyone would have guessed, Becket adopted an immovable stand in favor of an autonomous, independent Church—protected, but never interfered with, by the monarch.

Needless to say, Henry—who was equally implacable in his zeal to reform England's archaic legal system—was bitterly disappointed. In true Plantagenet style, rage followed closely on sorrow's heels. Two years of bitter dispute and acrimonious debate ensued, souring the closest of friendships and breeding the bitterest of rivalries. Henry was determined to make Thomas pay for his disloyalty, and the opportunity presented itself in October 1164. Ostensibly a citation for Thomas's refusal to swear allegiance to the "Constitutions of Clarendon," Henry demanded that Becket appear before the king's council at Northampton Castle . . . then used the opportunity to levy a laundry list of serious allegations against the archbishop. Declaring that Becket was still a feudal vassal of the Crown, the king demanded all of Thomas's financial accounts, then proposed staggering penalties as retribution for Becket's "misdeeds."

♦ ♦

☞ Did you know?

During his early career, Thomas was a bit embarrassed by his surname, thinking it didn't have quite the noble ring. He referred to himself as "Thomas of London." Once he became the Archbishop of Canterbury, tacking "London" onto his name made less sense. It was at this stage that he added the conceit of "à" to his name, becoming known as—despite the knowing smirks of his detractors —Thomas à Becket. (Perhaps if he'd foreseen his future title of "Saint," he would have been a tad less defensive!)

♦ ♦ ♦ ♦ ♦ ♦ ♦ ♦ ♦ ♦ ♦ ♦ ♦ ♦ ♦ ♦ ♦ ♦ ♦ ♦

Support for Thomas dwindled dramatically throughout the three-day trial; the temperature of the king was apparent to all who observed the proceedings, and neither churchman nor noble dared risk royal displeasure by falling on the wrong side of the debate. With no persuasive advocates, insufficient funds to pay the king's fines and too much pride to throw himself on Henry's mercy, Thomas fled Northampton in disguise, without waiting for the council's final judgment. Becket eventually made his way to France and lived the next six years in self-imposed exile.

By 1170, a tenuous peace was fostered between the adversaries and Becket cautiously returned to Canterbury, amid great fanfare from the citizens of Kent.

Then he rather *incautiously* excommunicated a handful of Henry's closest allies, including the Archbishop of York. For Henry, that was the last straw. Never one to mince words, the infuriated king ranted, "Will no one rid me of this turbulent priest?" Unfortunately for all involved, four knights took him at his word. On December 29, 1170, they entered Canterbury Cathedral and murdered the archbishop on consecrated ground in the nave. Within hours, throngs of mourners braved a sudden and violent thunderstorm to flock to the cathedral and pay their final respects. Two days later, the first of the "Thomas" miracles occurred—a mere three years after his assassination, Becket was canonized.

Henry's "Thomas Troubles" were far from over. No sooner was Becket's death announced than waves of protest rose against the king. In July 1174, Henry attempted to make amends: he donned a hair shirt and walked barefoot through the streets of Canterbury, was flogged by monks and processed on his knees down the cathedral aisles to the shrine of St. Thomas. There he publicly begged forgiveness and prayed that his former boon companion would intercede with the Almighty on the king's behalf. The furor abated after this act of contrition, but Henry II went to his grave tainted by the scandalous end to this most unusual political and personal entanglement.

◇ ◇

✝ Holdenby House
Holdenby

>>

PHONE
01604-770074

LOCATED
Off the A428 and the A5199, 7 miles northwest of Northampton

OPEN
1:00–5:00 p.m. Sunday, April–September
1:00–5:00 p.m. Sunday–Friday, July and August
Closed Saturday

Note: The house at Holdenby is very rarely open, except by prior appointment. However, Holdenby offers the rare opportunity to observe the medieval pastime of falconry. The following information pertains to the combined falconry demonstrations and garden tours.

ADMISSION
Falconry and Gardens
   £3.00 Adults
   £1.75 Children
   £2.50 Seniors

House
£5.00 Adults
£3.00 Children
£4.50 Seniors

>>>

Unless you happen to be lucky in your planning, it's very rare that you'll have the chance to observe the ancient sport of falconry. If you have never seen these magnificent birds of prey in action, plan to visit Holdenby. (*Although we've been known to wear our share of feather boas, we're not overly fond of birds . . . but we found the falconry demonstration thrilling.*)

Holdenby is yet another opulent mansion constructed for the express purpose of entertaining Elizabeth I in the manner to which she'd become accustomed. It was built in 1583 by one of Glorianna's favored courtiers (*a polite euphemism for an Elizabethan "Toy Boy"*) Christopher Hatton, known to history as the "Dancing Chancellor" due to the fact that he cut such a dashing figure on the dance floor. Hatton spared no expense in constructing this homage to his queen; there were 123 massive glass windows specifically dedicated to Elizabeth. Hatton took this veritable shrine so seriously that he refused to spend even one night at Holdenby until his queen made her official visit. That was unfortunate— he should have spent as much time as possible enjoying his extravagant home, for the project effectively bankrupted him. Hatton died penniless nine years

★ **Did you know?**

Holdenby is pronounced—and even sometimes spelled—"Holmby." That's another entry for the "beats-us-why" guide to Brit-speak.

★ **Did you know?**

If you're touring London, visit St. Etheldreda's Chapel at 14 Ely Place. The beautiful chapel is all that is left of Ely House, the once-magnificent London home of the bishops of Ely. One of the last ecclesiastic residences to be relinquished to the Tudor crown, the opulent Ely House became the city residence of Christopher Hatton—a man who clearly liked to live like a king and may well have aspired to become one! Today, St. Etheldreda's is distinguished as England's oldest Roman Catholic church.

later, and Holdenby passed to the Crown as collateral toward his massive debts. The manor became a palace of James I and a prison of Charles I before passing into private ownership.

The house at Holdenby is open only on rare occasions; that didn't disappoint us too much, since most of the manor home is a Victorian reconstruction, incorporating only the kitchen wing from Hatton's era. Nothing else remains of the Elizabethan structure, with the exception of two of the gatehouse towers. You will find them in a field alongside the residence as you stroll the Holdenby gardens.

Boughton House
Kettering

>>>

PHONE
01536-515731

E-MAIL
llt@boughtonhouse.org.uk

LOCATED
3 miles north of Kettering, past the junction of A43 and A14

TRAVEL
Trains depart St. Pancras Station for Kettering Station on a regular basis. Travel time is approximately 75 minutes. You will need to hire a car or taxi, however, to visit the sites in and round Kettering.

OPEN
2:00–4:00 p.m. daily, August and September

Note: In August, the state rooms are open only by prior appointment. You may phone or e-mail in advance.

ADMISSION
£6.00 Adults
£5.00 Children
£5.00 Seniors

>>>

Like so many of Henry VIII's cronies, Sir Edward Montagu, the king's Lord Chief Justice, profited tidily from the Dissolution of the Monasteries. In 1528, Montagu acquired the vast monastic estate of St. Edmundsbury Abbey. Using the monks' massive Great Hall as his centerpiece, Montagu proceeded to create one of the most lavish manor homes of the era. No fewer than seven courtyards were part of the first Boughton House. (*It's a wonder King Henry didn't snatch this palatial parcel, the way he did Wolsey's Hampton Court and Thomas Cranmer's Knole.*) An even more opulent, French-influenced expansion in 1695 earned Boughton House its reputation as the "English Versailles." Most of what you will see on your visit to Boughton House dates from this 17th-century conceit.

It's no wonder we found the monastic Great Hall to be the most interesting feature of our tour. It's a shame the original hammerbeam roof has been hidden beneath a garishly painted barrel ceiling. In fact, there is only one door that dates from Sir Edward's Tudor residence. However, displayed in the room are many beautiful portraits of luminaries from Henry's and Elizabeth's reigns, including our favorite: Glorianna herself. The late-in-life likeness dates from 1595. Along with various Montagu courtiers, you'll spot a portrait of Henry Wriothesley, fourth earl of Southampton. It is interesting to note that this painting was done while the earl languished in the Tower of London (1601–1603), where he was being held on charges of conspiracy for his role in the Essex rebellion (*posing for one's portrait is, we suppose, as good a way as any to pass time in prison*). Wriothesley was later released by Elizabeth's nephew and heir, James I.

• •

☞ Did you know?

The fourth earl of Southampton was one of Shakespeare's earliest and most generous patrons. The Bard's first two published works, *Venus and Adonis* and *The Rape of Lucretia*, are dedicated to him.

• •

While you're in the area . . .

✝ Rushton Triangular Lodge
Rushton
Kettering

>>>

PHONE
01536-710761

LOCATED
3 miles from the A6 on a back road, about 1 mile west of Rushton

OPEN
10:00 a.m.–6:00 p.m. daily, April–October

ADMISSION
£1.95 Adults
£1.00 Children
£1.30 Seniors

>>>

Hands down, this is one of the most remarkable buildings we've come across in our travels. In fact, we're hard pressed to describe it—you really do have to "see it to believe it."

As the name implies, Rushton is a triangular building. Minute (a mere 33 feet wide) and highly decorative, it was begun by Sir John Tresham in 1500. His son Sir Thomas Tresham resumed work on the Lodge in 1597, envisioning his home as an homage to the Holy Trinity. The three-walled, three-story structure sports triangular gables on all three ends and a trio of three-sided chimneys. Even the windows are—what else!—trefoil. It will take you all of, er, "three minutes" (*sorry!*) to tour the lodge, but this is one snapshot you can be certain your friends won't have in their scrapbooks!

• •
☞ **Did you know?**

You'll run across Sir Thomas Tresham and his peculiar architecture elsewhere in your Northamptonshire travels—he built the almost-as-odd (and never completed) Lyveden New Bield. A knight and an ardent Catholic, Tresham was also a frustrated (if quirky) architect. Elizabeth wasn't fond of his religious zeal—he was imprisoned for 15 years for his firebrand theology. That didn't stop him from peppering the countryside with what one brochure refers to as "the oddest collection of buildings in Britain."
• •

Ghost Alert!

Did you find yourself tapping your toes at Rushton? It must have been the merry melody of a gypsy fiddler who is said to haunt the Lodge.

~

Also while you're in the area . . .

 # Eleanor Cross at Geddington

Malting Lane at Bridge Street
Geddington
Kettering

>>>

PHONE
None

LOCATED
Off the A43 in Geddington, between Kettering and Corby

OPEN
Daylight hours daily, year-round

ADMISSION
Free of charge

>>>

When Eleanor of Castile, beloved consort of Edward I, died of a "slow fever" in 1290, her husband was bereft. The queen's remains were carried in great and solemn state from Harby, in Nottinghamshire, to their final resting place at Westminster Abbey. Numerous stops were made en route, so Eleanor's loyal subjects could pay their last respects. In 1291, King Edward commissioned a series of memorial crosses to mark each of the 12 stops made by the funeral cortege, including one at the (now vanished) royal hunting lodge at Geddington.

☞ Did you know?

Geddington was once the site of a royal residence, "Geiti's Settlement," built by Henry I in 1129. The property was a favorite Plantagenet hunting lodge before it became a more opulent palace. All that remains of the palace are its cross and the "King's door," both of which are displayed in the parish church.

Scholars tend to believe the Geddington Cross is the work of the master stone mason, "Garcia of Spain." This cross differs in significant ways from the other remaining Crosses (and from illustrations of the Crosses that were destroyed). An impressive 42 feet high, it is more richly ornamented than its counterparts—indicating that it was designed at the advent of the "decorative style," which profoundly influenced England's Middle Ages. Before you leave Geddington, wander across the square to **St. Mary Magdalene Church**. Dating from the 12th and 13th centuries, the church incorporates the decorative stonework of an earlier Saxon house of worship. There is an interesting effigy of a priest that dates from 1500, although it looks much older. You'll also want to note the bridge that runs over the pretty River Ise. It was constructed in 1250, and it's easy to imagine Eleanor's somber funeral cortege crossing this way on its way into the village.

☞ Did you know?

If you've visited London, chances are your medieval meanderings have taken you to the Eleanor Cross in the forecourt of Charing Cross Station. Unlike the cross at Geddington, the London cross is an 1863 replica, although true in both style and sentiment to the 13th-century original. In addition to Charing and Geddington, crosses were erected at Harby, Lincoln, Grantham, Stamford, Northampton, Stony Stratford, Waltham Abbey, Dunstable, St. Albans and Cheapside, London. The Victoria and Albert Museum in London has fragments of several of these crosses; only the crosses of Geddington, Northampton and Waltham in Essex remain extant.

ELEANOR OF CASTILE (C. 1244–1290)

I loved her in her lifetime . . .
I shall not cease to love her now that she is dead.
—King Edward I, upon the death of Eleanor of Castile

When you consider the highly fraught political machinations behind Eleanor's marriage to Edward I, you can't help but marvel that theirs was one of the period's great love stories. In an era when high-born women were valued first and foremost as alliance-building pawns and brood mares, theirs was a remarkable relationship: passionate, amicable, loyal, respectful, fruitful . . . and widely mourned when it ended.

The youngest daughter of Ferdinand III of Castile (pronounced "kastl") and his second wife, Jeanne of Ponthieu, Infanta Eleanor is believed to have been born in 1244. Her half-brother Alphonso X inherited his father's throne in 1252 and promptly set about adding the French territory of Gascony to his royal real estate portfolio. England's Henry III was furious and eventually went to war with Alphonso over the claim. The victorious Henry then demanded Eleanor as the bride for his son Edward—surety for Alphonso's future good behavior. Alphonso readily agreed; his only stipulation was that the marriage take place "five weeks before Michaelmas Day, 1254." The infanta had just turned 10 years old.

Eleanor of Castile and 15-year-old Prince Edward of Westminster were married at the convent church of Las Hueglas in Spain. Eleanor followed her young husband to England in 1255, where she lived under the protection and guidance of her father-in-law, Henry. Although custom would have allowed consummation of the royal marriage upon Eleanor's 14th birthday, it appears that the bride and groom did not live as "man and wife" until Eleanor was 18, or even 19 (their first child was born when she was 20). In 1263, she and Edward officially set up residence at Windsor Castle, where Eleanor remained until 1264. In June of that year, the monarchy's defeat at the hands of rebel barons during the Battle of Lewes resulted in the capture and imprisonment of King Henry and Prince Edward. Eleanor and her firstborn child fled to France, where she remained until Edward's escape and ultimate victory at the Battle of Evesham in August 1265.

The anxious days and lonely nights of that 15-month separation must have been enough to convince the couple of the depth of their love. Once reunited, the two were virtually inseparable. Eleanor left several young children behind to accompany her husband on crusade in 1270, a highly unusual act for a woman, especially one of noble birth. One child was miscarried while the couple was abroad; a year later, one of their most memorable children, Joan of Acre, was born in the eastern city of that name.

Henry III of England died on November 16, 1272. Edward, the new king of England, and his consort did not return from the Holy Land for nearly two more years. (*Apparently, the fact that Edward had been ipso facto "king" since the Battle of Evesham robbed the official title of some of its thrill.*) They landed at

◆ ◆ ◆ ◆ ◆ ◆ ◆ ◆ ◆ ◆ ◆ ◆ ◆ ◆ ◆ ◆ ◆ ◆ ◆ ◆

☞ Did you know?

Eleanor of Castile took a liberated step when she accompanied her consort on crusade. Of course, the real trendsetter—and eyebrow-raiser—in this arena was Edward's great-grandmother Eleanor of Aquitaine, who accompanied her first husband, Louis, King of France, to the Holy Land nearly 100 years before.

◆ ◆ ◆ ◆ ◆ ◆ ◆ ◆ ◆ ◆ ◆ ◆ ◆ ◆ ◆ ◆ ◆ ◆ ◆ ◆

Dover on August 2, 1274, and were crowned jointly at Westminster Abbey 17 days later.

During their 36-year marriage, Eleanor bore 16 children by Edward I; only six survived childhood, including their 14th child and the last of their four sons, the future Edward II. By the winter of 1285–86, years of continual pregnancy had begun to take their toll on Eleanor's health and she fell sick with her first episode of the mysterious fever that would recur each winter thereafter and eventually claim her life. (There is some speculation that this may have been tuberculosis; records of the time refer to her malady as a "slow fever.") Eleanor must have had some presentiment of her fate; in the years preceding her death, she commissioned drawings for her tomb and made arrangements for the Blackfriars monastery in London to receive her heart upon her death.

> **☞ Did you know?**
>
> Legend tells us that during their three-year adventure, Eleanor of Castile saved Edward's life by sucking the venom of an assassin's poisoned dagger from a wound in her husband's side.

At first, 1290 must have seemed a particularly auspicious year for the royal family. Eighteen-year-old Princess Joan of Acre was married to the preeminent Earl of Gloucester, and Edward, the 6-year-old Prince of Wales, was betrothed to 7-year-old Queen Margaret of Scotland. Following these summer festivities, the king and queen set off on an ambitious royal progress of the northern shires, despite the fact that Eleanor was still recovering from the stillbirth of their 16th child.

It was then that fate took a sudden turn for the worse. Young Margaret of Scotland died unexpectedly and her intended father-in-law, Edward I, hastened his northward pace, leaving Eleanor and her court to proceed on a reasonable timetable.

> **☞ Did you know?**
>
> Obviously, Edward I loved Eleanor of Castile deeply, but that did not prevent him from remarrying—albeit almost nine years later. On September 10, 1299, 60-year-old Edward "Longshanks" married 17-year-old Margaret of France. Margaret bore the aging king three children. Upon her death in 1317, she was buried at Greyfriars Church, London; Edward had long since been laid to rest in Westminster Abbey with his first queen and true love, Eleanor.

Sadly, the benefits of a more leisurely progress eluded the queen. It appears that by October, Eleanor's annual winter ailments were already troubling her. "Syrups" and medicines were purchased at Lincoln, where prayers for her recovery were offered at the Shrine of St. Hugh. On November 20, she was taken to the manor of Richard Weston in Harby, Nottinghamshire, about 8 miles outside of

Lincoln; her condition was grave. Edward was summoned to her deathbed, but Queen Eleanor died on the evening of November 28, with the Bishop of Lincoln—and not the king—at her side.

By all accounts, Edward was overwrought. Eleanor's body was taken to St. Catherine's priory in Lincoln and prepared for the arduous 172-mile journey back to London. Her viscera were interred in the Chapel of St. Mary at Lincoln Cathedral. The cortege bearing the rest of her remains stopped overnight 12 times en route to Eleanor's final resting place at Westminster Abbey; these 12 sites were eventually distinguished with the evocative Eleanor Crosses, commissioned in her memory by her bereft husband. The body of Eleanor of Castile was buried at the feet of her father-in-law, Henry III. True to her wishes, her heart was buried at Blackfriars in London.

◇◇

✝ Rockingham Castle
Market Harborough, near Corby

>>

PHONE
01536-770240

E-MAIL
rockinghamcastle@lineone.net

LOCATED
On the A6003, just south of the A6116, junction, 1 mile north of Corby

OPEN
1:00–5:00 p.m. Sunday and Bank Holiday Mondays, April–September
1:00–5:00 p.m. Tuesday and Thursday, July and August

Note: Special arrangements can be made for groups, year-round

ADMISSION
£5.50 Adults
£3.50 Children
£5.00 Seniors
Family ticket available

CONVENIENCES
Lunch and homemade teas; "Castle Under Siege" exhibit

>>

Although Rockingham has been the family home of the Watson clan since the 16th century, the castle was an important royal palace for nearly 500 years. Its commanding site, high atop a hill overlooking the Welland Valley, had been fortified since the Iron Age, with Roman and Saxon defenses in place well before it attracted William the Conqueror's attention. He ordered work begun on the current castle shortly after the Norman Conquest.

One can't help but wonder what strategic advantages Rockingham offered—it was not close to any major town, nor did it have an important waterway to defend. You can't argue, however, with the castle's bucolic benefits. The sprawling hunting grounds of Rockingham Forest and the glorious views of the surrounding countryside made the castle a favorite retreat for medieval monarchs and their families. Several kings visited so frequently, they left some of their personal effects behind; the castle displays King

> **Did you know?**
>
> Rockingham Castle entered the political spotlight in 1095, when the English bishops sided with William Rufus in his conflict with the Anselm, Archbishop of Canterbury. A council charged with resolving the matter was convened at Rockingham Castle. That council was one of the country's earliest recorded assemblies of state.

John's iron coffer (it once carried a significant chunk of the royal treasury) as well as a chest bearing the arms of Henry V. However, trends come and go even among the high and mighty. Edward I was the last monarch to invest time and capital on the castle's upkeep, reconfiguring the square entrance towers into the more defense-efficient curved style. By the end of Edward III's reign, Rockingham was not the popular getaway it had been for the early Plantagenets. Records

> **Did you know?**
>
> Charles Dickens was a regular visitor to Rockingham Castle. During his numerous stays there, he worked on his *Bleak House* manuscript.

show that by the 15th century, the castle was in great need of repair. Henry VIII sold it to Edward Watson in 1533; the Watson descendants live there still.

Unlike so many of England's grand houses that grew from castle origins, Rockingham retains significant vestiges of its ancient past. Although the Conqueror's motte is gone (the bailey is now the site of a rose garden), the castle's Norman walls are partially intact and the 1290 gatehouse still stands. Edward I's Great Hall serves as the core of the residence, although it is largely camouflaged behind a Tudor veneer. Other major portions of the manor home are Tudor, as well, and artifacts from all of "our" eras have been thoughtfully preserved as part of the home's decor. Among the special portraits in the Great Hall are that of Henry VIII's "favorite" wife, Jane Seymour, and one of her stepdaughter Elizabeth surrounded by her councilors Cecil, Howard and Dudley.

~

Kirby Hall

Deene
Corby

>>

PHONE
01536-203230

LOCATED
4 miles northeast of Corby; turn off the A43 at Corby to Stamford Road and proceed through the village of Deene. After Deene, make your first left onto an unclassified road and travel approximately 1 mile to Kirby Hall on the right.

OPEN
10:00 a.m.–6:00 p.m. daily, April–October
10:00 a.m.–4:00 p.m. Saturday and Sunday, November–March

ADMISSION
£3.30 Adults
£1.70 Children
£2.50 Seniors
Family ticket available

CONVENIENCES
Gift shop

>>

It's no wonder that Elizabethan chancellor Christopher Hatton died a pauper! This is another of his extravagant building projects, completed in 1575, before he took on his masterpiece, Holdenby House. Actually, work on Kirby Hall had begun in 1570 under the ownership of Sir Humphrey Stafford, on land that was once property of the Catholic Church. It is unclear whether Sir Humphrey's aspirations for the manor were as grand as Hatton's.

Although Kirby Hall is "not much more" than a shell, in truth it is *much, much* more. After touring countless manor homes that have been restored and gilded to the hilt, we found it delightful to see an intact Tudor mansion stripped to its barest essentials. Several important portions of the Elizabethan structure remain, including the Renaissance-style portico and the original Great Hall.

There are numerous elaborately carved friezes and a plastered vaulted ceiling that made us gasp (*believe us, it takes* a lot *for a ceiling to make us gasp!*). Likewise, if you're not prepared for the sudden screech of Kirby's roaming peacocks, that sound can make you gasp, too.

> **☞ Did you know?**
> Sir Humphrey Stafford's full name is cleverly carved into one of the parapets at Kirby Hall. If you're skilled at word puzzles, you'll be able to spot it . . . we don't want to give away the clue and spoil your fun! Christopher Hatton's initials can be found over the side entrance.

> **☞ Did you know?**
> Although the dandy "Dancing Chancellor" Christopher Hatton died childless, four successive heirs, each named Christopher Hatton, owned Kirby Hall from 1596 to 1706. His name, if not his gene pool, lived on.

While you're in the area . . .

If you are mad about manor homes and determined to visit all that can be seen, check out **Deene Park** in Corby, not far from Kirby Hall. Deene Park began life as a medieval courtyard home and evolved over six centuries into an interesting amalgam of architectural styles. Deene Park has very limited opening hours and no discernible connection to any luminaries from "our" period of history, but you may phone 01780-450223 if you'd like more information.

✝ Lyveden New Bield
Near Oundle

>>>

PHONE
01832-205358

LOCATED
4 miles southwest of Oundle, via the A427, off Harley Way; you will need to park along the roadside and walk the final half mile along a farm track.

OPEN
Ruins
9:00 a.m.–5:00 p.m. daily, year-round
Information Room and Elizabethan Water Gardens
11:00 a.m.–5:00 p.m. Wednesday–Sunday, April–November

ADMISSION
£2.00 Adults
£1.00 Children
Pay by the honor system

>>>

There is something strangely evocative about Lyveden New Bield. Not so much a *ruin* as a never-completed structure, this cruciform-shaped garden house was begun in 1595 by Sir Thomas Tresham as a testament to his Catholic faith. Tresham died 10 years later and work ceased on his sanctuary. To this day, it remains essentially unaltered from the way Tresham left it nearly 400 years ago. A more complete study of Tresham's aspirations can be found in the seasonal information room. The property also features a whimsical Elizabethan water garden.

☞ **Did you know?**

Just when we thought Tresham couldn't get any stranger, we discovered that his property, Lyveden *Old* Bield, is some 20 years younger than Lyveden New Bield. Go figure!

While you're in the area . . .

☩ Southwick Hall

Near Oundle

>>>

PHONE

01832-274064

LOCATED

3 miles north of Oundle, 4 miles east of Bulwick

OPEN

2:00–5:00 p.m. Sunday, July–September

Note: Southwick Hall operates on a variable schedule; it is important to call for details.

ADMISSION

£4.00 Adults
£2.00 Children
£3.00 Seniors

CONVENIENCES

Refreshment stand

>>>

Although its 11 public rooms are brimming with Victorian and Edwardian memorabilia, portions of Southwick Hall are far more ancient. By the mid 1300s, Sir John Knyvett, Lord Chancellor under Edward III, had completed work begun by his father and grandfather in the early 14th century. Between 1571 and 1580, a Knyvett descendant, George Lynn, rebuilt the south wing in the Elizabethan style atop the footings of the medieval Great Hall. Portions of this addition, as well as two 14th-century stair turrets and their adjoining rooms, can be seen by visitors today.

• •

☞ Did you know?

George Lynn of Southwick Hall was banner bearer for Mary, Queen of Scots.

• •

Also while you're in the area . . .

✝ **Prebendal Manor House**
Nassington

\>

PHONE
01780-782575

WEBSITE
www.prebendal-manor.co.uk

LOCATED
Off the A1 and the A605, 6 miles north of Oundle, 7 miles south of Stamford

OPEN
1:00–5:00 p.m. Sunday, Wednesday and Bank Holiday Mondays, May–September

ADMISSION
£4.00 Adults
£1.50 Children

CONVENIENCES
Homemade tea; "Living Middle Ages" interactive exhibitions

\>

Just when you think you've had enough of manor homes, you stumble upon one that truly amazes. Such is the case with the Prebendal Manor House, the oldest surviving residence in Northamptonshire and one of the longest continually occupied houses in all England.

As early as 1018, King Cnut built a royal timber palace on this Nassington site. The property stayed in the hands of the Crown until 1123, when King Henry I gifted the palace and its accompanying church to Lincoln Cathedral to use as its Nassington prebend.

The 13th-century stone home that serves as the set piece for your visit was built upon the authority of the Bishop of Lincoln. You'll also be able to enjoy an enclave of 15th-century lodgings and a 16th-century dovecote (the tithe barn is from the 18th century).

Interesting as the Prebendal Manor House and its accompanying buildings are, it is the property's grounds that attract the most visitors. These are the largest re-created medieval gardens in all Europe, and their unerring authenticity deserves to be lauded. The primary garden replicates a late 14th-/early 15th-century residential garden, with medicinal herbs, turf seating, arbors and a nut walk (*just the thing for all of us who are "nuts" about all things medieval!*). A medieval pleasure park (*hmm . . .*), a true-to-the-times vegetable garden, as well as the original medieval fish ponds, put the "great" in this attraction's "great outdoors."

◇◇

PREBENDS EXPLAINED

Many ancient cathedrals, such as Lincoln, benefited from numerous prebends, scattered throughout the diocese. These religious foundations provided lucrative income for the "mother church" and acted on behalf of the cathedral at the local level. Each prebend was overseen by a prebendary, who performed specially designated duties . . . including the daily recitation of a prescribed set of psalms, as dictated by the presiding bishop. Other prebendal duties included interceding on behalf of parishioners in areas of religious concern, disciplining errant clergy and maintaining the chancels in the local parish churches. One might assume that being a special envoy of the bishop had its benefits; apparently those benefits weren't great enough. More often than not, prebendaries spent as little time as possible in their assigned territories, hiring down-on-their-luck parish priests to fill in on a day-to-day basis. Although the prebend at Nassington had a long line of influential prebendaries, there is doubt that any of them spent much time in residence at the Prebendal Manor House.

◇◇

While you're in Nassington . . .

The roots of this ancient village stretch back to Roman times, but Nassington earned its archeological fame for the extensive Saxon artifacts found in the area. Once the site of a significant quarry, Nassington has yielded substantial amounts of pottery during digs. The Saxon cemetery has been discovered, and the parish church, **St. Mary and All Saints**, bears traces of late-Saxon architecture. The church also displays a handsome Saxon cross, and fragments of a wall painting depicting Doom can be seen above the chancel arch. Phone: 01780-782271.

✝ Barnwell Castle Ruins
Barnwell Manor, near Oundle

>>

PHONE
01832-274035

E-MAIL
Berengar@msn.com

LOCATED
Off the A605 at Barnwell

TRAVEL
There is sporadic train service from London to Oundle. Trains depart Kings Cross Station with one change of train before arriving at Oundle Market Place. Travel time varies from 90 minutes to 2½ hours.

OPEN
Barnwell Manor operates as a B&B. Your best chance of seeing the castle remains is to spend an evening here. Call the above number for rates and reservations.

>>

Barnwell Castle was built in 1266, during the reign of Henry III, by Berengar le Moine (a.k.a. Berengarius le Moyne). During the 14th century, the castle was used as a court of justice and execution grounds. Sir Edward Montagu purchased the castle in 1540, adding the adjacent—and suitably impressive—Tudor buildings.

Should you opt to spend the night at Barnwell Manor, you will be treated to a peek at the looming medieval bastion tower. A number of small vaulted rooms are believed to lie hidden within the 12-foot walls. (*Rumor has it that the remains of Berengar's hapless brother, Wintner le Moine, are buried in the walls as well!*)

Ghost Alert!

Believe it or not, there may be several different bodies buried within the walls and former dungeon of Barnwell Castle. In 1948, responding to numerous complaints of unexplained gale-force winds around the ruined northeast tower, a group of curious locals embarked upon a series of seances—and got rather more than they bargained for! One "correspondent" from the other side claimed to be Marie le Moyne, who referred to "horror and untimely death" and made oblique references to a chest in the castle's long-forgotten dungeon. When asked who had imprisoned her so cruelly, "Marie" refused to answer. "Secret," she is reported to have replied, "I can never betray my soul's secret."

❖❖

WEAK-WILLED MONTAGU

A close friend and trusted political ally of Henry VIII, Sir Edward Montagu was named in the king's will to the regency council of Henry's young heir, Edward VI. That was not the last association Sir Edward would have with Henry's "final word." In 1553, as the adolescent King Edward lay dying, Montagu succumbed to pressure from the Duke of Northumberland and altered Henry's royal will to favor the succession of the Tudor's Protestant cousin Lady Jane Grey. Montagu was savvy enough to sense a treasonable act when he saw one and he apparently voiced cursory reluctance to participate in the scam. However, promises of a parliamentary pardon induced him to draft the new will—and add his signature as one of the official guarantors. Unfortunately for him, the rightful successor, Henry's daughter Mary, was not amused by the tampering. Montagu was promptly thrown into the Tower, where he had sufficient time to sweat out various scenarios for his future. Much to his surprise (*and relief*), Mary eventually released Sir Edward . . . but not until he had paid a heavy fine and forfeited extensive lands "in apology" to the Crown. Neither Barnwell Castle nor Boughton House was among the lands relinquished to the queen.

❖❖

Fotheringhay Castle Ruins
Fotheringhay

>>

PHONE
None

LOCATED
Just outside the village of Fotheringhay, off the A605, about 25 miles southwest of Peterborough

TRAVEL
The closest station with direct service to and from London is Peterborough. Trains depart Kings Cross Station for Peterborough Station on a regular basis. Travel time is about an hour. From Peterborough, you will need to hire a car or taxi to take you to Fotheringhay.

OPEN
Daylight hours daily, year-round

ADMISSION
Free of charge
>>>

Let's make ourselves clear from the start: there's ancient rubble and then there's *ancient rubble* . . . rubble so saturated with the lifeblood of history that it takes on shrine-like importance (*at least to fanatics like us!*). Fotheringhay Castle is just such rubble: no more than a mound of earth and a pile of stones. But oh, what stories those stones could tell if they could talk!

It would have been unthinkable for us not to make the out-of-the-way pilgrimage to Fotheringhay. After all, this castle has strong associations with two of our favorite characters in English history, King Richard III and Mary, Queen of Scots. (*Just because Mary is one of our favorite characters doesn't keep us from wishing we could have given her a swift "smarten-up" smack upside her head from time to time!*) We assume that you, like us, will want to pay homage here, but we warn you: there's not a whole lot to see.

The manor of Fotheringhay predates the Norman Conquest, with records as far back as 1060. The *Domesday Book* refers to "Fodringeia," but apparently the property was not properly developed until the early 12th century, when one Simon de Senlis built the first substantial castle along the banks of the River Nene.

Fotheringhay passed through multiple owners for the next 200 years. At one point, it was included in the dowry of Princess Maud, the English bride of Scotland's King David I (reigned 1124–1153). By the mid-14th century, it was held by John of Brittany, Earl of Richmond and claimant to the crown of France.

Among his numerous honors, John was also the son-in-law of King Edward III, married (albeit, briefly) to Edward's daughter Mary. In 1377, the castle passed to Edward III, who in turn granted Fotheringhay to his son Edmund Langley, Earl of Cambridge.

When Edmund's nephew Richard II ascended to the throne, he not only ratified Edmund's possession of Fotheringhay, he also honored his uncle as the first duke of York. From that point on, Fotheringhay Castle would be one of the primary seats of the House of York. Edmund founded a handsome collegiate church on the

castle grounds, with chaplains and choristers designated to pray for the souls of the Yorkist clan. Improvements to the castle and village were continued by Edmund's son Edward Langley. Tragically, Edward was one of the only noble English casualties at the Battle of Agincourt in 1415. His body was returned from France and laid to rest in the quire of the collegiate church at Fotheringhay. In 1434, a separate parish church was built in the village, in a style mirroring Fotheringhay's religious foundation; it is the only substantial remnant from that era.

Although Fotheringhay wasn't the mightiest of castles—critics scoffed that instead of scaling the walls, one could merely leap over them—the Yorkists loved the place. It was the favorite home of Richard Plantagenet and Cecily Neville, Duke and Duchess of York, and it was here, on October 2, 1452, their fourth son, Richard of Gloucester, was born. The future Richard III spent his first six years at Fotheringhay and returned to it for extended visits, even after claiming the throne in 1483.

Whether by association with the tainted reputation of Richard III (*whose supposed crimes included the dubious deaths of his nephews, the ill-fated "Princes in the Tower"*), or because of its bleak, dark countenance, Fotheringhay Castle was not a property favored by the Tudors. They allowed the castle to fall in status from royal residence to state prison—a prison dedicated primarily to captives of noble birth. So dire were the implications of the name "Fotheringhay" that Katherine of Aragon grew nearly hysterical over the prospect of being sent there, declaring she'd have to be "cattle-tied and dragged thither." Queen Katherine had her way; alternate "accommodations" were found for Henry VIII's discarded wife.

Mary Stuart was not so lucky. After 18 years as the political prisoner of her cousin Elizabeth I, Mary was brought to Fotheringhay Castle on September 25, 1586. It was to be her final home. In a large room above the castle's Great Hall, a kangaroo court comprised of vehemently antipapist nobles sat in judgment of the Catholic queen of Scotland, whom they perceived as no small threat to Elizabeth and the stability of the Protestant English monarchy. After so long a captivity, it was a surprisingly speedy "trial," lasting only October 14 and 15, with a rather *unsurprising* guilty verdict. Elizabeth's decision to execute her cousin was not so hastily reached, however. The En-

---

☞ **Did you know?**

Apparently, the Yorkists' affinity for Fotheringhay was not shared by Duke Richard's son Edward IV. Once his kingdom was secure, Edward preferred not to venture beyond the Thames Valley, but he made an exception in 1475 for an act of family respect. Duke Richard, and Edward's younger brother, Edmund, Earl of Rutland, had been brutally slain at the Battle of Wakefield in 1460, and their defiled bodies were hastily buried in rudimentary graves at Pontefract priory. King Edward had his relatives disinterred and, with great splendor, made the solemn progress south to Fotheringhay. The bodies were then given a heroes' funeral and were laid to their final rest in the family vault at Fotheringhay's collegiate church. The entire royal family was on hand for the ceremony, and a lavish funeral feast was held afterwards—it is recorded that thousands of people from the surrounding villages benefited from the king's largess during the two-day banquet.

glish queen prevaricated for nearly four months over the wisdom of killing an anointed sovereign, pacing her floor and muttering *"Aut fer aut feri, ne feriare, feri"* (suffer or strike, strike or be struck). Succumbing at last to the inordinate pressure of her counselors—her chancellor William Cecil, in particular—Elizabeth signed Mary Stuart's death warrant. The queen of Scotland was beheaded in the Great Hall of Fotheringhay Castle on February 8, 1587. By law, the execution had to be a semipublic event; more than 300 people witnessed the horrible scene.

It is no wonder that the next ruler of England, James I, allowed Fotheringhay to molder. He was, after all, Mary Stuart's son, and although the two had been estranged for virtually all of his life, it seems only natural he would want no connection to the site of her execution. The castle was finally torn down in 1635; portions of it were "poached" and used in the construction of newer, nearby properties.

Today, a chain-link fence surrounds the small heap of earth and stones that once was Fotheringhay. In 1964, the Richard III Society adorned the fence with two memorial plaques, one in honor of the last Yorkist king, the other in memory of Mary, Queen of Scots.

∿

While you're in Fotheringhay . . .

✝ St. Mary Fotheringhay (a.k.a. St. Mary and All Saints)
Fotheringhay

≫≫

PHONE
   01832-226243

LOCATED
   In the village of Fotheringhay, not far from the ruins of Fotheringhay Castle

OPEN

The church is usually open during daylight hours daily. If you cannot gain access, seek out Ms. Juliet Wilson at Blacksmith's Cottage on the other side of the Falcon pub, about 200 yards from the church.

ADMISSION

Donation suggested

CONVENIENCES

The bookstall has an interesting collection of literature on Richard III and Mary, Queen of Scots. (*Time to tote out the tote bag!*)

>>

Begun in 1411 and completed in 1434, the parish church of Fotheringhay is all that remains of the ancient Yorkist seat. Thanks to the very active interest and support of the Richard III Society, the church has remained a well-tended memorial to the House of York. Here you will find the tombs of Richard Plantagenet and Cecily Neville, Duke and Duchess of York, parents of two Yorkist kings, Edward IV and Richard III. Along with them lies their son, Edmund, Earl of Rutland, who was killed with his father at the Battle of Wakefield in 1460. The Richard III Society also helped raise funds for the stunning stained glass windows, which show the arms and crests of the Yorks and their Warwick in-laws.

• • • • • • • • • • • • • • • • • • • •

☞ Did you know?

The handsome memorials to Richard Plantagenet and Cecily Neville were constructed under orders from Elizabeth I. The queen visited Fotheringhay in 1566 and was appalled to see the disgraceful neglect of her forebears' tombs.

• •

A visit to this church *almost* makes up for the fact that there is next to nothing left of Fotheringhay Castle. (*Okay, not quite, but it's pretty special.*) On the front porch, look for a stone lion that was once part of the castle architecture. There is also a bulletin board that honors Walter de Fotheringhay, first principal of Balliol College, Oxford, in 1282. But, without a doubt, the primary focus of St. Mary's is the House of York. Throughout the church, numerous tributes to the clan can be seen, from the stunning York stained glass window to the kneeler cushions, embroidered with Yorkist crests, symbols and arms. In addition to the tombs of Richard III's parents and brother, you'll find the striking tomb of Edward, second duke of York, who was killed on Friday, October 25, 1415, leading Henry V's vanguard at the Battle of Agincourt. The church tower features lovely fan vaulting and is adorned with the falcon and fetterlock emblem of the House of York, and the organ—although modern—is richly carved with Yorkist roses and the Scottish thistle . . . a nod, no doubt, to the ill-fated queen of Scotland.

•••••••••••••••••••••••

👉 Did you know?

The church you now see was originally conceived as the chantry chapel for the collegiate church on the Fotheringhay Castle grounds, but was ultimately re-located to the fields outside the castle walls. The surviving contract for construction of the church stipulates that the contractor, William Horwode, be sent to prison if he failed to deliver the project on time and within budget. (*Talk about "builder incentives"!*)

•••••••••••••••••••••••

RICHARD, DUKE OF YORK (1411–1460)

Henry IV set in motion the wheels that would turn into the Wars of the Roses by usurping the throne from his cousin Richard II. However, another royal cousin, Richard, Duke of York, was the catalyst that caused the smoldering fires of the dynastic struggle to burst into a raging conflagration that burned through England for 25 years.

Although Henry IV had jumped the queue, so to speak, in leaping over relatives with better claims to England's crown when he seized the monarchy, he and his successor, Henry V, were strong enough kings to quell grumblings—let alone revolts—from any disgruntled kin. The problems started when Henry V died young, leaving an infant heir who grew into the weak-willed King Henry VI. From the very beginning of his reign, Henry's court was riven by political struggles over who would be the power behind the throne during the king's minority. The vicious infighting didn't end when the king reached his majority. Unfortunately, Henry was not wise in his selection of advisors and generally relied on self-serving, greedy magnates. Their exploitation of the power granted them created factions that ultimately hardened into groups of followers of the houses of Lancaster and York, loosely ranked as those who supported the rule of Henry VI and those who opposed the advisors surrounding the king.

This second group was led by Richard, Duke of York. Richard was one of those pesky royal relations whose very existence was a continual reminder to

Lancastrian adherents that there might be *(ahem!)* something just not quite right with Henry VI's claim to the throne. By the strict laws of primogeniture, Richard's claim to the throne was superior.

Gradually, a group of lords disaffected with Henry's hapless rule and unhappy about the actions of his councilors gathered around Duke Richard. Their chance at managing the levers of power came in August 1453 when Henry fell into a catatonic stupor. For months, Henry's consort, Margaret, who was finally pregnant, and the king's adherents tried to keep secret the news of the king's incapacitation. They secluded him at Windsor Castle while Margaret awaited the birth of their child.

Such momentous news could not be kept secret long, however. Once Richard and his supporters got wind of the king's condition, they forced an assemblage of Parliament. A council was formed, with Duke Richard at its head, to rule England until the king recovered.

Henry suddenly emerged from his catatonic state on Christmas Day 1454 and the levers of power switched again. Margaret and her adherents were firmly back in control, their hold on the king now even more secure since the queen had at long last produced an heir to the throne. It was Richard's and his cronies' turn to be disgruntled and grow paranoid.

The situation erupted into open warfare in September 1459. An ill-prepared Duke of York confronted an army ostensibly led by Henry at Ludford Bridge near Ludlow. Hopelessly outmanned, York and his son Edmund of Rutland fled the scene and escaped to Ireland. They were not gone for long, however. They returned in June 1460 and ultimately were able to take control of London. For the first time, Duke Richard advanced his claim to England's crown. On October 10, before a session of Parliament in Westminster Hall, Richard placed his hand on the empty throne and declared his inherited right to it.

Queen Margaret and her supporters were not about to let this arrangement stand unchallenged. They harassed the duke's government throughout 1460 and, at the end of the year, gathered a large army in the north to challenge his rule. Duke Richard, again with his son Edmund at his side, left London in December to prepare for a confrontation with Margaret's forces. Instead of waiting behind the solid walls of his castle at Sandal, near Wakefield, until his army was at full strength, Richard rode out to meet the much larger force led by Margaret. The subsequent rout was quick and brutal. Both Duke Richard and Edmund were killed and their severed heads were displayed on pikes at the gates of York. The duke's head was adorned with a paper crown, mocking his attempt to claim the throne.

Margaret's victory was short-lived. She reckoned without the duke's eldest son Edward, Earl of March, an 18-year-old prodigy whose military and political skills far surpassed those of his father. Edward wasted no time in gathering adherents to the Yorkist cause and building a new army. He marched into England at its head and soundly trounced the royal forces at the Battle of Mortimer's Cross on February 2, 1461. Control of the crown switched again, this time with Edward claiming it as Edward IV, but Margaret and those nobles loyal to the House of Lancaster were not yet ready to cry "Uncle!" The bloody battles of Wakefield and Mortimer's Cross were just the beginning of the Wars of the Roses.

◇◇

Also in Fotheringhay . . .

The town of Fotheringhay has numerous ancient buildings dating from the late medieval and early Tudor times. Be on the lookout for **Old Inn**, c. 1400–1450, a cluster of five cottages that served as overflow lodging for the castle. **New Inn** (a.k.a. Garden Farm) was constructed during the reign of Edward IV in 1461; his heraldry can be seen on the gateway. Although the town bridge was heavily restored in 1722, it was originally built in 1498. Elizabeth I ordered the bridge reconstructed in 1573, and stone reclaimed from the ruined quire in Stamford was used in the construction.

> ☞ Did you know?
>
> In 1524, there were 100 families living in Fotheringhay. Today there are fewer than 40.

◇◇

MARY, QUEEN OF SCOTS (1542–1587, REIGNED 1542–1567)

Despite her shortcomings—and believe us, she had plenty!—Mary, Queen of Scots is among the most interesting women of her time . . . and the most frustrating. She's one of those people you just can't figure out—was she ill-advised, blinded by love, prone to sudden fits of insanity or just plain *dimwitted*? (*We don't disagree over much, but this is one topic that provides us with perpetual fuel for fussing!*) Whichever argument *you* endorse, there's no arguing the fact that Mary could have had it all, had she exercised a bit of foresight, patience, restraint, discretion or common sense.

> ☞ Did you know?
>
> It was upon Mary's marriage to Francis that her clan changed the spelling of their surname from "Stewart" to the more Franco-friendly "Stuart."

Mary inherited the crown from her father, James V, when she was six days old. The great-granddaughter of Henry VII, Mary was also runner-up for the

English throne, after the children of Henry VIII. Foreseeing complications in this dicey line of succession, Henry promptly started marriage negotiations between Mary and his son, the future Edward VI. The Catholic Scots had other ideas, and Mary was affianced to Francis, son of the French king Henri II and Catherine de Medici. (*Needless to say, the betrothal infuriated Uncle Harry Tudor, who embarked upon several years of "Rough Wooing": burning, plundering and pillaging his way through Scotland.*) Mary was reared at the French court from age six and, in 1558, married the physically fragile Dauphin of France. Within a year, the teenage couple would find themselves cast as king and queen of France.

* *

Did you know?

For all their rivalry and entangled history, Queen Elizabeth and Mary, Queen of Scots never met. The English queen was mighty curious about her cousin and extensively questioned those who knew her about Mary's beauty and charms. Yet Glorianna never let curiosity get the best of her. Despite Mary's pleas, Elizabeth refused a face-to-face introduction. This was more than a matter of pride and one-upmanship; Elizabeth knew that Mary's fate rested in her hands. The decisions the English queen had to make in that regard would no doubt have been even more difficult if the two women had established a personal acquaintance.

* *

From the start, Mary Stuart made truly wretched political decisions. As part of her dowry, she had willed Scotland to the French monarchy—along with her claim to the English throne—in the event she should die without heir. The Scots and the English were equally appalled. That same year, the English queen Mary Tudor died, leaving her throne to her Protestant half-sister, Elizabeth. Mary Stuart wasted no time in declaring *herself* the rightful heir to England's crown, citing Elizabeth's "illegitimacy" as the basis for her claim. She adopted the titles and style of the English monarch and quartered the arms of England and France—inflammatory steps that set the stage for all future relations between the cousins Mary and Elizabeth.

Elegant, sophisticated, worldly and quick-witted, Mary would, in all likelihood, have served France well (*assuming she had kept her political* faux pas *in check*). Unfortunately, her French reign was tragically short. Francis died within the year, leaving 18-year-old Mary widowed, with no French throne and beholden to her unpleasant de Medici mother-in-law.

Small wonder Mary returned to Scotland, by now in the throes of its own religious Reformation. Mary's decision to return to and rule a land she had not seen for 12 years, knowing that her religion was disavowed by the government and that the majority of her barons liked her not, was either incredibly courageous—or incredibly foolhardy. As far as Elizabeth was concerned, it was incredibly threatening. From the moment Mary sailed from Calais on August 15, 1561, she was kept under constant (if occasionally covert) scrutiny by her English cousin.

Unfortunately, Mary's attentions tended to focus on affairs of the heart rather than matters of state and religion. In 1568, personally disgraced and politically outcast, she fled to England, where she threw herself upon the mercy of Elizabeth.

Mary had grossly misjudged the depth of her cousin's dislike. Her "political asylum" came at a steep price: house arrest. For the next 18 years, Mary was held captive, not in dungeons and prisons, but against her will, guarded by a string of increasingly hostile Protestant caretakers. Petty jealousies and political insecurities did not completely cloud Elizabeth's sense of obligation to a fellow monarch. For several years, Elizabeth tried to negotiate Mary's restoration to the Scottish throne, but mutually agreeable terms were never reached.

Meanwhile, Mary became a convenient rallying point for England's malcontent Catholics as they plotted to overthrow Elizabeth in favor of the Tudor's Scottish heir. How actively Mary encouraged their schemes is unclear. There is convincing evidence that she agreed to marry the Catholic Duke of Norfolk and that she endorsed several plots to gain her freedom. In every instance, Elizabeth dealt harshly with Mary's co-conspirators, but declined to mete out a similar fate to her royal cousin. Elizabeth's Privy Council was not so lenient. Elizabeth ordered Mary moved to Fotheringhay Castle, where she was speedily tried and condemned to death.

Oddly, despite the turmoil, rivalry and ill will that surrounded Mary, Queen of Scots' relationship with the English queen, her tenancy in England served to cement a bond between the two kingdoms. Mary's Scottish enemies banded behind their Protestant English comrades to ensure that she remained as far from

♦ ♦
Did you know?

History has greatly romanticized the life of Mary Stuart. For years, the Catholic Church held her up as a persecuted paragon of faith. This fails to consider the fact that Mary was all too ready to turn her back on her religion when it served her political — or romantic — purposes. She essentially stuck her faith in the closet in order to rule Protestant Scotland. Her relationship with the earl of Bothwell was adulterous and their marriage was bigamous; Bothwell was married at the time of their union. Had the opportunity arisen for Mary to gain England's throne by making concessions to the English Protestants, there is little doubt those concessions would have been quick in coming. Passionate, impulsive, charismatic and (arguably) courageous she was. Virtuous? Probably not.

♦ ♦

Scotland's throne as possible. In the end, the long-sought unity of the neighboring nations was achieved when Mary's son, King James VI of Scotland, ascended the throne as Elizabeth's designated heir, James I.

◇◇

ANCIENT INNS AND EATERIES

~ Fawsley Hall
Daventry
01327-892000

Here's another in the list of "Elizabeth slept here," but in this case she really did. You can even sleep in the same room she did when she was feted during her 1575 summer progress by Sir Richard Knightley, the descendant of a Norman family that arrived in England with William the Conqueror. The room is called (*natch!*) the 1575 Suite. Check it out at *www.fawsleyhall.com*.

~ Barnwell Manor
Oundle
01832-274035

While the B&B itself is not an ancient inn, it is located on the grounds of the former Barnwell Castle. A stay here is your best chance of catching a glimpse of the castle's medieval bastion tower.

~ Talbot Hotel
New Street
Oundle
01832-273621

Although the hotel was rebuilt in 1626, it has strong connections to Mary, Queen of Scots (*reason enough, in our minds, to check it out!*). The hotel's staircase was moved here from the ruined Fotheringhay Castle, where Queen Mary was put to death. Legend says that her executioner spent time in this hostelry before the dire deed was done. Guests have reported that his spirit—as well as that of the misfortunate queen—haunt the Talbot to this day.

~ Slapton Manor
Chapel Lane
Slapton
01327-860344

Private-entrance B&B rooms on the property of a 12th-century manor house and working farm.

~ The Saracen's Head
Main Street
Little Brighton
01604-770640

Handsome 16th-century coaching inn; the hotel's restaurant specializes in seasonal game.

~ England's Rose
Upper Green
Moreton Pinkney
01295-760353

Traditional 16th-century coaching inn, restored to mirror its ancient roots.

~ The Brave Old Oak
104–106 Watling Street
Towcester
01327-358255

Comfortable hospitality in a 16th-century coaching inn.

~ Falcon Hotel
Castle Ashby
01604-696200

Beautifully restored luxury hotel with ancient roots. Cellar bar and garden dining.

CONTENTS

TRIP 3

Bedfordshire

Politics and Piety

his is a trip awash in religious houses founded by monarchs and other well-heeled and politically connected people, including Elstow Abbey, established by a niece of William the Conqueror. A highlight of the trip is Dunstable Abbey, founded in the 12th century by Henry I, but most closely associated with Henry VIII. It was here that the final drama in the divorce saga of Henry and Katherine of Aragon was played out. That alone is enough to make Dunstable Abbey a *not-to-be-missed* stop on any Tudor fanatic's schedule, but the church itself is quite lovely and surrounded by many other ancient structures that make a walk around Dunstable an exciting adventure.

✝ Dunstable Abbey (a.k.a. Priory Church of St. Peter)

Church Street
Dunstable

>>

PHONE
01582-477422

E-MAIL
prioryoffice@chewhouse.freeserve.co.uk

LOCATED
36 miles from London; take the M1 to junction 11; the church is close to the crossroads of A5 and A505.

TRAVEL
Trains are available from St. Pancras and Kings Cross stations, but they only leave late in the afternoon or at night, thus requiring an overnight stay.

OPEN
9:00 a.m.–5:00 p.m. daily, year-round

WORSHIP
Sunday: 8:00 a.m. Holy Communion
9:15 a.m. Sung Eucharist
6:30 p.m. Evensong

ADMISSION
Donation requested

>>

This church originally was the nave of an Augustinian priory established by Henry I c. 1131. Henry had founded the town of Dunstable around 1110 and built a palace, called Kingsburie, there. When he founded the abbey, he endowed it with his lands and property in Dunstable, although he continued to spend a great deal of time at his palace in the town.

It took somewhere between 70 and 80 years to finish construction of Dunstable Abbey. It was not until 1213 that the complete church was consecrated by Bishop Hugh of Lincoln. Apparently, the master masons of this project were not such "masters" after all. Just nine years after the consecration, in June 1222, the roof of the presbytery collapsed, and in December of that year, a howling storm knocked down the two western towers. The towers' collapse destroyed the front of the church except for the late 12th-century Norman doorway, which still exists. The front was rebuilt about 1240–1250—*sans* towers this time. The outer gatehouse of the original priory also survives.

In 1392, the monks' annoyance with the townspeople's invasions of their services caused them to retreat to other parts of the priory for worship. They turned the nave over to the town to serve as a parish church. It was the parishioners who corrected the deliberate oversight of the early 13th-century reconstruction program and added a tower to the front of the church in the early 15th century.

Dunstable Abbey hit its historic high point in the 16th century. It had the dubious honor of playing host to the ecclesiastical court headed by Archbishop Thomas Cranmer that finally granted Henry VIII his annulment from Katherine of Aragon. Cranmer convened his biased judicial panel at Dunstable on May 10, 1533. Katherine, who was staying at nearby Ampthill Castle, was summoned to appear before the

court. She declined, holding fast to her claim that only the Holy Father in Rome had the right to judge the validity of her marriage. The outcome of the session was a foregone conclusion, however. Although the members of the court took a few days to talk it over, they ultimately rendered a decision on May 23, declaring the marriage of Henry VIII and Katherine of Aragon to be "null and absolutely void." Legend has it that the verdict was

●●●●●●●●●●●●●●●●●●●●●●●

☞ Did you know?

For whatever reason, Dunstable was a popular site for medieval tournaments, especially among the Edwards. Edward I attended tournaments here in 1279 and 1280; Edward II came to one in 1308; and Edward III participated in tournaments in 1329 and 1341. The 1341 tournament brought so many nobles and their entourages to Dunstable that the priory was nearly bankrupted by the cost of hosting all of them. About 230 knights, including several of the great magnates of the land, took part in this tournament.

●●●●●●●●●●●●●●●●●●●●●●●

nailed to the church door for all to see, but there is no historical evidence to support this tale.

The fact that Dunstable Abbey had been converted into a parish church in the 14th century probably is what saved it from total destruction during the Dissolution of the Monasteries. After it was dissolved in January 1540, the priory was plundered and seriously damaged. Parishioners saved what is left by erecting walls to preserve the church nave and aisles.

Another part of the priory that survived is the former hostel, now heavily restored and converted into **The Priory House Inn**, located in High Street South.

While you're at the abbey . . .

Just across the street from Dunstable Abbey are two remnants of the palace built by Henry I. Both buildings now qualify as "Ancient Inns and Eateries." On the corner of Church Street and Kingsway, you will find **The Norman King** pub, which was most likely a storehouse for the palace. Next to it, on Church Street, is **The Old Palace Lodge**, which has been heavily restored over the years and is now part of the Hanover International Hotel chain.

◇◇◇

THE KING'S GREAT MATTER

The key to resolving King Henry's "Great Matter"—his need to divorce Katherine of Aragon so he could marry Anne Boleyn and thus beget a much-desired male heir to the throne—was found one night in 1529 during a convivial reunion of college chums.

Stephen Gardiner, the king's secretary, and Edward Fox, a doctor of divinity well versed in canon law, had stopped over in Essex, at a house owned by Waltham Abbey, on their return from Rome. There, they had once again been arguing the king's case before the Pope. At the house in Essex, they met Thomas Cranmer, who was studying and teaching at Cambridge University but staying in Essex to escape an outbreak of plague on campus.

Well, you know how it is when college friends get together—they drink, they have dinner, they drink, they talk, they drink—and Gardiner and Fox talked. Knowing how brilliant Cranmer was, they asked his opinion about the king's divorce. Cranmer said that it was a case to be decided by doctors of divinity at leading universities, not by the Pope.

The idea fell on receptive ears. From Gardiner's and Fox's perspective, this was the first positive suggestion anyone had offered in a long, long time. They wasted no time telling Henry, who (*no surprise here!*) promptly summoned Cranmer to court. Cranmer was ordered to write a treatise defining the legal arguments for his opinion.

Cranmer so impressed Henry that the king appointed the scholar Archbishop of Canterbury in August 1532. It did not take long for Cranmer to take up the matter of Henry's divorce. On April 11, 1533, the new archbishop formally requested permission to proceed with the "examination, final determination and judgment in the said great cause touching your Highness." Permission was granted immediately.

Of course, Anne and Henry already had been married secretly on January 25, 1533, because Anne was pregnant. No one seemed very disturbed by any question of possible bigamy here. Most likely, they had all managed to convince themselves that Henry's marriage to Katherine had never been valid—buying into Henry's argument that Katherine's prior marriage to the king's brother Arthur made their subsequent union incestuous.

Exercising the authority granted by the king, Cranmer called a special ecclesiastical court and summoned doctors of divinity and canon lawyers from all over England. They met at Dunstable Abbey on May 10. Their decision, issued on May 23, pronounced Henry and Katherine's marriage "contrary to divine law" and declared that the Pope had no jurisdiction in the matter.

To tidy up the little problem of Anne's and Henry's marriage occurring before the divorce was granted, Cranmer announced from Lambeth Palace in London on May 28 that he found their marriage to be good and true. Four days later, on June 1, 1533, Anne was crowned Queen of England at Westminster Abbey. Cranmer performed the anointing ceremony.

✧✧

✝ Woburn Abbey
Woburn

>>>

PHONE

01525-290666

E-MAIL

enquiries@woburnabbey.co.uk

LOCATED

Exit 13 off the M1 or take the A5 to Hockliffe for the A4012; drive is about 1 hour.

OPEN

11:00 a.m.–4:00 p.m. Monday–Friday, April–September
11:00 a.m.–5:00 p.m. Sunday, April–September
11:00 a.m.–4:00 p.m. Saturday and Sunday,
October and January–March
Closed November and December

ADMISSION

£8.00 Adults
£3.50 Children
£7.00 Seniors
Family ticket available

CONVENIENCES

Coffee shop, gift shops and pottery

>>>

Founded in 1145 as a Cistercian monastery by Hugh de Bolebec, Woburn Abbey was confiscated in 1538 after Abbot Robert Hobbes was found guilty of treason. In 1547, Edward VI gave it to John Russell, the first of that family to bear the title Earl of Bedford and an executor of Henry VIII's will. Since then, the property has been in the hands of the Russell family, who later became the dukes of Bedford. Although rooted in the early Middle Ages, Woburn has been heavily restored as an 18th-century mansion, and there is little to see of its medieval and Tudor past, with the exception of the "Armada Portrait" of Elizabeth I by George Gower.

✝ A lost treasure ...
Ampthill Castle

>>

This 15th-century castle was a favorite of Henry VIII. He purchased it in 1524 because it was famous for its "marvellous good health and clear air" and top-notch deer park. Not even the fact that his first wife, Katherine of Aragon, was sent to live here in 1533, when the turmoil over Henry's desire for an annulment of their marriage was at its peak, dampened his enthusiasm for the castle. It was at Ampthill where Katherine awaited the predetermined outcome of the ecclesiastical debate being conducted at Dunstable Abbey that was to judge whether their marriage would be annulled. Indeed, it was at this castle that she received the news on July 3, 1533—several weeks after the actual event had occurred—that the annulment had been granted. Still, Henry must have needed to wipe some memories clean because he had expansive new royal apartments built at Ampthill between 1533 and 1547.

The castle is long gone, but its presence and Katherine's stay here are commemorated by "Katherine's Cross," which marks the spot where Ampthill Castle once stood.

✺

✝ De Grey Mausoleum
Flitton
Bedford

>>

PHONE
01525-860094

LOCATED
1½ miles west of the A6 at Silsoe on an unclassified road

OPEN
Saturday and Sunday by appointment; contact the keeper of the keys at the above number

ADMISSION
Donation requested

>>

If you are a fan of the art of effigies, this is a must stop for you. The De Grey Mausoleum is said to contain one of the best Tudor effigy collections in the country. The first de Grey—John—was Sheriff of Bedfordshire in 1233. He was the progenitor of a powerful family that, through marriage and royal service, became the earls, and later, the dukes of Kent. The mausoleum contains effigies of de Grey family members dating from 1545.

✚ **Chicksands Priory**
Shefford

PHONE
01525-860497

LOCATED
Off the A600 near Shefford

OPEN
By appointment only, the 1st and 3rd Sunday of the month

TIP!
This is an important one: don't try your luck by just stopping by Chicksands Priory and hoping for a glimpse or a change in open hours. It won't happen. The priory is located smack dab in the middle of a military base, and the uniformed guards don't take kindly to the odd amateur historian dropping by for a casual stroll around the grounds. The only way you'll get access here is by signing up for one of the infrequently scheduled guided tours.

This priory of the Gilbertine Order was founded in 1150, when Payne de Beauchamp and his wife, the Countess Rohese, granted a manor to the order. It was one of the few monastic establishments in medieval England to house both monks and nuns. Leased to Thomas Wyndham during the Dissolution of the Monasteries, Chicksands was then conveyed to the Osborn family and has been owned by its descendants ever since. Traces of the original 12th-century building remain, but it was heavily restored in the 19th century in the Gothic style.

Ghost Alert!

Maybe because it was so rare in medieval times for cloistered monks and nuns to live together, the men and women who resided in Chicksands Priory apparently were reluctant to leave it. They are said to haunt the place.

 # Elstow Moot Hall
Church End
Elstow

>>>

PHONE
01234-266889

LOCATED
1 mile south of Bedford, off the A6 on the A5134; the hall is just off High Street

TRAVEL
Train from Kings Cross Station to Bedford; taxi to the Moot Hall

OPEN
1:00–4:00 p.m. Tuesday–Thursday and Sunday, April–September

ADMISSION
£1.00 Adults
50p Children

>>>

This medieval market house, dating from the late 14th or early 15th century, now houses exhibits associated with 17th-century author and fiery Puritan preacher John Bunyan. Bunyan, the author of *Pilgrim's Progress* and many other works, lived and preached in Bedfordshire.

✝ Elstow Abbey (a.k.a. Church of St. Mary and St. Helena)

Church End

Elstow

>>

PHONE

01234-261477

OPEN

A key is available at the vicarage or from the caretaker, or you may attend worship at 8:00, 9:00 and 11:00 a.m. and at 6:30 p.m. on Sunday.

ADMISSION

Donation requested

>>

This church was created around the nave of Elstow Abbey, a Benedictine nunnery founded in 1078 by Judith, a niece of William the Conqueror. One theory has it that Judith established the abbey as an act of atonement for betraying to her uncle her husband's role in a rebellion plot.

With such illustrious political connections, Elstow Abbey grew to be one of the largest and richest in England. Of the 106 Benedictine nunneries that existed by the mid-1500s, Elstow was the eighth-wealthiest with an income of £350 per year. However, the religious devotion of the 30 nuns who lived there seemed to be somewhat questionable. As early as 1270, bishops were admonishing the nuns for their licentious behavior and loose moral ways.

☞ **Did you know?**

Judith had been married to Waltheof, the Saxon earl of Northampton and Huntingdon. Her Uncle William had arranged the marriage c. 1070 in an attempt to buy Waltheof's loyalty. The effort failed miserably. Waltheof joined with other Saxon lords in 1075 to try to topple William's still somewhat precarious hold on the kingdom of England. Needless to say, they were not successful. Waltheof pleaded with William for forgiveness, but the Conqueror was not disposed to leniency when it came to rebellious subjects. He ordered Waltheof taken in chains to Winchester, where he was beheaded in 1076.

After the Dissolution of the Monasteries, the property was given in 1553 to Sir Humphrey Radclyff, brother of the Earl of Sussex. Radclyff lived in the abbey buildings until his death in 1566. His heirs were not as fond of the place and began demolishing everything but the church nave in 1580. The church still has many of its Gothic features, including some interesting corbels on the east wall, great floor brasses, a beautifully carved piscina and a 15th-century font with a 13th-century base that is still used for baptisms. One of the most intriguing items is a monument in the middle of the church de-picting the Radclyffs kneeling in prayer at the altar. Standing to the north of the church is a 15th-century bell tower. To the south, you will find what was once the outer parlor of the cloisters; it has some interesting 13th-century vaulting.

• •

☞ Did you know?

One of the brass floor effigies is of Elizabeth Hervey (d. 1527), the sec-ond-to-last abbess of Elstow Abbey. The effigy has the distinction of being one of the only two brass depictions in England of an abbess with her cro-sier. The most intriguing aspect of the tomb is that it is incomplete. The brass trimming surrounding it is in-scribed in Latin with the abbess's name and the phrase, "who died on ____ day in ____ year." Clearly, some-one was negligent and overlooked the need to fill in the date and year of Ab-bess Elizabeth's death.

• •

◤◥

A lost treasure . . .

✝ **Bedford Castle**
High Street
Bedford

≫≫

LOCATED
57 miles north of London on the A6

TRAVEL
Thameslink train service from London every 15 minutes or a direct train from Kings Cross Station; travel time is approximately 35 minutes.

OPEN

Daylight hours daily, year-round

ADMISSION

Free of charge

>>

Bedford Castle was one of the first built by henchmen of William the Conqueror as a means of solidifying Norman control over England after the Conquest. The early years of the castle's life seem to have been rather uneventful, at least for the time. That changed during the civil war between Stephen of Blois and Empress Matilda.

In 1138, Stephen appeared to be firmly in control of the crown he had usurped after the death of Henry I in 1135. Henry's daughter and anointed heir, Matilda, was marooned in Anjou with her little-loved husband Geoffrey, who refused to lead a campaign to help his wife gain her stolen throne. Despite appearances, Matilda's supporters were beginning to stir, and one of the initial sparks that lit the fire soon to engulf England for the next decade and a half came from Bedford Castle.

Stephen had created Hugh, the youngest brother of the powerful Beaumont family, Earl of Bedford and clearly intended for the castle, which the king considered a royal holding, to go with the title. The castle, however, was in the hands of Miles Beauchamp, who viewed it as a hereditary possession. He refused to yield it to the king. Despite the fact that this was happening during the holy days of Christmas, Stephen summoned his barons and laid siege to Bedford Castle. He managed to force a surrender of the garrison in just five weeks — a relatively quick victory, but one that cost him the loyalty of yet another vassal, who soon transferred his allegiance to Matilda's camp. Throughout the long struggle between Stephen and Matilda, Bedford Castle changed hands several times. When Matilda's son Henry succeeded to the throne after Stephen's death in 1154, he restored Bedford Castle to the Beauchamp family.

The death knell for Bedford Castle came in 1224. The castle

was held by Faulkes de Breaute, once a strong supporter of King John. De Breaute had captured the castle during the barons' revolt against John and held onto it when peace was restored after John's death. He greatly expanded the castle and strengthened its defenses. During the years of Henry III's minority reign, de Breaute grew increasingly arrogant and greedy. His continuous flouting of royal authority and the customs of the realm caused Henry's advisors to outlaw him in 1224. De Breaute's brother William then captured a royal judge who was conducting an assize in Dunstable and dragged him off to Bedford Castle as a hostage. Henry's regents had no choice but to respond to such a flagrant insult to the Crown and very soon Bedford Castle was under siege. The castle was taken by assault, and most of the 80 soldiers inside were captured. All of those who were captured, including a number of knights, were promptly hanged. This was a shocking event at a time when knights were generally offered the opportunity to pay a ransom for their release if they were captured in battle. No fewer than eight medieval chroniclers described the sorry spectacle; the preeminent chronicler Matthew Paris even went so far as to draw a picture of the horrifying scene.

After the fall of the castle, orders for its destruction were issued in great detail, and the castle was dismantled stone by stone. Only the motte and the base of a square tower mark the spot where this castle once stood. Bedford Museum, located close by the castle remains, has a model of the castle and the story of its history.

While you're in Bedford ...

If you feel compelled to pay homage to the site where Bedford Castle once stood, close by you will find the ancient church of **St. Paul**. It dates from the early Middle Ages and retains some medieval and Tudor features, but most of its treasures date from the 17th century on.

While you're in the area . . .

✝ # Willington Tudor Dovecote
Willington
Bedford

>>

PHONE
01234-838278

LOCATED
4 miles east of Bedford, just north of A603

TRAVEL
Train from London to the Sandy rail station; taxi to the dovecote

OPEN
By appointment only

ADMISSION
£1.00
>>

If your obsession with medieval and Tudor history compels you to seek out each and every site with the remotest connection, then here is one in the "weird, but wonderful" category for you. This is a 16th-century dovecote built by Sir John Gostwick, Master of the Horse for Cardinal Wolsey. The dovecote contains nesting boxes for 1,500 pigeons. (*We admit it. We failed to see the charm of this site. Our passion for all things medieval and Tudor does not include pigeons. We see enough of those daily in Washington, D.C.!*)

✝ Bushmead Priory Refectory
Colmworth

>>>

PHONE

01234-376614

LOCATED

Take the M1 to A6 through Bedford to B660; the priory is located 2 miles south of Bolnhurst on an unclassified road.

OPEN

10:00 a.m.–1:00 p.m. and 2:00–6:00 p.m. Saturday and Sunday, July and August only

ADMISSION

Free of charge

>>>

Bushmead Priory was founded in 1185 as a house of the Augustinian order. What remains intact today is the 13th-century refectory, and the timber-framed roof of the building is original. The stained glass windows are from the 16th century. There also are some intriguing medieval wall paintings.

ANCIENT INNS AND EATERIES

~ **The Bull**
High Street
Dunstable

A 16th-century coaching inn.

~ **The Crown Inn**
High Street North
Dunstable

A 16th-century structure that most likely once served as a beerhouse for the servants of more exalted travelers.

~ The Norman King
Church Street
Dunstable

This pub was once part of the 12th-century palace built by Henry I.

~ The Old Palace Lodge
Church Street
Dunstable
08457-444123

Also a building that was part of Henry I's palace of Kingsburie.

~ The Saracen's Head
High Street South
Dunstable

A 14th-century inn probably built to accommodate overflow guests from Dunstable Priory.

~ The White Swan
High Street South
Dunstable

Built in the 14th century by William Dyve, Lord of the Manor of Sewell, to accommodate the many travelers who passed through Dunstable.

~ St. Helena Restaurant
High Street
Elstow
01234-344848

Dating from 1550, this country-house style restaurant features English food and garden seating.

~ The Swan
High Street
Elstow
01234-352066

Sixteenth-century pub.

~ The Emplins
Gamlingay
01767-650581
Fifteenth-century house with en suite bedrooms and a garden restaurant.

~ Rose Cottage
Broughton Road
Salford, Milton Keynes
01908-582239
Sixteenth-century B&B located close to Woburn.

~ Orchard Cottage
1 High Street
Wrestlingworth, Sandy
01767-631355
B&B in a 16th-century cottage with a modern extension.

CONTENTS

TRIP 4

Hatfield

Royal Real Estate

rime parcels in Hertfordshire have gilded the property portfolios of England's royalty at least since Saxon times. Your visit will lure you into ruins, welcome you into churches and sweep you through hallways owned by—or treated as if they were owned by—Harold and William I, Stephen and Matilda, most of the Plantagenet kings and their consorts and, of course, Elizabeth I and her Tudor forbears. The history of Hatfield House and both Hertford and Waytemore castles (a.k.a. Bishop's Stortford Castle) makes for great armchair reading and will whet your appetite for your day in Hertfordshire ... less than an hour from London!

∾

 ## Hatfield House
Hatfield

≫≫

PHONE

01707-287010

LOCATED

21 miles north of London; take the M25 to junction 23 and proceed 7 miles, or take the A1 to junction 4 and continue 2 miles

TRAVEL

Trains depart from Kings Cross Station every 30 minutes and take you directly to Hatfield; travel time is about a half hour.

OPEN
House (March–September only)
Noon–4:00 p.m. Monday–Friday (guided tours only)
1:00–4:30 p.m. Saturday and Sunday (no guided tours)

Note: The park and gardens operate on separate schedules.
Please phone ahead for details.

ADMISSION
£6.20 Adults
£3.10 Children

CONVENIENCES
Restaurant, gift shop

TIP!
Hatfield House holds Elizabethan banquets in the Old Palace
throughout the year. The costumed staff, entertainment and
bill-of-fare are reminiscent of a Tudor feast. Although we have
not personally indulged in this merriment, you may do so by
calling 01707- 262055 for reservations.

>>

As much as we enjoyed our visit to Hatfield House, we feel compelled to preface our statements with a couple of caveats. Although this was the primary childhood home of Queen Elizabeth I, very little of the Tudor royal palace still exists. The only
building on the site from that era is the Old Palace, and the only
way you can see the inside of the Old Palace is to while away an
evening at a "merrie olde banquet," a pastime for which you can
expect to pay dearly. However, several of Elizabeth's possessions
are on display in the Jacobean Hatfield House, as are the glorious *Rainbow Portrait* by Isaac Oliver and Nicholas Hillard's *Er-
mine Portrait*. We feel these masterpieces alone are worth your
visit. Try your hand at this Tudor treasure hunt and see if you
can spot the following swells among the portraits on display:
William Cecil and his various family members, Mary, Queen of
Scots and a particularly sour-faced Margaret Beaufort, Countess of Richmond and great-grandmother of Elizabeth I.

Our second caveat is that if you intend to include the
grounds in your visit, the schedule can be more than mildly

confusing. We strongly urge you to phone ahead if the gardens and park are an important part of your tour.

Hatfield manor had long been an ecclesiastic retreat for the bishops of Ely. The dowager queen Katherine of Valois gave birth to her second Tudor son, Jasper, at Hatfield in 1431 (her first Tudor son, Edmund, was born in 1430 at nearby Much Hadham Place). In 1497, Cardinal Morton of Ely and Westminster replaced the ancient manor with a brick edifice that featured a massive interior courtyard and a distinctive multicolored tile roof.

In the 1530s, Hatfield fell the way of most of England's church properties: into the hands of Henry VIII. Apparently, it was never high on the monarch's list of preferred homes, although it proved to be a handy nursery palace for his children. Indeed, Elizabeth's adolescence propelled Hatfield into the limelight.

Relations between Elizabeth and her sister, Mary, were always strained, at best. Mary's bitter regard for the daughter of the woman who had displaced her own mother turned into outright hostility as Catholic Mary sought to protect her crown from Protestant agitators perceived as promoting Elizabeth for the throne. Elizabeth spent much of her time during Mary's

◆◆◆◆◆◆◆◆◆◆◆◆◆◆◆◆◆◆◆◆◆◆◆

☞ Did you know?

Practical in matters of both state and heart, Elizabeth indulged her whimsical side when it came to her personal attire. In fact, despite her austere dress as a princess, as queen, Glorianna was nothing short of a clotheshorse. Garrett Johnson, her personal shoemaker, provided her with a new pair of shoes each week . . . that's well over 14,000 pairs of shoes throughout her 40-year reign. An inventory of her wardrobe in 1600 revealed 198 cloaks or mantles for cold weather outerwear. She had an affinity for expensive silk stockings and was prone to bedecking herself with such quantities of pearls, precious stones and gold thread that, had sunglasses been invented by the 16th century, they would have been a boon to those who happened upon her in bright light. Both of the formal portraits at Hatfield House show Elizabeth adorned in fantastically lavish style. (*We believe that dressing over the top is one of the best perks of Queendom—we just wish today's women rulers were so inclined!*) Items from Elizabeth's wardrobe on display at Hatfield include a pair of her silk stockings, a wide-brimmed straw hat and her long-fingered gloves.

◆◆◆◆◆◆◆◆◆◆◆◆◆◆◆◆◆◆◆◆◆◆◆

turbulent reign essentially confined to the house and gardens at
Hatfield . . . and although it surely beat the accommodations
at the Tower of London (where

◆◆◆◆◆◆◆◆◆◆◆◆◆◆◆◆◆◆◆◆◆

☞ Did you know?

One of Hatfield's more poignant inci-
dents seems to have set the stage for
the impassioned rivalry Mary Tudor
felt with her younger half-sister. In
January 1534, Henry (*ever the dutiful
father!*) popped into Hatfield to spend
a moment or two with 4-month-old
Elizabeth. Papa Tudor did not, however, extend the same courtesy to his
elder daughter, Mary. In fact, Princess
Mary was confined to her room at the
top of the palace for the duration of
Henry's visit. Unbelievably, this did
not extinguish Mary's desire to see her
father. Despite his displacing her in favor of baby Elizabeth, Mary still nur-
tured great affection for dear old Dad.
As Henry prepared to leave, Mary
stood at her bedroom window, waving
forlornly, desperate to catch Henry's
eye. Various courtiers noticed and
no doubt were moved by the scene;
however, none thought it politic to ac-
knowledge the *princess non grata*. At
the last minute, Henry rewarded Mary
with a perfunctory lift of his plumed
hat. His much-relieved attendants
followed suit, with enthusiastic cap-
lifting of their own. No one recorded
Mary's reaction.

◆◆◆◆◆◆◆◆◆◆◆◆◆◆◆◆◆◆◆◆◆

Princess Elizabeth also endured an enforced residency),
you can be certain that the willful, active Elizabeth harbored
a fair amount of resentment at
being kept in the rather cloistered atmosphere of Hatfield.
In fact, Hatfield would join
Hampton Court on the list of
studiously avoided royal residences during Elizabeth's early
years as queen.

Elizabeth's memories of
Hatfield House cannot have
been all bad, however. On November 17, 1558, while reading
under a tree on the verdant Hatfield lawns, Elizabeth received
official word that the Crown of
England was hers. The news
did not come as a total surprise;
Mary had been quite ill for
some time and, in recent days,
a steady stream of courtiers
had fled the dying queen's bed-
side to pledge allegiance to the
presumed heir, Elizabeth. Still,
uncertainty about Elizabeth's
rightful inheritance had loomed large. Up until her final hours,
Mary had continued her threats to deprive Elizabeth of the
crown. Prepared as she may have been in theory, the magnitude
of the proclamation "The queen is dead. Long live the queen!"
rendered Elizabeth speechless. Momentarily overcome, she

fell to her knees stammering in Latin, "This is the Lord's doing; it is marvelous in our eyes."

Of course, Elizabeth was not one to give way to "womanly" emotions for long. In a matter of moments she had regained her composure and, in true regal style, proceeded into the palace of Hatfield to officially begin her reign. Wasting no time on pleasantries, she called her closest councilors to assemble in the Great Hall, where she commenced her first official Council of State, mapping out her early plans for ruling England.

That Great Hall (today known as "Old Palace") is all that remains of Elizabeth's Hatfield House; the rest of the palace was pulled down during the early years of James I, and the bricks were used in construction of the new, refined home. Although the Old Palace interior is closed except during once-a-week theme dinners, you can get a fairly good peek from the outside. From the main house, follow the Arbor Path, which will bring you alongside the palace. Straight ahead, under what appears to be a side porch, is a most remarkable carved frieze depicting Elizabeth and her first Great Council.

Innumerable trees grace Hatfield's sprawling 4,000 acres; which one may have had the honor of supporting Elizabeth while she awaited news of her ascension is anyone's guess! The curators, however, have designated one massive oak along North Park Avenue as "Queen Elizabeth's Oak."

◆ ◆

☞ Did you know?

Between his properties in Scotland and those he inherited with the English crown, King James could afford to be picky. Hatfield House was clearly not to his liking. A man of more "modern" sensibilities, he cast his eye, instead, on the beautiful estate of nearby Theobold's Park, owned by his chief minister, Sir Robert Cecil. In the finest Cecil tradition (his father, William, made a career out of accommodating Elizabeth), Robert agreed to trade Theobold's for Hatfield. In 1608, Cecil undertook a massive renovation of Hatfield House, which, unfortunately for all of us amateur historians, included the demise of most of the Tudor palace. The home has been in the Cecil family ever since.

◆ ◆

◆◆

WILLIAM CECIL, LORD BURGHLEY (1520–1598)

Stunned though she may have been by the reality of being named queen, Elizabeth had done no small amount of planning for taking control of the monarchy. For more than a month, she had been giving considerable thought to her choice of chief advisors. By mid-afternoon on her ascension day, she was ready to announce the key positions; the first of those named was her Secretary of State, Sir William Cecil. Some may have pointed out that this position was not, on paper, the most powerful title a courtier could hold. No matter. Both Cecil and Elizabeth knew that with Cecil serving as Secretary of State, an exceptionally close working relationship could be fostered. Elizabeth had infinite trust in Cecil, and keeping him close at hand was ultimately of more value to her than honoring him with powers that would keep him farther afield.

Cecil was no newcomer to Tudor politics. He entered the service of Protector Somerset (guardian to Edward VI) in 1547 and a year later held a seat in Parliament as the representative for Stamford. Guilt by association touched many of those surrounding Somerset; on the heels of the Protector's demise, Cecil found himself spending part of 1550 in the Tower of London. It was a mercifully short residency. Within two months, he was free and serving as Principal Secretary of State, appointed by the Duke of Northumberland.

Once again, Cecil would find himself uncomfortably close to a treasonable plot. Northumberland's role in placing the "Nine Days Queen," Lady Jane Grey, on Mary Tudor's throne could well have implicated Cecil had Sir William not taken extraordinary care to distance himself from the intrigue. It is a testament to his political savvy, as well as to his upstanding character, that Mary gave him a general pardon and restored him to his position of Justice of the Peace for Lincolnshire. On at least two separate occasions, the queen employed Cecil on diplomatic missions, and he participated actively in the 1555 Parliament.

When exactly Sir William caught the attention of Princess Elizabeth is unclear. Certainly, by the time she had chosen him to serve as Secretary of State, she held Cecil in very high regard. It was an esteem that did not diminish with time. The 40-year working relationship between the queen and her chief advisor is believed to be the longest in English history. And although it was not without its rocky periods, the unfailing trust and respect that was the bedrock of their partnership prevented any discord from doing long-term damage.

From 1558 to 1598, Cecil served in three official capacities. As Principal Secretary of State (1558–1572), he oversaw administration of all English foreign policy, including diplomatic relations, defense and finance. In 1561, he added the responsibilities of Master of the Court of Wards, an important, powerful and lucrative position that provided Cecil with a substantial boost to his income. In 1572, he was promoted to Lord Treasurer, presiding over the Court of Exchequer and administering all royal finances.

Along with his political titles and duties, Cecil added personal honors. In 1571, he became the only one of Elizabeth's ministers to be elevated to the peerage, when he was titled Lord Burghley. The following year, he became a Knight of the Garter, an honor he had first received in 1552, but had to relinquish during Mary Tudor's reign.

If his 40-year partnership with Elizabeth was unique in both its duration and its productivity, Cecil himself was unique among the politicians of the era. In an age when mistrust, intrigue, disloyalty and arrogance were hallmarks of life at court, Sir William maintained a reputation that was virtually flawless. Almost universally well liked, he was renowned for his loyalty, hard work, common sense and uncommon devotion to God, Elizabeth and England . . . a devotion that seems to have fueled his uncharacteristic venom toward Mary, Queen of Scots. So virulent was Cecil about the threat posed by Elizabeth's Catholic cousin that he became the driving force behind Mary's execution. Torn between the desire to protect her throne and her sympathetic regard for a fellow anointed sovereign (and a family member at that), Elizabeth lashed out at Cecil in a guilt-induced rage after Mary's beheading. For a long period, Sir William avoided court. Yet, even this emotionally fraught issue was not enough to drive a permanent wedge between Elizabeth and the man who was probably her closest friend in the world.

Cecil's last years were far from pleasant. The death of his beloved wife, Mildred, in 1589 began a slow, steady physical decline for Sir William. Although he never lost his exceptionally keen mental faculties, he was tormented by a series of painful illnesses that left him so debilitated he eventually had to be carried in a litter wherever he went. In 1596, his highly capable son Robert was named Principal Secretary, a move that relieved Cecil of the bulk of his governance responsibilities.

William Cecil, Lord Burghley, died on August 4, 1598. In the days preceding his death, Elizabeth had sat with him, comforting him with their most pleasant memories and feeding him with her own hand. In one of her last letters to him, the queen reassured him that he was "to [her] in all things, and ever shall be, Alpha and Omega." To England, he was certainly one of the finest statesmen the country would ever know.

❖ ❖

✝ Hertford Castle
Hertford

>>>

PHONE

01992-584322 (Tourist Information Centre)

LOCATED

East of the A1/M6 on the A414; follow the signs from the center of Hertford

OPEN

Daylight hours daily, year-round

Touring of the postern gatehouse is limited to one Sunday per month, 2:30–4:30 p.m., May–September. Please phone 01992-552885 (Town Council) for the current schedule.

ADMISSION

Free of charge

>>>

The ancient town of Hertford dates from the reign of King Edward the Elder (872–924 CE), who established the burgh after England's victory over the second Danelaw in 911. The double-moated motte-and-bailey castle was built by William the Conqueror soon after the Battle of Hastings. The River Lea was too strategic a site to leave unprotected; the responsibility of safeguarding the waterway conferred along with the castle to Peter de Valoignes, Sheriff of Hertfordshire and Essex, one of William's Norman stalwarts.

Every monarch from William I through Henry III spent considerable time at Hertford Castle. Under the custodial care of Roger de Valoignes, the castle and town of Hertford supported Empress Matilda in her struggle to wrest her rightful inheritance—the Crown of En-

* * * * * * * * * * * * * * * * * * * *

☞ Did you know?

The First General Synod of the English Church was held in Hertford on September 24, 673 CE. A marker on the grounds of Hertford Castle tells that Theodore of Tarsus, seventh Archbishop of Canterbury and first Primate of All England, presided. The bishops of East Anglia, Rochester, Mercia, Wessex and Northumberland were in attendance.

* * * * * * * * * * * * * * * * * * * *

gland—from her cousin Stephen of Blois. The castle only engaged in active warfare once during the Middle Ages, however, surrendering after a month-long siege to the Dauphin Louis during the French invasion of 1216. The castle was restored to England when the French retreated in 1217.

Embattled or not, Hertford Castle served the Crown well in other ways. Edward III began the tradition that distinguished Hertford as a "lady castle" when he gifted Hertford to his mother, Isabella, the "She-Wolf" of France. Edward also laid the groundwork for Hertford's other key function: cushy confines for political prisoners of note. Two of the king's prize "trophies," John II of France and David II of Scotland, were held in far-from-unpleasant accommodations at Hertford.

Nor were the only royal prisoners at Hertford of foreign blood. The deposed English King Richard II was held here in 1399 before his final incarceration at Pontefract. Ironically, Richard had once owned Hertford, albeit under less than scrupulous circumstances. After the death of Edward III, the castle had been granted to the king's second son (and Richard's uncle), John of Gaunt, Duke of Lancaster; it quickly became a favored residence of both Gaunt and his son Henry Bolingbroke. Family relations were strained throughout Richard II's reign; at one point the king seized Hertford during a quarrel with Gaunt, but he restored it in fairly short order. Upon Gaunt's death, the castle was part of the Lancastrian estate inherited by Bolingbroke, who was living in exile—another victim of family feud, Richard-style. Taking advantage of his cousin's absence, Richard snatched up Hertford (along with the rest of the extensive Lancastrian holdings) and promptly established his 8-year-old-bride, Isabella, as lady of the castle. It was just the sort of crass, greedy and ill-advised move that had already cost Richard his popular support and would ultimately cost him his crown . . . and his life.

Henry IV—for such was the title conferred upon Bolingbroke as the result of his successful 1399 palace coup—continued Hertford's history as ladies-palace-cum-prison. He gave the castle to his second wife, Joan of Navarre, and then proceeded to use it as a jail for the son of his enemy, Robert III of Scotland. Nor did the roster of queenly residents stop there.

In 1418, Henry V awarded the castle to his queen, Katherine of Valois. Their son, Henry VI, inherited the throne at the age of 10 months, but most of his infancy was spent at Hertford, venturing to Westminster only for state occasions. As an adult, Henry VI conferred the castle on his consort, Margaret of Anjou. It was not, alas, a peaceful tenancy. The armed conflicts of the Wars of the Roses led to Hertford's confiscation by Yorkist forces. With the coronation of the first Yorkist king, Edward IV, Hertford passed into the hands of yet another queen, Elizabeth Woodville; Edward's 1465 gatehouse is still evident as you tour the castle today.

It was Edward's brother Richard III who temporarily broke the queenly pattern at Hertford. He gifted the castle to one of his closest friends and supporters, the Duke of Buckingham, Humphrey Stafford. Buckingham, however, was caught in the myriad allegiance shifts of Richard's reign, ultimately losing his head—and Hertford Castle. As we all know (*we will not insult you by assuming otherwise*), Richard did not fare much better. His brief four-year reign ended at the Battle of Bosworth in 1485; the medieval era ended and the Tudor era had begun.

Not much of an original thinker, Henry VII gifted Hertford castle to the first Tudor queen, Elizabeth of York. It was their son, Henry VIII, who elevated Hertford from a fairly pedestrian royal residence to a true "palace," one of several devoted to the upbringing of his children Mary, Edward and Elizabeth. All spent a considerable part of their childhood at Hertford during their formative years. Young Edward was living at Hertford when news of his father's death—and his own accession—first reached him. During his reign, his sister Mary Tudor remained at Hertford, while Elizabeth resided primarily at nearby Hatfield.

As queen, Mary Tudor gave a rather grim twist to Hertford's role as jail for political prisoners. The zealous Catholic monarch used the castle as a holding bin for persecuted Protestants awaiting trial for heresy. One can only surmise that their residency was far from the benign imprisonment experienced by various royalty previously under house arrest at Hertford.

Hertford Castle lies in ruins now. Edward IV's tall, brick gatehouse is the dominant feature; unfortunately, it is only open intermittently. Several minor Tudor-era (and later) buildings adjacent to the structure house the Hertford town council offices and are not open for touring. Portions of the castle walls, dating from 1170, form the border of a pleasant neighborhood park, anchored by two of the old castle towers.

While you're in Hertford . . .

Before you leave Hertford, take a moment to enjoy two more ancient buildings. The first is the Norman church of **St. Leonard's**, built in 1120. You may reach it by a charming riverside walk. You'll typically find the church open on summer weekends, between 2:30 and 4:30 p.m. Also check out **Verger's House** on St. Andrew's Street. The oldest residence in Hertford, the building dates from 1450. It's now an antique shop (*presumably none of the shop's wares dates from the building's inception*).

✝ Bishop's Stortford Castle (a.k.a. Waytemore Castle)

Bishop's Stortford

>>

PHONE
01279-655261

LOCATED
On Bridge Street in the center of Hertford, on the A414

OPEN
Daylight hours daily, year-round

ADMISSION
Free of charge

>>

Although Waytemore Castle was in ruins by 1520, it had already enjoyed a long and somewhat romantic history. It is believed that the property originally belonged to Edith Swan-neck, mistress of Harold, the last Anglo-Saxon King of England. Local legend asserts that Edith retrieved Harold's body after the Battle of Hastings and brought it to Waytemore for burial. Such a story probably would have been debunked as folklore by now, had it not been for the 1850 discovery of an ancient stone coffin in nearby St. Michael's Church; the coffin revealed the remains of an ancient corpse of tremendous stature, certainly fitting the common image of the mighty Harold.

Whether it was associations

• •

🐾 Did you know?

Despite the fact that Geoffrey de Mandeville, Earl of Essex was a foul political weathercock, both Stephen and Matilda bent over backwards to purchase his ever-changing loyalty. In 1141, Matilda issued a series of charters designed to guarantee de Mandeville's support. In addition to confirming him as castellan of the Tower of London and upholding his extensive powers in Essex, the empress named him Sheriff and Justiciar of London, Middlesex and Hertfordshire. She sweetened the pot by throwing in the bishop of London's castle, Bishop's Stortford—a move that did little to endear her to the London powers-that-be.

• •

with Harold or the strategic fording of the River Stort that prompted the Conqueror to action, William wasted no time building a castle at Waytemore. This he granted to Maurice, Bishop of London. Despite its prominent location, the castle was never called upon to defend—or defend against—the local populace. Rather, it became a favorite holiday house for the bishops of London until the 15th century, when the "modern" amenities of nearby Much Hadham competed for—and won— their patronage.

The 11th-century castle was expanded in the 1100s when the long, rectangular tower with twin corner chambers was built. Today, all that remains of Waytemore Castle are the foundations of the keep, which sit atop a 40-foot-high mound. The moated grounds have been incorporated into the whimsical Castle Gardens, a decidedly pleasant resting spot for footsore amateur historians.

While you're in Bishop's Stortford . . .

~ St. Michael's Church
Windhill

This stunning church looms majestically over the medieval town of Bishop's Stortford. Although the present church dates from the 15th century, evidence of earlier Saxon and Norman structures have been found on the site. Legend has it that the bodies of King Harold and his common-law wife, Edith, were buried in St. Michael's.

~ Bishop's Stortford Museum
Apton Road

Bishop's Stortford has been associated with the bishops of London since well before the Norman Conquest. The interesting history of this ancient hamlet is explored in the museum's rotating exhibitions. The museum is open on summer Fridays and on the first Sunday of the month.

While you're in the area . . .

Close by Bishop's Stortford is the historic hamlet of **Much Hadham**. Although nothing significant remains of Edmund Tudor's birthplace—the bishops of London's summer palace—it's worth a walk around the neighborhood. Elizabethan cottages pepper the streetscape, and the parish church, with its remarkable "spike" spire, dates from 1225. By the way, it is interesting to note that two churches—the Roman Catholic Holy Cross Church and the Anglican St. Andrew's Church—share this large parish building (*my, how times change . . .*).

ANCIENT INNS AND EATERIES

~ The George
High Street
Bishop's Stortford
Built in the 1400s, the inn also sports Jacobean and Georgian renovations.

~ Ashford Cottage
Chipping, near Buntingford
01763-274163
Sixteenth-century thatched-roof guest house with a one-acre garden and orchard.

~ Hadham Mill Stables
Much Hadham
01279-842768
The guesthouse, with rural setting, dates from 1550.

~ Bush Hall Hotel
Mill Green
Hatfield
01701-271251
Built in 1574, this hotel offers 25 updated guest rooms.

~ The Roebuck Inn
Old London Road
Stevenage
01483-365445

Charming 15th-century inn with hearty traditional fare.

CONTENTS

St. Albans

All Roads Lead to Rome

he town that bears St. Albans's name was originally a significant Roman settlement. Known as Verulamium, it died out after the fall of the empire and was never restored. Rubble from its ancient buildings was used during the 8th century to build King Offa II's abbey in memory of St. Alban, the predecessor of today's impressive cathedral. Still, there are considerable vestiges of the town's Roman heritage to be investigated just across the River Ver from the town of St. Albans. Together with St. Albans's well-preserved medieval streetscape and famous cathedral, this makes for one of Hertfordshire's most fascinating visits.

St. Albans is an especially pretty city to stroll through, with many ancient sites to admire along your way. Of particular interest is French Ros, just off the centrally located Marketplace. This street has changed very little from the Middle Ages. Be sure to look for the Fleur de Lys Inn—one of many "resting spots" enjoyed by Edward III's 1356 prisoner of war, King John II of France, following the Battle of Poitiers. Also of note is the massive flint Clock Tower (c. 1412), one of England's last remaining curfew towers. If those long hours on the Stairmaster™ have paid off, treat yourself to the climb and enjoy wonderful views of the surrounding countryside. The Clock Tower is open on summer weekends; phone 01727-860984 for details.

✝ St. Albans Tourist Information Centre

Town Hall
St. Albans

>>

PHONE
01727-864511

E-MAIL
tic@stalbans.gov.uk

LOCATED
20 miles north of London off the M1, junction 6

TRAVEL
Regular train service (although somewhat limited on Sunday) departs from Kings Cross Station; travel time is about 30 minutes.

TIP!
We have found that Sunday is not the best time to visit St. Albans, unless a church service at the cathedral tops your list. Several sites are closed on Sunday, and the cathedral has limited touring, out of respect to its worshipers.

◆◆

ENGLAND'S FIRST PATRON SAINT

Thomas à Becket may hold the title of Britain's most famous martyr, but he certainly wasn't the first. That honor is bestowed upon St. Alban, a Roman soldier who, in 209 CE, was beheaded not only for embracing Christianity, but also for harboring a fugitive priest. St. Alban was adopted as the patron saint of England in fairly short order (later to be upstaged by St. George), and the site of his execution became one of the most important pilgrim destinations of the Middle Ages.

For years, there was considerable controversy regarding the exact whereabouts of the remains of St. Alban. Tradition had it that during one of the early Danish invasions, the saint's body had been removed to Ely for safekeeping. According to the story, the monks of Ely became rather attached to the saint and refused to return the body after the Danes withdrew. The monks

• •
☞ **Did you know?**
St. Albans and London have more in common that one might imagine. Not only were they originally Roman outposts, but both had the dubious distinction of being burned to the ground by the fiery Icenian queen Boudicca.
• •

of St. Albans, however, had a different spin on the tale: they claimed to have sent a duplicate corpse as a decoy, keeping their resident saint safe in the confines of the church that bears his name. Edward II particularly revered St. Alban and decided to personally investigate the rival claims. He ordered the opening of the Ely tomb and witnessed the removal of a rough-hewn garment, which appeared to be splattered with fresh blood. It was declared that Ely held the tunic of the martyred Alban—the well-preserved blood was believed to be a sign of a miracle—while St. Albans possessed the actual corpse. To the delight of all involved, St. Alban could be officially venerated at both sites.

✧✧

✝ St. Albans Cathedral and Abbey Church
Abbey Mill Lane

»»

PHONE
01727-860780

LOCATED
Just beyond the central Marketplace; you can't miss it

OPEN
9:00 a.m.–5:45 p.m. daily, year-round
Limited touring during worship

ADMISSION
Donation suggested

»»

As England's first martyr and patron saint, St. Alban was one of the most fervently admired figures of medieval church history. The site of his execution became a popular pilgrim destination for England's early Christians, but it was not until the 8th century that a shrine to his memory was officially dedicated. Construction of an abbey church in honor of St. Alban was commissioned by King Offa II of Mercia on the site of the present cathedral. This Saxon structure—built largely from the Roman rubble of nearby Verulamium—was re-built shortly after the Norman Conquest and re-modeled extensively throughout the ensuing ages. Despite all this attention, the abbey church did not become a cathedral until 1877; by then, most of its ancient heritage had long since vanished from the interior.

Still, we found St. Albans to be exceptionally beautiful and deeply moving—one of those special places we found hard to leave. If you are patient and persistent, you'll find important attractions within the cathedral worth exploring. Among these are the medieval wall paintings. Savagely whitewashed by Puritans in the 17th century, these remarkable pieces of ancient art have been splendidly restored and offer a hint of St. Albans's original demeanor.

Another significant feature is the 14th-century shrine of St. Alban. You'll find it located in the chapel immediately behind the altar screen. Incredibly, this shrine was also demolished by the Puritans. In 1872, all 2,000 pieces of the desecrated monument were painstakingly reassembled, an outstanding tribute to England's first martyr.

Depending on how you approach the cathedral, there are two separate-but-related exterior buildings you will want to scout out. The first, on the High Street side of the building, is Waxhouse Gateway; its name is a reminder of the era when offertory candles were sold here to pilgrims approaching the abbey shrine. The second structure is Abbey Gateway (c. 1361); once the town jail, it is now part of St. Albans School. The school, by the way, is no Johnny-come-lately. It was founded in the 10th century, making it one of England's oldest educational institutions.

Try to plan enough time to enjoy the rare, peaceful ambience of St. Albans. The atmosphere alone makes this a *not-to-be-missed* attraction.

While you're in St. Albans . . .

✝ Museum of St. Albans
Hatfield Road
St. Albans

>>

PHONE
  01727-819340

OPEN
  10:00 a.m.–5:00 p.m. Monday–Saturday, year-round
  2:00–5:00 p.m. Sunday, year-round
>>

Amid the displays of local crafts, industry and geology, the museum offers a smattering of insight into St. Albans's ancient roots.

∿

✝ Verulamium Roman Wall and Ruins
St. Albans

>>

PHONE
  None

LOCATED
  From the cathedral, take Abbey Mill Lane past St. Albans School;
  cross the River Ver via the footbridge to the ruins on the opposite
  bank.

OPEN
  Daylight hours daily, year-round

ADMISSION
  Free of charge
>>

After London and Colchester, Verulamium was the largest of Rome's British outposts, a city of such stature that the emperor designated it as a *municipum*, or "municipality," which, in effect, conferred Roman citizenship on the locals. Burned to the ground by Queen Boudicca in 61 CE, the town was rebuilt and became a thriving commercial and civic hub, until the Romans evacuated it around 410 CE. Although much of the rubble left behind was used to construct the Saxon abbey dedicated to St. Alban, you will still find considerable remnants of the Roman village to explore. In addition to major sections of the Roman wall, you can visit the *Hypocaust*, where large residential traces—including a floor mosaic and an innovative central heating system—have been preserved in a contemporary structure.

You will also want to investigate the remains of the massive **Roman Theatre**. In its day, this semicircular venue could accommodate an audience of 1,600; no other structure of this type still exists in England. The Roman Theatre is open 10:00 a.m.–5:00 p.m., daily; phone 01727-835035 for details.

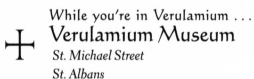

While you're in Verulamium ...
Verulamium Museum
St. Michael Street
St. Albans

>>
PHONE
01727-751810

OPEN
10:00 a.m.–5:30 p.m. Monday–Saturday, year-round
2:00–5:30 p.m. Sunday, year-round

ADMISSION
Fee charged; phone for details.
>>

This museum boasts one of England's most important displays of Roman artifacts, including wall paintings, domestic items, pottery, statuettes and jewelry.

Old Gorhambury House
St. Albans

≫≫

PHONE
  01604-730320

LOCATED
  From the A4147 at St. Albans, travel north approximately 2 miles and
  look for the private signposted driveway.

OPEN
  Daylight hours daily, year-round

ADMISSION
  Free of charge

≫≫

Although this former Elizabethan manor is essentially a ruin,
portions of the home bear witness to the Renaissance influence
in Tudor England. Pay particular note to the porch that graces
the Great Hall—it is a fine example of Italian inspiration.

~

Berkhamsted Castle
Berkhamsted
St. Albans

≫≫

PHONE
  01442-871737

LOCATED
  Just beyond the Berkhamsted Station

TRAVEL
  Regular train service from Euston Station to Berkhamsted; travel
  time is approximately 30 minutes.

OPEN
  10:00 a.m.–4:00 p.m. daily, year-round

ADMISSION
  Free of charge

≫≫

Berkhamsted was yet another castle built in the post-Conquest defensive frenzy by William the Bastard's half-brother Robert, Count of Mortain and Earl of Cornwall. Robert had been well rewarded for his loyalty and service during the Norman invasion, and Berkhamsted was just one of many properties in the earl's impressive "Spoils of War" portfolio. His son, however, was not as astute. He made the unfortunate choice of siding with Robert of Normandy against Henry I in the family feud for England's crown . . . the crown and the castle went to Henry.

Although Berkhamsted remained a royal castle for most of its existence, it was usually held in safekeeping by a trusted minion of rank or power. Thomas à Becket was its landlord during the reign of Henry II (after Becket's demise, Berkhamsted briefly served as a prison for Henry's feisty queen, Eleanor of Aquitaine). In October 1216, the castle had its first—and only—brush with warfare, surrendering to Louis of France after a particularly vicious two-week siege. Like Hertford Castle, it was restored to England when the French retreated the following year.

Berkhamsted's association with the earldom of Cornwall was renewed when Henry III granted the castle to his brother Richard—who traded as "King

---

☞ Did you know?

Edgar Atheling, great-nephew to King Edward the Confessor and a claimant to the throne of England, surrendered to William the Conqueror at Berkhamsted—despite the fact that he had been chosen as king by the London magnates following the death of King Harold at Hastings.

☞ Did you know?

One of the first honors bestowed on Piers Gaveston by the newly crowned Edward II was the castle of Berkhamsted. It was here that the king's favorite celebrated his marriage to Edward's niece Margaret of Clare. A highlight of the festivities was a magnificent tournament on the grounds of nearby Wallingford, in Berkshire. Gaveston was no friend of the older nobility—jealous of his royal perks and scandalized by the "excessive affection" between Edward and Piers, they rallied against Gaveston at the tourney. Gaveston was forced to rely on the talents of younger, stronger men whose lack of rank and resources would only be assuaged by a major win. Gaveston and his motivated supporters carried the day.

of the Romans" as well as "Earl of Cornwall." During the Hundred Years War, King John of France was held briefly at Berkhamsted, but the castle's poor repair made it ill-suited for such a royal hostage. He was transferred to the more accommodating Hertford Castle for the remainder of his involuntary English holiday. Berkhamsted was to see yet another royal "prisoner" in 1330, when Queen Isabella was briefly confined to the castle. It was here she awaited her son Edward III's decision on her fate for the role she played in her treasonous lover's crimes against the state—including the foul murder of Edward II. (The younger Edward proved to be surprisingly lenient, permitting his mother, the "She-Wolf of France," a graceful retirement at Castle Rising.) While staying at Berkhamsted with his wife Joan, the Black Prince—eldest son of Edward III—first fell ill with the wasting disease that would eventually bring about his early death, throwing England into one of its many medieval accession crises.

By the reign of Elizabeth, Berkhamsted Castle was completely abandoned. Today, you can poke around the extensive earthworks and trace major portions of the curtain wall. Foundations of three semicircular towers remain; these are believed to date from Becket's tenure. There is also an oblong chunk of the three-story tower built by Richard, Duke of Cornwall, in 1254.

∿

A lost treasure . . .
✝ King's Langley

American presidents escape to Camp David when the frenetic pace of the nation's capital becomes too much to bear. Queen Elizabeth II has Balmoral, where she slogs across the moors in her Wellies. And the medieval monarchs of the 13th and 14th centuries had Langley, the out-of-town hideaway where England's leaders rested from affairs of state.* Conveniently located between the royal castle of Berkhamsted and the important abbey at St. Albans, just 20 miles from London, Langley was neither castle nor palace, but an "at ease" royal residence, held by Queen Eleanor of Castile on behalf of Edmund, Earl of Cornwall, her husband's cousin. In time, the manor became the favored winter residence for Eleanor and Edward I's sizeable brood of children.

Considerable effort and expense went into making Langley a restful retreat befitting the royal family. Surrounded by rolling meadows, crystalline ponds and lush gardens, Langley managed to retain its idyllic rural atmosphere, even while offering the most impressive modern luxuries. There were vineyards and a working farm, a renowned game park with its own hunting lodge and two working watermills. Strolling the grounds, whiling away an afternoon fishing or wooing, it would be easy for a weary statesman to imagine himself well insulated from the cares of the world.

Still, Langley was no rustic "cabin in the woods." The home itself was the height of sophistication as the result of its first remodeling, completed in 1289. Vast amounts of timber, tile, stone and iron had been ordered for the impressive renovation, which included luxurious private apartments for the king, queen and their then-eldest son Alphonso. The exterior walls were whitewashed with accents of brilliant red and sunny yellow. Inside, the walls were decorated with exquisite hand-painted murals, like the one in the Great Hall, which depicted knights en route to a tournament. Colorful renderings of 54 heraldic shields continued the chivalric theme. In addition to the usual public rooms, there were extensive suites of private apartments for noble visitors—rooms made more commodious by the generous use of fireplaces and tapestries.

Of all of Eleanor and Edward's children, it was the future Edward II who held Langley closest to his heart. When his un-

---

* The manor did not become known as "King's" Langley until 1428.

cle of Cornwall died in 1302, young Edward Caernarvon inherited the manor, and as both prince and king, he remained actively involved in the property. An avid gardener, he took great interest in cultivating rare flowers and blossoming fruit trees, further enhancing Langley's pastoral charm. His stables were reportedly magnificent, housing a camel in addition to the finest horseflesh money could buy. Fond of entertaining in the grandest possible style, Edward earned the ill will of the townsfolk who complained that he helped himself to whatever produce and livestock were needed to laden his table (with a rumored 200 dishes a day), never bothering to pay a farthing in exchange.

Among those frequently in the young king's company at Langley was the controversial courtier, Piers Gaveston. An intimate and near constant companion of the king, Gaveston had been honored with the vacant earldom of Cornwall — just one of many moves that enraged Edward II's court. The fact that the two men spent an extended and virtually sequestered Christmas at Langley in

Did you know?

The burials of Piers Gaveston and Richard II were both tinged with political intrigue and tainted by unconscionable delay. Gaveston was executed by order of the Earl of Warwick in 1312. His body was sent to the Dominicans at Oxford, who refused to bury the corpse in consecrated ground. It took Edward II over two years to receive the necessary papal dispensation to have his friend buried properly. Gaveston was moved to the Dominican friary at Langley in 1315 and given what amounted to a state funeral. Nearly 100 years later, the deposed King Richard died (under exceedingly suspicious circumstances) at Pontefract Castle. The usurper Henry IV ordered Richard's body sent to King's Langley, perhaps to subliminally underscore the less-than-positive association between Richard and his great-grandfather, Edward II. Richard's express wish, however, had been to be buried with his beloved first queen, Anne of Bohemia. In fact, Richard already had commissioned his own elaborate tomb at Westminster Abbey. It was not until 1415 that Henry V made amends for his father's harsh treatment of Richard by moving the body from King's Langley to London. Like Gaveston's, this second burial was accorded all due pomp and circumstance . . . a case of too little, too late.

1309 prompted the nobility to appear at the next Parliament fully armed; they claimed the king was fraternizing with an enemy of the state. Yet, despite his reputation for dissolute living, Edward was actually rather pious. He established a major Dominican friary at Langley—never suspecting it would become the final resting place for both his lover, Piers Gaveston, and his deposed great-grandson, King Richard II.

Long after Edward II's murder in 1327, Langley continued to be a favorite Plantagenet residence. The new king, Edward III, undertook a major expansion plan, enlarging the royal apartments, upgrading the hunting facilities and adding a state-of-the-art bathhouse. His grandson and heir, Richard II, spent less time at Langley than his ancestors, but the property still enjoyed a fair amount of royal favor. Richard's elder brother, Robert of Angouleme, was buried at the manor's friary, and the king traditionally paid his respects during Lent. Richard also added private apartments for his favorite courtiers, Robert de Vere and Thomas Mowbray—houseguests who were no more popular among their peers than Piers Gaveston had been!

For reasons that seem unclear, Langley ceased to be occupied in the mid-1470s, and eventually fell into decay. All that remains are scattered remnants of masonry.

ᴧᴧ

 ## Knebworth House
Near Stevenage

≫≫

PHONE
   01438-812661

E-MAIL
   info@knebworthhouse.com

LOCATED
   Off the A1, junction 7, approximately 28 miles north of London

TRAVEL
   Trains depart Kings Cross Station for Stevenage; Knebworth is approximately 2 miles from the station, with taxi service available.

OPEN
Noon–5:00 p.m. daily, April–September

Note: There are occasional summer closings; please be sure to call ahead for current schedule.

ADMISSION
£7.00 Adults
£6.50 Children and Seniors
Children under 4 admitted free of charge
Family ticket available

>>>

If you're looking for a way to combine a bit of 15th-century touring with 21st-century diversions for your children, Knebworth may well fit the bill. Although light on actual history (or actual Tudor-era relics for that matter), Knebworth is a magnificent home to admire, truly "larger than life." Perhaps that's why so many films—including *The Shooting Party, The Canterville Ghost, Jane Eyre, Wilde* and (oddly) *Batman*—have chosen Knebworth for location.

Aside from film-making, Knebworth is a favorite venue for major rock concerts. There's also the wildly popular Adventure Playground and an equally child-pleasing miniature railway. (*Have we given you fair warning?*)

The vast Knebworth lands are believed to have once housed a Saxon settlement, perhaps "Cnebba's camp," home to a 5th-century Saxon prince by that name. Certainly there were a manor and a fort here during the reign of Edward the Confessor, for it is recorded that he made a gift of both to his thane Aschill. Aschill was just one of Knebworth's many blue-blooded tenants. Over the next 400 years Robert de Hoo, Thomas de Brotherton, Walter Manny and Thomas Bourchier each added noble panache—and their architectural imprint—to Knebworth House. Sir Robert Lytton purchased the estate in 1490. The few "ancient" bits and pieces left at Knebworth House today date from Sir Robert's massive reconstruction of the manor house. Robert Lytton was a close friend of the usurper king Henry VII, fighting alongside the Tudor hopeful at the Battle of Bosworth and later becoming Under Treasurer of the Royal Household. You'll find Sir Robert's portrait in the Banqueting Hall and a memo from Henry VII in the Minstrel's Hall. Queen Elizabeth was also close to the Lytton clan. She visited Sir Roland Lytton at Knebworth House on August 21, 1571; records from her four-day stay are on display in what is aptly named Queen Elizabeth's Room.

✝ Royston Cave
Royston

>>>

PHONE
01763-245484 (Royston Town Council)

LOCATED
Royston is located off the A10 and the A505, near the Bedfordshire border. The well-marked cave is in the middle of Melbourn Street in the Royston Town Center.

OPEN
1:00–5:00 p.m. Saturday, Sunday and Bank Holiday Mondays, April–October

ADMISSION
Phone for details

TIP!
Royston Cave is well worth a visit, but it really is far-flung from the other Hertfordshire sites. You may want to save this excursion for the day you spend touring Bedfordshire.

>>>

You will never, *ever* see another medieval attraction quite like Royston Cave. Depending on how you feel about dark, dank, subterranean spaces, you might consider that a good thing! The only other known cave of this ilk has been found in the Czech Republic, a place unlikely to work its way into the *Amateur Historian's* repertoire. Still, we found Royston Cave to be incredibly fascinating, as much for the questions it raises as for the remarkable findings it displays.

Royston Cave is man-made, not a natural formation. No one

knows for certain when the circular, bell-shaped chamber was built, by whom or for what purpose. Discovered in 1742, during the expansion of Royston's Butter and Cheese Market, the cave soon became a popular attraction for scholars, archeologists and tourists. They came to admire—and ponder over—the unusual medieval friezes that decorate the cave's walls. Some of the detailed carvings are readily identifiable as biblical characters: the psalm-writing, giant-slaying King David, martyred St. Catherine, a repentant Mary Magdalene. Others are possibly figures from England's medieval past, perhaps Henry II and Richard the Lionheart. But many of the etchings are enigmatic, slightly pagan and somewhat disturbing.

◆◆◆◆◆◆◆◆◆◆◆◆◆◆◆◆◆◆◆◆◆◆
☞ Did you know?
Royston is believed to take its name from a Norman woman of noble birth, Lady Rohesia (Rose). For many years there was speculation that Royston Cave was the burial site of the town's foremother, but that fable has been debunked.
◆◆◆◆◆◆◆◆◆◆◆◆◆◆◆◆◆◆◆◆◆◆

The current "best guess" theory is that the cave was constructed by a local chapter of the Knights Templar. The original construction featured two separate floors, one of which might have been used for cool storage (Royston has been known for its butter and cheese since ancient times). The second story was, perhaps, a secret temple of worship. There is considerable justification—although no absolute proof—for this speculation. The chamber's bell-shaped curve could be interpreted as a model of the Holy Sepulchre. Even more convincing, many of the etchings on Royston Cave's walls resemble carvings found in the dungeons of Chateaux de Chinon, where members of the French branch of the Templars were imprisoned, following their 1312 suppression by Pope Clement V. One character, originally thought to be a bishop in his mitre, is now believed to be Templars' Grand Master Jacques de Molay, who was burned at the stake in 1314.

While you're in Royston . . .

In 1998, excavations at the entrance to Royston Cave revealed an unrelated set of 15th-century cellars, once belonging to a local inn. Records reveal that the cellars were purchased in 1523 by local Samaritan William Lee, who offered the chambers as refuge for Royston's paupers before the advent of the workhouse. You will also want to take a moment to mosey over to the **Town War Memorial**, farther along Melbourn Street. In addition to the usual tributes to veterans from "recent" wars, you'll spot stone figures of an Agincourt bowman, a medieval knight in armor and an Elizabethan Armada soldier. Clearly, the boys of Royston have seen many a battlefield over the centuries.

• • • • • • • • • • • • • • • • • • • •

☞ Did you know?

Melbourn Street was once known as Ickenfield Way—or *Via Icenia* to all you Romaniacs. This was the passage used by the ancient Celtic tribe, known as the Iceni. The most famous Icenian was Queen Boudicca (d. 61 CE), whose most *in*famous act was burning a swath through southeast England in retaliation for Rome's gross mistreatment of her kin and countrymen. Apparently, Melbourn Street was spared this fiery woman's rampant road rage!

• • • • • • • • • • • • • • • • • • • •

ANCIENT INNS AND EATERIES

~ Ye Olde Fighting Cock
   Abbey Mill Lane at River Ver
Hearty pub fare at one of England's very oldest inns.

CONCLUSION

When we first conceived of the *Amateur Historian's* series, our motive was, to be honest, twofold. On the one hand, following the ancient kings and queens, knights and nobles, monks and merchants, do-gooders and ne'er-do-wells on their merry romp through the English countryside was a powerful lure. At the same time, we were strongly attached to London and eager to find ways to satisfy our historical cravings while subsidizing our yearning for our favorite city.

Three years—and three books!—later, we marvel at how successful we've been, balancing castles and cathedrals by day and the charms of London by night. We have managed to visit nearly 250 medieval and Tudor sites . . . some more than once . . . while spending only two nights outside of London during our travels. Sure, we've logged some major mileage along the English motorways, but we've enjoyed every minute. Without a doubt, we've had the best of both worlds, ancient and new.

The challenge we face is: what next? Attached as we still are to London, there are cities and sites farther afield in England that beckon to us as well. One of the options we are exploring is *East Anglia*, which offers Cambridge University, myriad manor homes, cathedrals and castle ruins, *plus* the pleasure of being largely London-based. Also under consideration are *Richard III's York* (and surrounding counties) and the evocative *West of England*, where the scenery is as rich as the history. Each possibility intrigues us; in time we plan to visit—and write about— them all!

We hope you've enjoyed the *Amateur Historian's Guide to the Heart of England*. As always, we welcome comments, suggestions and tales from your own historical adventures.

Happy travels.

Carole and Sarah
The Amateur Historians
www.amateurhistorian.com

GLOSSARY

After years of lapping up medieval literature and lore, we find ourselves sprinkling our own writing with medieval and Tudor "lingo" as if they were household words. Here are some terms you might run across that could otherwise give you pause.

Abbey: A religious enclave headed by an abbot or abbess. Also known as a *monastery, cloister, priory* or — if housing female monastics — *convent, nunnery* or *convent monastery.*

Attainder: An Act of Parliament that sanctioned execution of a noble without trial. The heirs of an attainted noble lost the rights to inherit that person's lands or titles.

Aumbury: A cupboard or recess in the wall for storing sacred vessels.

Bailey: The protected outer courtyard of a castle, also known as a *ward.*

Baron: A tenant-in-chief of the monarchy who held land and titles specifically granted by the king or queen.

Bastion: A flanking tower used exclusively for defensive purposes.

Bosses: Carved ornaments that disguise the joint between rib vaults; often gilded or painted.

Buttress: A vertical stone projection from a wall that strengthens (or resists) the lateral thrust of a roof.

Calefactory: The warming house of a monastery or abbey; this was the only room, besides the kitchen, in which the strictest orders allowed a fire.

Canon: An ordained, non-monastic priest living communally with others in observance of a Rule, typically that of St. Augustine of Hippo. A canon's main role was to officiate at religious services.

Cathedral: Christian house of worship that contains a *cathedra* or bishop's chair/throne. The bishop (or archbishop) is the presiding religious authority at a cathedral.

Chancel: The east end of a church or cathedral closest to the high altar; reserved for clergy.

Chantry: A small chapel (in some cases simply an altar) endowed with funds to maintain a priest to pray for the repose of the founder's (or loved one's) soul.

Charter: Formal written record of the royal transfer of rights or property.

Clerestory: The part of a building that rises above standard roof level and contains a window that lights the core of the building. Also, the upper story of a church nave, providing light to the center of the church.

Corbel: A stone or timber wall projection that supports a beam or overhead platform.

Crenelation: Parapets of a castle that are divided into distinctive solid chunks of wall (used as shields), interspersed with gaps ("crenels") used for aiming weapons at one's enemy. Also known as *battlements*.

Crosier: Also *crozier*. A staff with a crook or a cross at the end, reminiscent of a shepherd's staff. A crosier is carried by (or in some cases precedes) an archbishop, bishop or abbot.

Curtain Wall: A (typically) freestanding wall with interval towers that encloses a castle courtyard.

Donjon: The keep or great tower of a castle.

Dovecote: Your basic pigeon condominium.

Excommunication: Punishment levied by the Pope that denied the offending party the right to receive Holy Communion, thereby putting the individual's soul in jeopardy of eternal damnation, unless papal pardon was received.

Friar: A member of one of the mendicant orders who has taken a vow of material poverty.

Garderobe: Your basic medieval loo or latrine.

Gothic: A style of architecture popular from the 12th through the 15th centuries. It is characterized by pointed arches, rib vaulting and flying buttresses. The word Gothic is also often used as a synonym for *medieval*.

Grotesque: Used to describe a style of medieval wood carving, found particularly in church decor. Although some of the faces depicted are, indeed, "gross," the word really stems from the Latin word *grotto*—the Roman grottos serving as the inspiration for this art form.

Guild: Also, *gild*. Organizations that oversaw regulation of trade in a particular town. Many also had religious functions as well.

Hammerbeam: A horizontal beam that projects at right angles from the top of a wall to support a wooden roof.

Interdict: A censure by the Pope that prohibits a person or group of people from participating in the sacraments of the Church.

Lady Chapel: A chapel dedicated to the Blessed Mother, usually located in the east end of a major church or cathedral.

Minster: A large church served by a clerical community, not necessarily monastic.

Misericord: A ledge located beneath the hinged seat in a choir stall, allowing the seat to be adjusted for the comfort of its occupant. These ledges and their brackets are often intricately engraved.

Monastery: A community of persons who have retired from the world under religious vows. When referring to collected monastic buildings, *monastery, abbey* and *priory* are frequently interchanged.

Motte: The rounded castle mound.

Nave: The west wing of a church or cathedral.

Oriel: A round, protruding window.

Perpendicular: The swan song of Gothic architecture, this uniquely English style of design is characterized by uniform, parallel lines, as opposed to the flowing tracery of early Gothic work. Popular in London and urban centers from the mid-1300s until the reign of Elizabeth I.

Piscina: A sink, set into the recesses of the altar area, used exclusively to wash sacred vessels.

Portcullis: Heavy grate that slides vertically, designed to close off a passageway.

Prebend: An estate belonging to the Church that was granted to a canon to provide income. In return, the canon paid some taxes and agreed to offer a set number of psalms each day—a task usually subcontracted to a poor priest.

Presbytery: The east wing of the church, where the high altar is located; also known as the *sanctuary.*

Priory: A religious house headed by a prior or prioress. Although a prior is technically one step below an abbot (making a priory subordinate to an abbey), the terms *priory, abbey* and *monastery* are commonly interchanged when referring to an enclave of monastic buildings.

Progress: The monarch's official tour of the realm, usually conducted annually.

Quire: Portion of the church between the presbytery and the pulpit. The quire comprised stalls where monks sat to sing the Offices; modern use: *choir.*

Rape: A governing jurisdiction created after the Norman Conquest that empowered Norman nobles with military power and administrative control, centered in an English castle.

Relic: A part of a saint's body or an article of possession, believed to be a medium of intercession to God; relics of holy people were often preserved in ornamental caskets known as *reliquaries.*

Reredos: Decorative screen or hanging on the wall behind an altar.

Romanesque: Architectural style very similar to Norman; popular in the 11th and 12th centuries and characterized by rounded arches and groined or barrel vaults.

Rood Screen: An ornamental division between the nave and the quire of the church, adorned with a crucifix.

Sanctuary: 1. The area of a church or cathedral containing the high altar (see *presbytery*). 2. The medieval practice of granting refuge to fugitives who sought official shelter within the church walls.

Sarcophagus: Stone coffin, typically adorned with an effigy and inscription.

Sedilia: Trio of recessed wall seats made of stone for officiating clergy; located on the south side of the quire and usually topped with a decorative canopy.

Seneschal: Official deputy in a medieval great house.

Shield Wall: A virtually impregnable defensive stance formed by warriors standing shoulder-to-shoulder and shield-to-shield.

Shire: The main territorial subdivision of England. Derived from the Anglo-Saxon *scir,* meaning bit or part. Although England is now divided into counties, many still retain the shire designation, such as Leicester*shire,* Oxford*shire,* etc.

Transept: Transverse (north-south) part of a cruciform church or cathedral, set at a right angle to the main axis; the transept links the nave and the chancel.

Translation: Solemn ceremony in which the remains of a dead person are moved from one burial site to another.

Undercroft: Vaulted underground room or cellar, supporting the principal chamber above; Carole's favorite part of any medieval building (*not!*).

Vault: An arched stone ceiling or roof, sometimes punctuated with ribs; a *barrel vault* is an arched, semicylindrical vault.

Wall Walk: The fighting platform directly behind the parapet of a curtain wall.

Ward: A castle's courtyard or bailey.

Writ: The written command of the Crown, signed and sealed by the monarch. By the 12th century, these official documents were required to initiate any proceedings in the royal courts of justice.

INDEX

Bold type indicates sites highlighted by the authors.

The Amateur Historians,
Sarah Valente Kettler (left) andCarole Trimble.

ABOUT THE AMATEUR HISTORIANS

Professional writers by trade and historians by hobby, authors Sarah Valente Kettler and Carole Trimble discovered their shared passion for medieval and Tudor England through their work with the Shakespeare Theatre in Washington, D.C. Their combined fascination with fact-finding, insatiable love of London, and extensive background in their "favorite" period of history gave rise to this book — inspiration assisted by post-Tower libations in a Knightsbridge pub.

Carole Trimble is the founder and president of Communications Management Strategies, a Washington-based public relations/public affairs consulting firm. Sarah Valente Kettler is the former owner and creative director of the award-winning advertising agency Valente Associates, Inc. Voracious readers, intrepid travelers, enthusiastic theater patrons, and fans of old movies, Carole and Sarah are best friends as well as co-authors of two previous Amateur Historian's Guides: Volume 1 — *The Amateur Historian's Guide to Medieval & Tudor London* and Volume 2 — *Medieval & Tudor England: Day Trips South of London*, both published by Capital Books.